Modern Travel in World History

Modern Travel in World History uses three themes—technology, mass movements and travelers—to examine the history of the modern world from the fifteenth-century transatlantic explorations to the impact of the global COVID pandemic of the twenty-first century.

This book focuses on both the evolving nature of travel, from land and sea routes in the 1500s to the domination of planes and cars in the modern world, and the important stories of travelers themselves. Taking a global perspective, the text places travel within the larger geopolitical, social, religious and cultural developments throughout history. It emphasizes not only the role of technology innovation in the ways people travel but also how those changes affect social structures and cultural values. Tom Taylor explores the journeys of well-known travelers as well as ordinary people, each with different perspectives, through the lens of gender, social class and cultural background, and considers how fictional travelers define the importance of travel in the modern world. Why people set out on the sojourns they did, what they experienced, who they met and how they understood these cross-cultural encounters are important to not only understanding the travelers themselves but the world they lived in and the world their travels made. Several maps help illustrate important routes and destinations.

This book will be of interest to students of world history and literature.

Tom Taylor is an associate professor of history at Seattle University, where he teaches a wide variety of courses focusing on travel and travelers in the modern world.

Themes in World History
Series editor: Peter N. Stearns

The *Themes in World History* series offers focused treatment of a range of human experiences and institutions in the world history context. The purpose is to provide serious, if brief, discussions of important topics as additions to textbook coverage and document collections. The treatments will allow students to probe particular facets of the human story in greater depth than textbook coverage allows, and to gain a fuller sense of historians' analytical methods and debates in the process. Each topic is handled over time—allowing discussions of changes and continuities. Each topic is assessed in terms of a range of different societies and religions—allowing comparisons of relevant similarities and differences. Each book in the series helps readers deal with world history in action, evaluating global contexts as they work through some of the key components of human society and human life.

Happiness in World History
Peter N. Stearns

Peasants in World History
Eric Vanhaute

Childhood in World History *(Fourth Edition)*
Peter N. Stearns

Nations and Nationalism in World History
Steven Grosby

Gender in World History *(Fourth Edition)*
Peter N. Stearns

Modern Travel in World History
Tom Taylor

For more information about this series, please visit: www.routledge.com

Modern Travel in World History

Tom Taylor

Routledge
Taylor & Francis Group

NEW YORK AND LONDON

Cover image: Eric Gevaert / Alamy Stock Photo

First published 2022
by Routledge
605 Third Avenue, New York, NY 10158

and by Routledge
4 Park Square, Milton Park, Abingdon, Oxon, OX14 4RN

Routledge is an imprint of the Taylor & Francis Group, an informa business

Library of Congress Cataloging-in-Publication Data
A catalog record for this book has been requested

ISBN: 978-0-367-76824-9 (hbk)
ISBN: 978-0-367-76599-6 (pbk)
ISBN: 978-1-003-16869-0 (ebk)

DOI: 10.4324/9781003168690

Typeset in Times New Roman
by Apex CoVantage, LLC

Contents

Maps

Introduction

When I was in high school in the early 1970s, I had to choose a language to study. I selected Latin. I knew nothing about Latin aside from the fact that it was used in Catholic Mass (I was attending a Catholic school) and in science terminology. I had a few friends who had also decided to take it, so why not? I thought, why learn a foreign language? I did not imagine ever traveling abroad. Fast forward a number of years. I have now traveled to forty-plus countries, sailed around the world twice with Semester at Sea (a comparative global study-abroad program) and spent months living abroad.

My experience is not particularly unique for my generation and socioeconomic background. When I was growing up, the idea of foreign travel was foreign. Going abroad, unless we canoed across the Canadian border, was a rare experience. Planning a trip was expensive and challenging—working with a travel agent was necessary to determine available flights and prices, add to that figuring out how to get around and where to stay. Guidebooks like the *Lonely Planet* or *Europe on $10 Day* were just beginning to be published.

Several years later, I had the opportunity to go abroad in college, and it was a big to-do. Arrangements for transportation and housing were done via mail or expensive phone calls. Aside from a passport, traveler's checks had to be purchased and carefully managed; losing them was like losing your luggage but worse. I did not have a credit card or ATM card, so replacement was difficult (done in person during business hours and usually took several days). In Europe, each country had its own currency, so I exchanged money every time I crossed a border. The idea of losing my passport created even greater angst, and I kept it in a money belt tucked inside my shirt.

When I left home, the goodbyes were difficult. I was away for almost four months and had little contact with family and friends. I sent aerograms (flimsy pieces of blue paper) because regular letters were too expensive. International phones were almost non-existent. (There was one phone that could make calls to the United States in the German town where I studied. It was in the post office, and you had to reserve it well in advance. I made one call home in four months. It lasted three minutes.) My faulty German was helpful because in many of the places where I went, no one spoke English.

DOI: 10.4324/9781003168690-1

Today (at least until a global pandemic brought travel to a virtual halt), international travel for many people has become more common. In 2019, pre-COVID, over one billion people traveled abroad. Students cross the globe to study in different countries. Approximately 350,000 US students studied abroad in 2019, and international students are part of university communities around the world. Cell phones and the internet have allowed us to become our own travel agents, and trips can be booked in a matter of minutes using a credit card. For better or worse, the globalization of English as a primary or secondary language has made communication easier. Translation is available through a cell phone.

For many in the world, travel is very difficult. Millions flee wars, political and religious persecution. Others are forced to move by droughts, floods and fires caused by climate change. They often leave suddenly, with little, and they face dangerous conditions, negotiating gangs who prey on people in need. Journeys require crossing vast deserts and turbulent waters to find refuge. Massive numbers of refugees have created instability and, by many accounts, burdens on potential host countries who are unable to accommodate the influx. This has exacerbated negative reactions against those attempting to immigrate.

The Importance of Travel in World History

Travel is defined as going from one place to another, usually over some distance, and in many ways the modern world is defined by people traveling around the world. Humans have traveled ever since Homo sapiens began to walk out of Africa and populate the world. The modern era is differentiated by the number of people who traveled, where and why they traveled and how modes of travel have evolved. Migrations, whether forced like the Atlantic Slave Trade or voluntarily like the immigrants in search of new lives, have increased exponentially during the last half of the millennium. Tourism (travel for leisure or business) was an experience reserved for a few elite in the pre-modern world. Today, at least before the COVID pandemic, it is the largest industry in the world, with over a billion people traveling annually.

Distances that used to be insurmountable are now easily bridged. In the early fourteenth century Ibn Battuta, one of the most famous travelers ever, set out to perform his Islamic religious obligation, the *Hajj*—a pilgrimage to Mecca, home of the Prophet Mohmand. His trek from Morocco to Mecca took months, and his subsequent travels across the expansive Islamic world spanned decades. Now, those performing the Hajj can fly from almost anywhere in the world and be on their pilgrimage in a matter of hours.

Travel is not always measured in miles or kilometers but sometimes through life experience. Nelson Mandela's journey from prisoner to president of South Africa is one of these stories. Robbin Island, where he spent the majority of his almost three decades of incarceration, lies just across the bay from Cape

Town, less than 6 miles away. For him it was it was a distance measured by the repression of millions of black South Africans denied human rights by a racist state. For Mandela, this *Long Walk to Freedom*, as he calls his memoir, was therefore a voyage of personal and public transformation. Travel is also about geography, moving across oceans and borders, and through different cultural, social, philosophical, psychological and theological spaces.

In addition to people who travel, this book also considers 'imagined travel' as it offers important insights into the modern world. During the late nineteenth century, for example, the most popular literature in the world was Jules Verne's fictional travel writings. Whether taking his readers on an imagined journey to the center of the earth or 20,000 leagues under the sea or around the world on a flying ship, Verne's work captivated millions who never left their homes or cities. It stimulated as much intrigue and fascination with the unknown as Columbus did, landing in the Bahamas in 1492.

This book examines the impact and experiences of travel in the modern world using three themes: first, development of the technology of transportation from ocean-going vessels to railways and steamships to cars and planes; second, understanding significant travel movements such as the Atlantic Slave Trade, patterns of immigration and refugees fleeing one place for another; and last, personal perspectives from travelers and how their accounts and records are important to understanding the history of the modern world.

Theme 1: Transportation Technology

The evolving nature of transportation influenced how people moved around the world, who and what moved, where and how fast. New shipbuilding technology in Europe made crossing the Atlantic possible, bringing together and dividing worlds in profound ways. The development of steam engines brought about an industrial and transportation revolution. Railroads and steam ships moved goods and people faster and further than ever before, and those who controlled these technologies shaped economies and held power. The twentieth century saw the development of the internal combustion engine and later the jet engine. Cars took to the roads and planes to the skies. Cities and countries were reconfigured to accommodate these new ubiquitous modes of transportation and travelers.

The development and adaptation of new technologies did not happen in a vacuum. At the beginning of the fifteenth century, China had ships that could navigate any waters and the financial and military resources to do so. Yet, those ships only sailed for a few decades and then were called home and scuttled. China focused on its inland borders rather than transoceanic possibilities. The opportunities this presented for Europeans were, in part, predicated on China's decision not to use the maritime technology it had developed. The impact of Columbus' voyage was because of the political, social and religious agendas he carried with him across the Atlantic.

Theme 2: Migrations and Mass Movements

This second organizing theme is focused on how mass movements of people—immigrants, laborers, slaves and refugees—were part of modern world history. The Transatlantic Slave Trade forcibly moved 12 to 13 million Africans from their homes to the Americas. Well over a hundred years have passed since the end of that brutal system, and it continues to profoundly impact the countries involved. Similarly, it is impossible to understand the modern world without taking into account the role that migrants, immigrants and refugees have played historically. Foreign laborers and immigrants have built the railroads and harvested the crops that make up the modern global economic system. Their movements have also led to debates about citizenship and human rights, ultimately who belongs in and out of any given country. War, economic dislocation and environmental catastrophes have pushed people out of their homes in desperate searches for survival. The movement of refugees is an important part of the history of the modern world.

Theme 3: Travelers

The third theme relies on the perspective of individual travelers, who they were, where they traveled and what they experienced to understand history. Travelers are agents of historical events, i.e. they make history, and they are also witnesses to those events. They provide insight into places through the lens and bias given where they come from. How travelers tell their stories, to whom and what their experiences tell us about the circumstances are in many ways as meaningful as the journeys themselves. Jesuit missionaries' recorded encounters between Europeans and indigenous peoples are often the only written records we have about these seismically important meetings. Matteo Ricci spent years trying to assimilate and understand Chinese culture and his journals influenced western views of China for centuries.

The letters of Lady Wortley Montagu, the wife of a British diplomat serving in Istanbul in the early eighteenth century, provide important insights into the Ottoman Empire and help us understand how the British interpreted issues of gender and political power. These letters offer very different perspectives from the reports of Indians like the social reformer Behramji Malabari, who wrote about his experiences in London at the end of the nineteenth century. His views of English family life and politics are filtered through his lens as a colonial subject.

Some of the travelers referenced in the book are likely familiar, such as Christopher Columbus and the Beatles. Others are perhaps less well-known, such as Cornelia Sorabji or Annie Moore. Their travels and relationships were just as critical as Prime Minister Churchill's sojourns to allied conferences in Teheran and Yalta during World War Two. History is not only the story of the famous and powerful; it is also the stories of ordinary people and how they were influenced by world-changing events.

It should also be noted that many travelers referenced remain nameless. Of those millions of Africans forcibly taken from their homes and transported across the Atlantic Ocean as slaves, we know the names and actual stories of a very, very few. Understanding their experiences is exceedingly difficult, but groundbreaking historical work is beginning to give those people and their experiences a voice.

Chronology

World historians debate the dates that delineate the beginning of what is referred to as 'the modern world.' In 2018, the College Board (whose role in teaching and administering advanced placement courses makes it a major player in world history circles) decided to split world history into two sections: pre-modern history and modern history. The date 1450 was chosen to begin modern history so that the modern era is not predicated on a Eurocentric perspective that would lead with the voyages of Christopher Columbus in 1492. Rather it considers the rise of the Ottoman Empire and the Fall of Constantinople in 1452 as a key markers.

This decision, in turn, sparked a new round of chronological debates. Some argued that 1450 did not capture any key transformations in East Asia, Africa or the Islamic world. Others countered that 1200, a time of Mongol expansion linking much of the Afro-Eurasian worlds together made more sense. That date captured a time when Europe was moving beyond its Roman past and key developments were taking place in the Americas. In the end the College Board, while recognizing the validity of these debates and alternative chronologies, decided to move forward recognizing the mid-fifteenth century as the divide between the pre-modern and modern worlds.

This book uses mid-fifteenth century to mark the beginning of the modern world for several reasons. First, the prequel to this book *Early Modern Travel in World History* by Stephen Gosch and Peter Stearns covers many of the critical events and travels in the preceding era. Moreover, 1450 aligns with significant developments in the technology of transportation and the emergence of transregional movements that were revolutionary. For example, the era of the Chinese treasure fleets plying the waters of the China Seas and Indian Ocean had come to an end by the 1430s. Given the technology being used, the Ming Dynasty was clearly poised to become a global empire, however the emperor's decisions to scuttle the fleets in the 1430s and to refocus on securing its northern and western borders indirectly opened the door to others.

Another point of reference considered was the emergence of the Ottoman Empire as both a land and a maritime power. In 1453 the empire captured Constantinople, which set the foundation for the control of Western Asia, the Eastern Mediterranean and the North African region. Beyond control of vast domain, the sultan became protector of the key Islamic holy cities of Mecca and Medina, sites that were critical to the religious travels of tens of thousands of Muslim faithful across Dar-al-Islam, 'the abode of the Islamic faithful.'

The mid-fifteenth century also saw the emerging Iberian powers of Spain and Portugal finally succeed in their centuries-long struggle against the Moors, the Islamic peoples of the Peninsula. These victories enabled these European states to cast their eyes and ambitions further afield to the coasts of Africa and the Indies, fueled by aspirations to lead a global Catholic movement.

These victories for Spain and Portugal coincided with new innovations that had come about through centuries of technological borrowing. Compasses, maps and other developments in oceanic navigation, along with the dramatic improvements how ships were built, allowed them to venture out of the Mediterranean and off the African coast. New technology charted the way for Christopher Columbus to sail across the Atlantic Ocean in 1492, followed by the Portuguese sailor Vasco de Gama's voyage rounding of the southern tip of Africa and the Cape of Good Hope in 1497.

The Structure of the Book: Chapter Briefings

The emergence of Spain and Portugal as global powers changed the world, particularly from a travel perspective, and they are the focus of Chapter 1. Columbus' voyage established interaction with the Americas and Afro-Eurasian world that was unprecedented. Vasco de Gama's entrance into the Indian Ocean gave Europeans direct access to the peoples and riches of Asia, which they had sought for centuries. Land travel was still common, but its importance on the world stage had diminished. The global impact of what was carried on these voyages—plants, animals and diseases—reshaped the ecology of the western hemisphere and decimated the peoples of the Americas who had no immunity to viruses and microbes that had come ashore.

Europeans also carried their culture, values and religion with them on these voyages. The Jesuits, a Catholic religious order founded to combat the rise of religious revolution in Europe in the 1540s, traveled with the Spanish and Portuguese to their distant empires in the Americas, Africa and across Asia. In their effort to win the hearts, minds and most importantly souls of the peoples, Jesuits became important and controversial interpreters of these encounters. Their story is told in Chapter 2.

Chapter 3 examines the global impacts of the emergence of three Islamic Empires in the early modern world: the Ottomans, the Mughals of India and the Safavid Empire of modern Iran. Their military and economic power attracted many travelers to their markets and courts. As protectors of Islam, they drew to holy sites pilgrims and western Christians who were anxious to convert them. Their cultural and artistic achievements attracted students and admirers from afar.

The Atlantic Slave Trade, over three hundred years of forced migration of millions of Africans taken to the plantations of the New World, is the focus of Chapter 4. Examining the slave trade considers not only the magnitude of the trade but also how little we know of those who experienced it. New research is informing how we continue to understand this movement. As singular as the Atlantic Slave Trade was, it was not the only transoceanic slave trade of the era as slaves were bought, sold and moved across the Indian Ocean as well. Finally, comparing the nature of these two systems of slavery and what we know about them brings an invaluable perspective to the horrors of both.

As Europeans moved into unchartered waters they encountered plants, animals and societies that challenged previous conceptions of the natural world and where humans fit into it. Attempts to make sense of this knowledge prompted an intellectual and cultural revolution. The Age of Enlightenment, as it became known, heralded many of the scientific, philosophical, social and political ideas that framed the modern world. Through key travels that gathered this new information and an examination of the ways that these new insights were disseminated through scientific journals and imaginative novels, Chapter 5 looks at how travel shaped developments in science, political philosophy and social theory during the eighteenth century.

Chapter 6 examines the changes in world travel brought about by the development of the steam engine and the Industrial Revolution. The engine was used for everything from automating the textile industries of Manchester to powering trains and steamships. The new transportation technologies changed in exponential ways how we moved, where we moved, how fast we moved, why we moved and who moved. Continents were wrapped with ribbons of iron rails connecting cities well as other places used for farming, ranching, mining and forestry. Tourism, travel for leisure and personal edification, became more common.

Millions of people used these new modes of travel, and the nineteenth century witnessed migration and the global movements of people on an unprecedented scale. Their travels and experiences are examined in Chapter 7. Railroads encouraged the settlement of the Americas, and Europeans traveled across the Atlantic, eager to take advantage of new opportunities. These new migrants settled lands that had been lived on by native peoples for centuries. The story of migration is closely linked to the story of displacement in many places. Immigrants changed the cultural and social dynamics of the places they came to work and provoked ethnic and racial backlashes by those who did not welcome their arrival.

The nineteenth century also witnessed political and social upheaval on many continents as new ideas coming out of movements like the Enlightenment spurred revolutions across the Atlantic world. Global migrations and immigration also exacerbated debates on citizenship and ethnic identity. Through a look at key revolutionaries and reformers Chapter 8 investigates the changes that travel had on the social and political landscape of the nineteenth century.

The trains and steamships that carried tourists and migrants also carried colonizers who intended to establish their control in distant lands. Chapter 9 first examines the role that transportation technology played in facilitating the Age of Imperialism. Then it looks at how travelers to and from the colonies shaped the nature of colonialism and how their travels help us understand the Imperial Age from both the perspective of the colonizer and the colonized.

The internal combustion engine, using oil-derivative products as its fuel, entered the scene in the early 1900s and is the subject of Chapter 10. Car and plane travel evolved from a novelty to become the dominant means by which people and goods moved around the world. After World War Two cars reshaped where people lived, and suburbs became normative in many parts of the world. Cars also became important cultural symbols of personal freedom and individual choice. For the Futurists, an artistic movement that originated in Italy, they represented speed, power and a future dominated by the power of these new technologies. Planes connected people with places in unprecedented ways and revolutionized twentieth-century travel. By the 1950s people were flying across the Atlantic or Pacific non-stop, and tourism became, by some estimates, the largest industry in the world. The role that these new technologies have played in shaping the contemporary world is not, however, without its drawbacks, as pollution and climate change have become major concerns today.

Chapter 11 looks at World War One and the revolutions that followed. Internal combustion engines were put in tanks and taken to the trenches of the Western Front. Planes went from being used for reconnaissance to dropping bombs on distant enemies. Ships and planes transported soldiers and laborers from all corners of the world into the battles fought in Europe and the Near East. The aftermath of the war saw revolutions erupt across Europe and topple the tottering empire of Tsarist Russia. This revolution heralded the beginning of new global ideology, communism, which changed the trajectory of the modern world.

The world's fragile recovery after World War One was shattered by the collapse of the global financial system in the late 1920s. As banks closed and stock prices plummeted, first in the United States and then across the world, industries closed and millions were unemployed and on the streets and highways looking for work. Some, like the American welder John Scott, headed abroad in search of a job and a future. The Great Depression, in turn, weakened governments that were unable to meet the skyrocketing social needs of their citizens and prompted the emergence of radical solutions to the crisis. In Germany, the Depression led to the emergence of the Nazi state, which promised its citizens a return to the good old days. Those promises were hollow, as it ultimately delivered war and the Holocaust.

The transportation revolutions of the twentieth century became the armored tanks and bombers of World War Two. The Depression crippled many economies but strengthened elements in Japan bent on war and expansion. As Japan attacked China and soon launched assaults across the Pacific, it not only brought the United States into the conflict, but it also forced many innocent civilians into forced labor and detention camps.

Chapter 13 looks at the way travel shaped the end of World War Two and the global developments that would dominate the world for the rest of the century. As the battles of World War Two raged, the leaders of the Allied powers—Great Britain, the Soviet Union and the United States—held a series of meetings to coordinate the post-war peace. Although as allies they shared a common enemy, it was obvious that they did not share common goals. When the war was over, those differences and mutual distrust shaped political and international relations for much of the rest of the century. The Cold War, as it became known, played out in ideological debates and proxy wars. It spurred young men like the Argentinean Che Guevara to abandon a medical career and take up the weapons of revolution in Cuba and Africa. Demographics shifted, and the voice of younger generations demanded to be heard. The Beatles, perhaps the most famous musicians of all time, became an iconic symbol of change. The end of World War Two also saw movements to decolonize countries in Africa and Asia. Newly independent countries like Ghana on the west coast of Africa drew many to its promises of hope and freedom.

By the end of the twentieth century, the Cold War ended and so did most colonial regimes. Yet, despite those changes many of the challenges of the twentieth century persisted, and Chapter 14 considers the issues of change and continuity that mark world history in recent decades. Communist regimes collapsed in Eastern Europe and the Soviet Union but remained entrenched in places like China. The end of the apartheid regime in South Africa signaled an end to the system of racial injustice that had plagued that country for decades, but building a post-apartheid society has proved difficult. Many hoped that the end of the Cold War would see an era of peace. Sadly, wars and injustice have resulted in more refugees on the move than ever before. More people work abroad than ever, but the challenges of rights and security that are often part of migrant laborers' experiences remain numerous.

The year 2021 marks a world well into the second year of a global pandemic that has closed borders, shuttered global travel and crippled global supply chains in ways few would have imagined. Climate change is precipitating arguments about the future of the internal combustion engine; electric cars and clean energy are well-placed in conversations. Some now argue that new communication technologies, especially the internet and cell phones, are creating a future where people will be less inclined to travel at all. The Afterword of this book will take a look at how travel is shaping and being shaped by current events.

The history of the modern world is in many ways reflected in the history of travel in the modern world. Evolutions in transportation technology played a major role is shaping what the French historian Fernand Braudel called 'the limits of the possible'—where people could go, what they could do and how they lived. Migrations and forced movements of peoples altered the demography of continents and changed the historical trajectories of nations and empires. Travel changed people's understanding of the world they lived in and the values and goals they should aspire to. It has brought worlds long separate together and has made us more interdependent than ever. It has helped solve some of humanity's common challenges and created new ones.

Works Quoted

Philp, Paul, "What's in a Date: Starting a World History Course at 1200 CE," *World History Connected* (June 2020). https://worldhistoryconnected.press.uillinois.edu/17.2/forum_philp.html (Accessed November 11, 2021).

1 Global Travel and the Making of the Modern World

Introduction

For many years, October 12 was observed as the Columbus Day holiday across the Americas. In Latin America it is now celebrated under different terms. It was a day to commemorate when the small Spanish flotilla, captained by Christopher Columbus, landed on the shores of the Bahamas in 1492. Today, it is a day of reflection and remembrance. In Mexico it is now called Indigenous Peoples and Intercultural Dialogue Day. Venezuela heralds it as the Day of Indigenous Resistance. It no longer celebrates worlds coming together but rather worlds and peoples lost by the consequences of that day.

Even though the history of that day has been called into question, it is a day that changed the world forever. The Atlantic Ocean, a vast body of water that had separated the American and the Afro-Eurasian continents, was bridged, and continents were now connected. Europeans viewed the Columbus voyage as pivotal in order to reposition themselves in the larger world, to gain access to the wealth and trade of Asia that had largely alluded them. Although Columbus never expected to discover new worlds, his voyage did succeed in creating unfathomable opportunities that aligned with European colonial ambitions. In the wake of his voyage, France, England, Holland and others joined the exploration and colonial fray into the Americas and Asia.

By the end of the sixteenth century, travel across the Atlantic and Pacific Oceans, that was once infrequent and often accidental, had become regular and intentional. The European empires that dominated the Atlantic world carried with them a zealous ambition to discover, convert, colonize and conquer new worlds. This effort fundamentally reshaped the history of the modern world.

Ocean Travel and World History

World historians now consider the role that oceans have played in shaping global events through a field of study known as Thalassology. Rather than being seen as vast blue spaces between the land, they are increasingly analyzed as connectors not barriers. David Armitage's *World History as Oceanic History: Beyond Braudel* offers an introduction to this evolving field. When

DOI: 10.4324/9781003168690-2

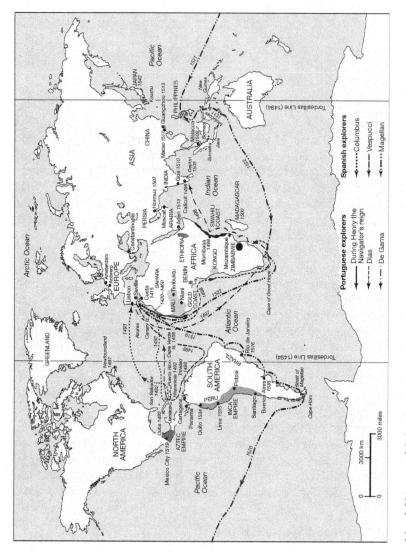

Map 1 Voyages of Columbus and Magellan

Thalassology first took hold, it focused on the Mediterranean world, the Atlantic World or the Indian Ocean. It has evolved to better understand relevant connections between bodies of water, peoples from distant lands and shared experiences. "The English East India Company," Armitage notes, "could not have functioned in the Indian Ocean without its Atlantic outpost on St. Helena. Until the opening of the Suez Canal, the Cape of Good Hope was the pivot between the Atlantic world and the Indian Ocean, a 'tavern of the seas' where empires joined, and oceans connected."

Transoceanic travel radically transformed the world during this period, building on land-travel routes that existed. The fabled Silk Road connecting Europe, the Near East and East Asia, while diminished in importance nonetheless continued to be used by traders, missionaries and travelers. The Inca roads that traversed the Andes continued to be used by Spanish conquistadors long after the Incan empire was destroyed. The peoples of North America traveled routes across the Rockies, across the Great Plains and into the Mississippi River Valley. Many Saharan routes continued to be used to as conduits for goods and ideas across Africa.

Setting the Stage: Oceanic Travel in the 1400s

Prior to the Spanish and Portuguese, in the late fifteenth century China was positioned to indeed become the global maritime power. In the early 1400s, a new Ming Emperor Yongle (r. 1402–1424) decided to enhance his prestige by establishing contact with and influence in territory outside of China. He did so by building a massive fleet of Chinese junks and ordering them to explore the Asian and Indian Ocean worlds. The voyages were referred to as the Chinese Treasure fleets.

Many of the ships were huge vessels that dwarfed other ships afloat. The largest ships of the fleet measured 400 feet long and over 150 feet wide with four decks and watertight chambers. Nine masts with sails of silk rose high above the decks. (By comparison, Columbus' ship, the *Santa Maria*, built close to one hundred years later, was 80 feet long and had only three masts.) Some voyages used over sixty of these ships and numerous support vessels; there were seven voyages in total that sailed between 1405 and 1433.

Carrying precious goods produced by the empire—silks, porcelains and tea—the fleet hoped to impress the distant kingdoms it sailed to with the wealth and sophistication of the Chinese. The ships also carried soldiers, thousands of them. Their presence was intended to also make the wider world aware of the empire's military strength and for it to be acknowledged accordingly. It is important to note that these fleets did not attempt to establish colonies or seize lands; they were more interested in establishing trading connections and proving their power rather than expanding China's empire.

The Treasure fleet brought back medicines, spices and other precious commodities. Three of the six expeditions sailed across the Indian Ocean to the coasts of East Africa; some brought back giraffes to be displayed in the imperial court. While they largely succeeded in fulfilling the Emperor's goals when he died in 1424, a new emperor, with new concerns and priorities, began to ignore and later abandon the fleets. The last voyage was in 1433, and when it came back to Nanjing Harbor it was ordered scuttled. Historians continue to debate the reasons why the new emperor turned away from the opportunities China had to be a transregional/global naval power, but what is clear is that that decision opened the doors for the emerging European maritime empires to fill the void left by China.

Europe Enters the Global Stage

Transoceanic travel was not new, but the developments of the second half of the fifteenth century and into the sixteenth century were different. New maritime technologies in ship design, navigational methods and cartography facilitated travel in unprecedented ways. These developments reshaped global trade, cultural exchanges and systems of political and military power that still influence the world over a half a millennium later.

Prior to the 'voyages of discovery' by Portuguese and Spanish adventurers in the later 1400s, Europeans had largely been limited in their transcontinental exploration. Various African kingdoms controlled key ports along the West and Swahili Coasts. The rise of the Ottoman Empire, marked by the capture of Constantinople in 1543, effectively shut off any direct access between Europe and the lucrative land routes that had been traveled by Marco Polo and others in prior centuries. Arab, Indian and Asian traders sailed on the monsoon winds across the Indian Ocean and South China Sea, largely controlling and benefiting from profitable trades in spices, medicines and other highly desired products.

Europe's changing position in the world was predicated by three key developments. First, Spanish and Portuguese military success against the Islamic states along the Iberian Peninsula freed them to pursue transregional goals, convinced that their Catholic/Christian dominance over Islam was divinely ordained. When Christopher Columbus wrote to the Spanish crown trying to convince them of the opportunity to make connections with the riches of the Indies, he was inspired by such thinking. He penned his letter while looking over the recently breached walls of the last Muslim stronghold on the Peninsula, Granada. "The present year of 1492 after Your Highnesses had brought to an end the war with the Moors who ruled Europe. . . ," he wrote, "had now made the Peninsula free 'of all idolatries and heresies.' Please consider sending me, Christopher Columbus, to the said regions of India . . . and to see how their conversion to our Holy Faith may be undertaken." Similarly, the Portuguese were successful after decades of incessant warfare against Muslim forces in gaining footholds along the West African coast and offshore islands. Success led to even greater hope that expansion would garner heavenly favor and earthly riches. Eventually, rivalry between these two Iberian powers spurred desire for expansion in order to outmaneuver and ultimately defeat the other.

Ambition and religious conviction were not sufficient to accomplish the global domination that Spain and Portugal desired; they also needed the technology to traverse open oceans. In the minds of most mid-fifteenth-century Europeans, the Atlantic Ocean was, "a desolate place." Even though Scandinavian Vikings had sailed across the Atlantic using the bridges of the North Atlantic islands centuries before, that knowledge had been largely forgotten, replaced with ancient tales of monsters and danger that lurked beyond the safety of the coast.

Given the challenges of navigating the ocean and the inadequacies of their ships, these treacherous conditions did not augur well for sailors who ventured outside the relative safety of coastline travel in the Mediterranean and Baltic Seas. Whether powered by oarsmen or by a single sail, galley ships used in these areas were simply not designed for longer open water voyages. Rough ocean conditions rendered small side-oar rudders useless as they had limited contact with the sea.

Poorly designed ocean-going vessels were only one of the technological impediments that European seafarers faced; they also needed better methods of navigation. Most medieval maps were highly schematic and tended to represent the world in relationship to the divine plan rather than with geographic accuracy. There were accurate maps of some trades routes frequented by European merchants, but these maps, called *portolan charts*, while useful for navigating Europe's coastline, were worthless if one lost sight of land. A quadrant coupled with knowledge of the constellations visible in the northern hemisphere gave European sailors a good sense of latitude (their north-south position), but this knowledge was of little use once they sailed south of the equator, and the often stormy, cloudy weather made celestial observation impossible.

Over the course of several centuries, European sailors developed or borrowed the technology and knowledge necessary to make ocean travel possible. Historians debate exactly which innovations came from where and when. For example, they know that the magnetic compass that allowed sailors to determine direction in any kind of weather was first used by the Chinese and probably came to European travelers via their contacts with Arab sailors. They still speculate, however, as to whether the rear-keel rudder, which allowed ships to sail in rough waters and against the wind, came to Iberian sailors through contacts with Baltic sailors or possibly through knowledge of Arab ships in the Indian Ocean; both had used them for centuries. They wonder whether use of multiple sails and lateen, or triangular sails, which allowed their ships greater maneuverability, was developed from a process of trial and error or whether it came via sources that had seen Arab and Chinese ships in the Indian Ocean. Although questions remain, historians are confident that by the late medieval period Iberian fisherman and sailors developed the caravel, which eventually made transoceanic travel a reality. The caravel, a relatively small ship holding a maximum crew of fifty, could sail against the wind and was maneuverable enough to sail tight to the coast and even up larger rivers. Its rounded bottom also made it faster and therefore able to withstand longer voyages. Speed of travel, in turn, lessened at least some of the maladies—scurvy and tensions from the cramped, fetid conditions—that scuttled earlier voyages.

The Voyages of Christopher Columbus

The Christopher Columbus fleet was comprised of three caravels that sailed across the Atlantic in 1492. Columbus was named admiral of the venture, but given the size of the three caravels and a crew of eighty-seven men, the title seems every bit as exaggerated as his later claims of success. Columbus had a less-than-accurate understanding of geography. As his son later wrote: "The Admiral inferred that since the whole sphere (world) was small, of necessity that space of the third part which Marinus [a geographer who adopted Ptolemy's maps] left as unknown had to be small and therefore could be navigated in less time."

Columbus and his crew left their Spanish port of Palos de la Frontera on August 3, 1492, and headed south to the Canary Islands where they resupplied. From there, they headed west across the Atlantic. As days ticked by, with endless water ahead, his crew became increasingly nervous and questioned whether he knew what he was doing. Threats of mutinies surfaced but finally, after thirty-five days at sea, in the early morning hours of October 12, 1492, the crew of the *Pinta*, the fastest of the fleet's ships, issued the signal that land had been sighted. A faint light, indicative (the crew surmised) of fires from a distant village or town, had been spotted. Together with the captains of the other ships and a small crew, they splashed into the water and walked to the beach. They thought they were in the Indies, but they were somewhere in the Caribbean, in the Bahamas.

Most of what we know about what happened that day comes from a version of Columbus' diary. The original diary does not exist. The copy we have, while based on his original journal, was excerpted and summarized by his friend Bartolemé De Las Casas some thirty years later. The entries/journals abstracted by Las Casas challenge how historians understand the first encounters by Columbus. However, even given these caveats the journal remains an indispensable source for understanding these historic events.

According to the journal, as they approached land the admiral "called the two captains and to the others who had jumped ashore . . . and said that they should witness, in the presence of all, he would take, in fact he did take, possession of the said island for the king and queens his lords." It was a gesture that would be repeated by European explorers over the next decades and centuries as they ventured further into the world. This act of declaring possession of a foreign land is widely known as colonization.

On January 4, the *Niña* set sail for home. A few months later Columbus pulled into safe harbor in Spain and presented the wonders of his voyage to King Ferdinand and Queen Isabella. It was not much, some gold, but not nearly the amount they likely anticipated. A few samples of cotton, spices and fauna were put on display. So, too, were several Indians that Columbus had kidnapped and dragged back to Spain. They were presented as symbols of the exotic voyage he had undertaken, with the hope of using them as interpreters for the return trip he had already started to plan. Despite the meager treasures he brought home, Ferdinand and Isabella agreed to finance another trip.

Shortly after Columbus returned and word of his success leaked out, the Portuguese crown appealed to the pope to protect the land claims that the papacy had previously granted them in return for their fight against Islam. In 1494, the Treaty of Tordesillas drew a line of demarcation 370 kilometers west of the Canary Islands. Everything to the west was to be Spanish territory and everything east, Portuguese. The race to stake claim was on. Amerigo Vespucci captained a Spanish fleet a few years later that sailed much of the South American Atlantic coasts. His widely published reports earned him the title 'Discoverer of the Americas.' Not to be outdone, the Portuguese renewed their efforts to find a sea route to the riches of the East.

The Columbian Exchange

Columbus returned to the Indies in 1493 to stake claim to lands promised him by the Spanish crown and to continue his search for the wealth of the East that he was convinced must be close at hand. The crown supplied him with seventeen ships and twelve hundred men, most of them heavily armed and ready for battle. Five priests went along to serve the needs of the crew and begin the process of converting the indigenous populations. This voyage was clearly one of conquest, conversion and colonization more so than exploration.

Also on board Columbus' fleet were two dozen horses and unknown quantities of cattle, pigs, goats, chickens, seeds and plantings for wheat, sugar and more. Hundreds of years later, it is difficult to imagine how dramatic the introduction of Old World livestock was to the New World, but think of Argentina without cattle or the American plains without horses. These large, hoofed creatures that were unloaded from his ships in 1493 were unknown in any part of the New World (with the exception of the relatively isolated llamas of the Andes Mountains), and they rapidly became adapted to their new environment. In Mexico, for example, a small number of cattle were first introduced around the time of Cortés' landing on Veracruz in 1517. By 1579 the conquistadors had spread throughout Mexico and so had their cattle. Some ranches in the north reported herds as large as 150,000 head. Horses also spread rapidly, and by the time European explorers found their way into North America they encountered vast herds of horses roaming the plains. Pigs adapted to the Caribbean climate and became abundant on many islands within a few generations.

In other ways, seeds and plant cuttings were equally important in the Columbian Exchange. In 1493, the plant cutting carried by Columbus' fleet that most radically altered the Caribbean was sugar. Sugar plantations were already profitable businesses in the Spanish and Portuguese islands off Africa, and Columbus wanted to transplant that success to his new colony. The cane, itself a grass, literally grew like a weed; and, in a matter of decades after being planted at

Columbus' colony, Isabela (now known as Dominican Republic), it was cultivated throughout the islands and on the east coast of South America (Brazil).
Profits from sugar made his successors on Caribbean plantations some of the
wealthiest men in the early modern world. Soon after, the sugar industry's
intense labor needs ushered in the enslavement of indigenous peoples and later
Africans.

The Columbian Exchange was certainly not a one-way street. Ships returning to Spain in 1494 carried many agricultural products that transformed the
European diet and lifestyle, and over time they spread into Eurasia and Africa.
Columbus had been offered tobacco when he first set foot in the New World,
but after nibbling it he threw it away. By the second voyage it was one of many
plant products shipped back to Europe. Peanuts, pineapples, cacao (source of
chocolate), papayas, manioc (a key carbohydrate of Africa), and a variety of
peppers and beans were all 'discovered' by Europeans and sent back across the
Atlantic. As explorers made their way to the American mainland, tomatoes,
potatoes, pumpkins and corn (maize) were added to the Old World diet.

The exchange of food impacted much more than the palate. Cattle and pigs
provided significant sources of protein and calories for indigenous populations. Horses made it possible for Indians in North America to hunt buffalo on
the plains. In West Africa, manioc, a bush that grows in almost any temperate
soil became the dominant source of calories. In Europe, the introduction of
the potato rivaled the role of the manioc in Africa by providing a calorie-rich
food source that could be grown in soils often inhospitable to other crops. The
potato also played a significant role in the growth of the European population
that, in turn, developed into the labor pool necessary for industrialization.

Much of the Columbian Exchange was intentional, but much of it was not.
Ships also carried rats, insects and, most importantly, pathogens. This was the
case with Columbus' second voyage. Reports from fellow colonizers indicated
that illness was rampant on the voyage, plaguing both animals and humans.
Columbus himself was laid low with a high fever shortly after they established
Isabela (Hispaniola in Hatti). Disease that plagued the crew soon passed to the
local populations. In a letter to his benefactors in early 1494, Columbus apologized for not being able to send more gold back with the fleet, but, he said, "the
greater part of the people we employed fell suddenly ill."

The introduction of diseases such as small pox, malaria, yellow fever, influenza and even the common cold had devastating consequences for the Native
American populations of people previously sheltered from many of the diseases that for centuries had ravaged the Eurasian and North African worlds.
Each was a killer in the Old World, but in the Americas (where genetic resistance to them had not been built up over centuries of exposure) their effects
were close to genocidal—especially combined with war, servitude and starvation. A German traveling to Hispaniola in 1529 noted the extent of the disaster: "[O]f five hundred thousand Indians or inhabitants of various nations and
languages that existed on the island forty years ago, there remain fewer than
twenty thousand living."

Sadly, diseases often traveled faster than humans. By the time British explorers began to penetrate the coastal regions of North America in the late seventeenth century, they found few indigenous peoples living in these 'virgin territories.' This was not because peoples had not lived there; it was because European diseases had already made their presence known and much of the indigenous population had been wiped out.

Like other aspects of the Columbian Exchange, pathogens also made their way from west to east. The most notable was syphilis, a sexually transmitted disease that crew members most likely got though relations with indigenous women. Women made up only five to six percent of all Europeans traveling to the New World around 1540, and thereafter they remained a small minority, less than thirty percent of all immigrants. Many conquistadors, whether married in Spain or not, took up relationships with indigenous women—some through marriage, more likely as concubines or through rape. Sexually transmitted diseases were not unknown in the Old World, but the introduction of these new strains of syphilis had devastating consequences in the decades after Columbus' ships returned to Europe.

Rounding the Cape

Columbus originally sought a direct route to the riches of the Indies to secure trading opportunities with China and the Great Kahn. While, in some ways the Americas got in the way, the goal to find a route to the riches of the East never faded for the Spanish or for their European rivals. In fact, as news of the discoveries filtered back through the courts of Europe, the race to not only claim new lands in the Americas but to find new routes to the East intensified. Portugal soon took the lead when Vasco de Gama led a small fleet around the Cape of Good Hope and into the Indian Ocean in 1497.

Unlike European sailors who first made their way to the west coast of Africa or the Americas, the Portuguese voyages into the Indian Ocean and beyond sailed into a world accustomed to foreigners and international commerce. For centuries Arab traders and Islamic scholars had been sailing monsoon winds on semiannual journeys around the Indian Ocean and though the China Seas. Marco Polo had sailed back to China via these routes, and Islamic travelers had plied these waters during the fourteenth century. Nevertheless, the Portuguese expeditions into these waters were especially significant.

Why, if travel and commerce appeared to be well established in this part of the world, did the arrival of Portuguese and Spanish ships have such an impact on world history? Why, if the peoples of this part of the world were accustomed to encounters with languages, ethnicities and cultural customs other than their own, did the initial contacts with these Europeans make such a lasting impression?

The simplest answer is that, in rounding the Cape and entering the Indian Ocean, the Portuguese opened up a direct trade route for the first time between their homeland and the East. No longer did Arab traders and, for much of this period their Mediterranean counterparts in Italy and Greece, enjoy the crucial and profitable role as commercial middlemen. No longer did Europeans have to depend on Arab traders or merchants and caravans on the Silk Road for access to the luxuries of China. For the first time, Europeans—especially Europeans based on the Atlantic seaboard—could directly participate in the global economy, and for the Portuguese, that direct access meant incredible wealth. Even though Da Gama's first trip around the Cape did not go according to plan—Arabs unhappy with his meddling in their profitable world forced him to return to Portugal with only a few spices bought at inflated prices—he still made a three thousand percent profit.

Acquiring access to more of this rich trade potential in the Indian Ocean world was not going to be easy for the Portuguese. For centuries, Muslim and Hindu merchants had created a mutually beneficial trading network. The Portuguese, when they first arrived, could offer little in the way of goods or services to trade. The weapons they had sold in West Africa were already in use in the Indian Ocean. Indian spices, cloth and porcelains (many of which were of better quality and cheaper than those offered by the Portuguese) were readily available. Quickly, Da Gama and his followers surmised that the only way they could get in on the action was through brute force. They were motivated by the desire for wealth with a crusade-like religious zeal—especially against Muslims, who dominated much of the Indian Ocean trade.

Religious zealotry, military aggression and poor quality of trading goods made the first Portuguese expeditions into the Indian Ocean and China Sea world less than welcome by others already moving and trading in the region. Some locals were willing to see what the newcomers had to offer, and others saw opportunities in Portuguese guns and ships that could play to their advantage in their own quest for land and trade. Portuguese ships were much better designed and equipped for naval engagement than most local vessels. This was likely the case in the more remote islands of Indonesia, where firearms and large vessels were rare. Still, many locals quickly learned to mistrust the avaricious interlopers.

The Portuguese responded to the indifference and rejection with more forceful attempts to destroy their rivals and establish a hegemonic control of the area. The challenge was that they had neither the people nor resources to achieve such brazen goals. Instead, they established a series of forts and factories (merchant posts) in key ports throughout the Indian Ocean and sent out their fleets to destroy rivals and demand tribute from allies. These tactics worked only as long as there were no more-powerful opponents on the horizon.

Portugal's lead in the race to Asia was short-lived. By the 1520s a Spanish fleet under the command of Ferdinand Magellan had succeeded, barely, in rounding the tip of Cape Horn in South America and sailing into the Pacific. For the next three-and-a-half months it struggled across the vast ocean, its crew wilting under the intense sun, the relentless waves and lack of food and water. "We ate biscuits," one crew member recorded, "which was no longer biscuit, but powder of biscuits swarming with worms for they had eaten the good. It stank strongly of the urine of rats. We drank yellow water that had been putrid for many days." Scurvy, the malady of sailors who do not get enough vitamin C, afflicted many. Gums softened and teeth fell out.

Somehow, even after the fleet survived the transpacific journey, disaster struck Magellan's fleet. As they landed on the island of Cerbu in the Philippines, the local leader got into a squabble with the Spanish captain, and Magellan ordered retaliation. According to a diary kept by one of the crewmen on board, Magellan's crew of forty-nine men found themselves confronted by over a thousand armed and angry locals. After an hour-long struggle, Magellan was slain and the remnants of his force fled. Eventually a skeleton crew of the voyage that had left Spain years before returned home. It was indeed the first noted circumnavigation of the globe.

The Manilla Galleons

The Spanish believed that the true glory of Magellan's accomplishment was the opportunity that came from his claim of the Philippines archipelago. The Philippines became a valuable colony and ultimately a very key point for the transportation of Spanish gold and silver between the New World and Asia.

Transferring wealth from the Spanish Empire in the Americas to Asia, where it was used to trade for the riches of the region, required extensive use of earlier-established networks together with transoceanic travel. After the Spanish conquistadors took control of the Incan Empire, they used the vast road system the Incas had built to extract the resources of the former empire. *Cerro Ricco*, which means "rich mountain," was a silver mine in modern Bolivia. During its heyday it produced four-fifths of all the silver mined by the Spanish. The 'rich mountain' was an arduous ten-week mule trek from the capital of the Spanish Empire in South America, Lima.

At first, Spanish colonists used the tried and true system of forced local Indian labor to mine Cerro Rico. Such labor in this remote landscape with little agricultural resources quickly exhausted the surrounding population, and the Spanish overlords began to import forced labor from farther afield. They also needed to import food and other resources, and gradually the town of Potosi emerged. As word of the riches got out, more and more colonial adventurers made their way across the mountains hoping to stake their claim on the silver or to make their fortune serving the needs of the growing town. Potosí grew, and by 1600 over 160,000 people were crammed in the often haphazard and ramshackle buildings of what was now the world's highest and largest city, on a par with London and Amsterdam. One observer, circa 1570, noted, "New people arrive by hour, attracted to the smell of silver."

The wealth generated by the mines of Cerro Rico fueled a dramatic transformation of the world economy. During its most productive era, Potosí produced four-fifths of all the Spanish empire's silver (another major source of production was Zacatecas in Mexico)—an amount that practically doubled the amount of silver available worldwide. In Europe, this influx of wealth triggered an era of Spanish political and military dominance. The King of Spain, Charles I, and his successor, Ferdinand II, used it to finance wars of religion against the Protestant kings of England and the Holy Roman Empire and to support the ongoing struggle against the Ottoman Turks.

Potosí silver also changed the relationship between Europe and the Asian World. For a long time Europeans merchants had been hampered in their attempts to penetrate Asian markets, particularly those in China, because Europeans had few goods to interest them. But Chinese merchants and rulers as well as Spice Island kings and traders had a strong desire for silver, and the mines of Potosí gave them all they wanted. In return for the silver, Chinese porcelains, silks, cloves and nutmeg became available to the European world in quantities previously unknown. To facilitate the transfer of Andean silver and Asian luxuries between the two worlds, Spain developed an elaborate system of moving goods. Once the silver made it to Lima it was loaded on ships and sailed north to Acapulco, Mexico. There, along with silver and gold collected from Mexican mines, it was held until the favorable late winter winds made travel feasible to carry valuable cargo across the Pacific. The Marianas Islands, Guam and especially the Philippine Archipelago became important supply stations for the fleet, and Spanish imperialism spread into those areas. Manila became a key point of access. The return voyage in the summer would sail north to pick up the favorable winds, taking the ships close to Japan and then across the Pacific to the shores of California before returning to Acapulco.

Conclusion

The Manilla Trade filled the Spanish coffers and helped fund continued expansion of the Spanish empire in Europe and around the world. It also encouraged other European powers like England, France and Holland to launch their own global initiatives. By the end of the century these European countries would be sending out expeditions of discovery and conquest. They would send merchants to gain access to the benefits of global trade, scientists to discover new flora and fauna, missionaries to bring the peoples of foreign lands to their God and settlers to make distant lands their own. Global expansion led to the unprecedented movement of peoples around the world. Lands and peoples that had been significantly separate were now bound, for better or worse, inextricably together.

End Materials Chapter 1

Works Quoted

Armitage, David, "World History as Oceanic History: Beyond Braudel," *The Historical Review/La Revue Historique*, vol. 15 (2019): 343–364.

Cook, Noble David, *Born to Die: Disease and the New World Conquest, 1492–1650* (Cambridge: Cambridge University Press, 1998).

Dunn, Oliver and James E. Kelly, Jr., eds., *The 'Diaro' of Christopher Columbus's First Voyage to America, 1492–1493* (Norman, OK: University of Oklahoma Press, 1989).

Pigafetta, Antonio, *Magellan's Voyage: A Narrative of the First Circumnavigation* (New York: Dover Publications, 1969).

Pomeranz, Kenneth and Steven Topik, *The World That Trade Created: Society, Culture and the World Economy, 1400 to the Present*, 4th ed. (New York: Routledge, 2018).

Additional Readings

Benjamin, Thomas, Timothy Hall and David Rutherford, eds., *The Atlantic World in the Age of Empires* (Boston: Houghton Mifflin, 2002).

Crosby, Jr., Alfred, *The Columbian Exchange: Biological and Cultural Consequences of 1492* (Westport, CT: Greenwood Press, 1972).

Davidann, Jon Thares and Marc Jason Gilbert, *Cross-Cultural Encounters in Modern World History* (Boston: Pearson, 2013).

del Castillo, Bernal Diaz, *The True History of the Conquest of New Spain* (Indianapolis, IN: Hackett Publishing, 2012).

Gosch, Steven and Peter Stearns, *Premodern Travel in World History* (New York: Routledge, 2008).

Kearny, Milo, *The Indian Ocean in World History* (London: Routledge, 2003).

Lunenfeld, Marvin, *1492: Discovery, Invasion, Encounter* (Lexington, MA: D.C. Heath & Co., 1991).

Mann, Charles, *1491: New Revelations on the Americas Before Columbus* (New York: Vintage Books, 2005).

Padgen, Anthony, *European Encounters with the New World* (New Haven: Yale University Press, 1993).

Roy, Tirthankar and Giorgio Riello, *Global Economic History* (London: Bloomsbury Press, 2019).

2 The Jesuits and the Making of a Global Missionary Order

Introduction

The Society of Jesus, more commonly known as the Jesuits, was founded as a Catholic religious order in 1540 during a time of tremendous religious upheaval in Europe. For the better part of a century the papacy, the central symbol of the Catholic Church, had been roiled in controversy as many popes had eschewed their heavenly calling for earthly desires. Moreover, many of the faithful were calling into question the basic practices and tenants of the Church that had long been irrefutable. In 1517 a common German monk, Martin Luther, precipitated what would become a religious revolution when he publicly challenged the Church to defend its practices. Luther's provocation resonated with many who felt, like him, that the Catholic Church was threatening their chance for eternal salvation. Others joined in, raising their voices against the Catholic Church, and by the time Ignatius of Loyola asked Pope Paul III for permission to establish a religious order dedicated to restoring the universal Catholic Church, Europe was fractiously divided.

The founding of the Jesuit order coincided with the push for European colonial outreach around the globe. Spanish and Portuguese Catholics legitimized global expansion as part of an ongoing struggle against Islam after their success at in pushing the Muslim Moors out of the Iberian Peninsula. Colonizers saw religious conversion of indigenous peoples as a central part of their imperial mission and as rationale for taking control of territories across the globe.

Ignatius and his followers hoped to play a role in this emerging global religious quest, vowing "to go anywhere His Holiness [the pope] will order, whether among the faithful or the infidels, without pleading an excuse and without requesting any expenses for the journey for the sake of matters pertaining to the worship of God and the welfare of the Christian religion." It was a promise that would see Jesuit priests traveling around the world in the coming decades and centuries. One of the first Jesuit missionaries, Francis Xavier, accompanied the Portuguese to colonial enclaves throughout the Indian Ocean and into East Asia. They followed the Spanish to Central and South America, to the Philippines and to the Pacific Ocean archipelagoes, and the French to Canada.

DOI: 10.4324/9781003168690-3

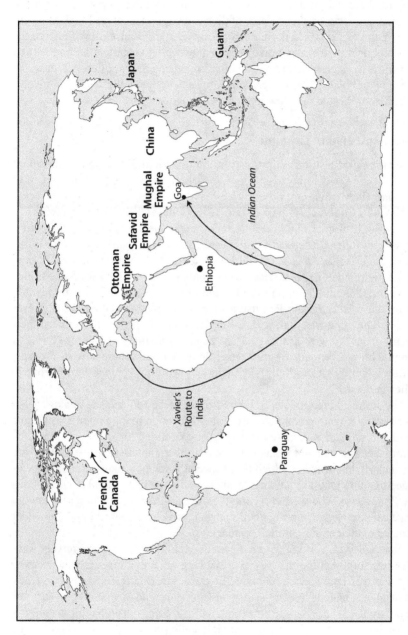

Map 2 Key Places for the Sixteenth Through Eighteenth Centuries

The Jesuits were prolific writers, and the journals and letters documenting their extensive travels provide vital information about the early modern world and the cross-cultural encounters they had in different places. They have become, for better or worse, some of the most important sources we have about many parts of the world during this period. Better because often they are the only reports we have, and worse because they were European missionaries and and wrote through a distinctly Catholic European lens that often left the voice of the other unheard. Nonetheless historians have found the Jesuits an invaluable, if complicated, window into the early modern world.

The Jesuits Go to Ethiopia

One of the first Jesuit missions, a mission that highlights both the important role that the Jesuits played in shaping early modern cross-cultural encounters and their often-conflicting views and treatments of peoples in other lands, is in Ethiopia. As part of one of the oldest Christian communities in the world, Ethiopians had been traveling to the Near East and Rome to converse with other Christians for centuries. In the sixteenth century, as Europeans began to take a greater interest in Africa, Europeans began to journey to the highlands of East Africa. Their goals were to unite with these Ethiopian Christians in the hope that it could build on their victories in pushing Islam out of the Iberian Peninsula by now pushing Muslims out of North Africa. The hope was that, with Ethiopian support, they could squeeze their enemy from the west and east. They began to identify the land's Christian kings with a legendary figure Prester John, a ruler somewhere in the East who was committed to fight Islam and was awaiting contact with European allies to do so.

The Jesuits were anxious to be part of this renewed crusade against Islam and quickly volunteered to be part of the delegation that traveled to Ethiopia. As the missionaries prepared to leave, Loyola urged his envoys to learn the local languages and not to take "away from them anything in which they are particularly interested or which they especially value . . . and without any violence to souls long accustomed to another way of life." He also encouraged the Portuguese, who were directing the expedition to bring along people with practical knowledge in bridge building and medicine to demonstrate the wider benefits of the coming of the foreigners.

This policy of working with indigenous peoples rather than coercively forcing them to accept the missionary's teaching became known as accommodation and was famously summarized by the Jesuit Duarte de Sande: "In truth, among these nations that are so distant from ours, and have laws and customs so different it is necessary to enter with theirs to come out with ours, accommodating ourselves to them in what our Holy Faith permits, in this way to divulge and teach our holy doctrine, which they would receive in no other way." Jesuits have been praised by many for their more tolerant attitudes toward the other and their less aggressive approach to missionary work.

There were clear limits to accommodation, however, as Duarte's definition reveals. Accommodation stopped where it conflicted with the Holy Faith. This principle was also clear in Ignatius' instructions to the Jesuits going to Ethiopia, and in the end the Jesuits refused to accept Ethiopian Christianity as anything but heresy. And when Ethiopians refused to give up their faith and values, the Jesuits turned against them. Later missives became more denigrating of the Ethiopians and clearly demonstrated an elitist superiority to them. Near the end of the mission, in the early 1600s, some Jesuits were advocating armed intervention to bring the Ethiopians to Catholicism.

While the Jesuits did convert some key leaders in the beginning, their missionary work soon provoked religious and political backlash by many elements of Ethiopian society. By the early seventeenth century, new rulers expelled the Jesuits, and the empire, torn now by religious factionalism, descended into civil war. It was a story that would be repeated in many other places as the Jesuits developed their global missions. It is a story that reflects the importance of the Jesuits in shaping encounters in the early modern world and that often resulted unforeseen consequences for all sides.

Francis Xavier and the Founding of the Jesuit Mission in India

As the Jesuits were making their way to Ethiopia, they were also beginning missions across Asia. In 1540 King John of Portugal requested their help in Goa, the center of his emerging empire in the Indian Ocean. One of the Jesuits ordered there was Francis Xavier. On April 7, 1541, he sailed with the annual Portuguese fleet from Lisbon. The first part of the journey was slow and miserable. The fleet stalled for over a month off the coast of Guinea in West Africa when the doldrums hit and the favorable winds died. The heat was oppressive, the conditions crowded, the food and water fetid, and the bugs a great nuisance. Finally, Xavier says, "by the grace of God" the winds returned, and they made their way to the Portuguese enclave of Mozambique, on the east coast of Africa.

Because of the delayed start, the whole crew was forced to wait for six months in Mozambique as they once again awaited favorable sailing conditions. The tropical climate plagued the crew. Xavier reported that eighty crewmembers died during this period. In a letter to Ignatius, he apologized for the delay in writing because he had been sick since his arrival, noting that he was just that morning being bled for the seventh time.

By the end of February 1542, they finally left Mozambique. The ship made its way up the east coast of Africa, stopping at ports where Portuguese merchants had set up shop. On May 6, 1542, Xavier finally landed in Goa, a journey that had taken thirteen months. Typically, although nothing was typical during early modern oceanic travel, it was supposed to take half that time.

In one of Xavier's first letters back to Rome he describes Goa as a "completely Christian city," but, in fact it was anything but. It was one of the central *entrepôt* of the whole Indian Ocean region and, as such, incredibly diverse. A Jesuit missionary in 1560 noted that the population [of Goa] includes:

> Chaldaeans, Hebrews, Greeks, Armenians, Janissaries, Russians, Arabs, Persians, Moors, Jews, Brahmans, Yogis, Sannyasis, Fartakis, Nubians, Khorassanians, Moguls, Gujaratis, Dekhanis, Canarim, Kanarese, Malabaris, Singhalese, Malays, Peguans, Bengalis, Kaffirs, Japanese, Chinese, Malucos, Pathans, Makassars and many others.

At first, Xavier was sent to minister to the Portuguese Catholics but soon turned to a broader effort to proselytize across the region. It was a challenging task, to say the least, since most had little interest in his religion and he had little to convince them of its value.

He was also trying to manage the mission; he had few Jesuits with him, and support in Rome was far away. During the early years the founder of the Jesuits, Ignatius of Loyola, spent countless hours in his small study in Rome writing letters to his followers, approving budgets, consoling and exhorting them. Many of those letters, however, never made it to intended destinations. It was common for Xavier, for example, to write several versions of the same letter back to his superiors, expecting that most would never make it. Even when they did, so much time had passed that the information they contained was almost worthless. "Two years and nine months ago I sailed from Portugal," he wrote on January 15, 1544, to Rome from Cochin, India. "During that time I have been in India I received only one letter from you written on January 13 1542."

Many Jesuits did not make it to their destinations either. Luke Clossey, in his study of the early Jesuit organization, for example, notes that between 1600 and 1623 there were thirty-four Portuguese ships with Jesuits aboard sailing from Lisbon to Goa. Of those thirty-four, eight were wrecked, two captured and nine forced to return home; more than half never made it. Liam Brockey's investigation of the Jesuit missions to China concluded that "the sea voyage caused the death of half the prospective missionaries who embarked." In the same letter noted earlier, Xavier reminisced that "in these regions my dearest brothers, my recreations consist in frequently calling you to mind and the time when, through the great mercy of God our Lord, I knew you and conversed with you." Xavier must have sensed that he may never return to his European home, that he may never see those with whom he founded the order. He died in Macao, Asia, ten years later. Death abroad was so common, Clossey notes, that martyrdom was a recruiting pitch for those called to the global missionary order.

The Jesuits had to balance their goals as missionaries with the goals of their benefactors, who were often more interested in establishing empires and colonies. In Xavier's case this benefactor was the King of Portugal, John III. In his letters Xavier often complained that the Portuguese treatment of the peoples of South Asia was wrecking his chances to bring them to the Catholic faith.

In a letter dated 1544, he goes on to say that he excoriated the Portuguese merchants/pirates who were fighting for control of Sri Lanka. "They must be deleted from the book of life and not reckoned with the just. Wrongdoing here is so common here that I see no remedy for it, since all go the way of '*rapio, rapis*' [I steal, you steal]."

Xavier was also willing to call out the king if he felt his benefactor was failing in his duties to the Jesuit mission. In a 1549 correspondence he castigated the king directly. "Your Highness is not strong enough to spread the faith of Christ in India, though strong enough to take and possess all of India's temporal wealth. . . . I am therefore fleeing to Japan."

Xavier Travels to Japan

The missionary's reasons for "fleeing to Japan" were more complicated than just his frustration with King John's policies. By 1549 Xavier was also frustrated with his inability to win more converts in the Indian Ocean world. A chance meeting with a Japanese man in Indonesia who was fleeing murder charges from his native land convinced Xavier that Japan had more potential for missionary work. He understood it to be a unified land with one ruler, a single language and an educated populace. For the European Xavier, this model of a single ruler who could hold sway over a vast populace, with only one language to master and one culture to dissect, seemed both comfortable and propitious. After all, the Jesuits had focused a lot of their early energies in Europe and on ingratiating themselves with royalty in the hopes of getting both financial support and religious influence. Moreover, as a fledging global religious order, the chance to convert the emperor and win the whole of his subjects held great appeal.

Traveling from the Jesuit missions in Goa, India, to Japan was every bit as complicated as getting from Lisbon to Goa. Ships had to sail with the seasonal monsoon winds that begin blowing from the northwest in the spring. In a couple months, if all went well, one would arrive in Malacca, Malaysia, for a quick resupply. Later, Xavier advised those who followed that under no circumstances should they stop to trade in China; if you do, he warned, the four-to-five-month trip could easily take a year and a half.

Xavier spent three-and-a-half years in Japan, during which time he found it far from the unified ordered society he had been promised. Instead Japan was in the midst of a violent civil war between warring samurai factions. While some liked his religious ideas as a solace to their unsettled lives, more of them likely wanted access to guns that his European connections provided. He remained discouraged by his limited successes and was frustrated that he was never able to meet the emperor. He soon discovered that the emperor was a ruler in name only and it was the shoguns, the regional military leaders, who really ruled.

As Xavier spent more time in Japan, he came to understand that missionary success depended on fully understanding the culture and values of the peoples he sought to convert. In Goa his methods had often been superficial. He would arrive in a community, teach a few willing locals essential prayers and basic creeds and be gone, hoping the seeds he planted for future Jesuits would bring about a garden of Catholic faithful. Japan was a different matter. Buddhism was rooted in society, and he quickly realized that he needed to engage and convert Buddhist leaders if he was to have any chance to make inroads. That meant learning the languages, the theology of Buddhism as well as its social and cultural norms. Over time, this deep understanding of local culture became one of the key markers of the Jesuit missionary playbook of conversion strategies. The Jesuits also realized that these studies would help them win support in Europe, where their reports on the peoples they encountered were used to legitimize their missions. In places like Japan and China, where the Jesuits were few and the power dynamics of the region limited European influences, missionaries adapted their approach, allowing for local customs to be retained by converts.

Matteo Ricci in China: Conversion and Accommodation

Perhaps the most famous practitioner of the Jesuit principle of accommodation was the Italian Jesuit Matteo Ricci. The young priest had gone to China in 1582. His lofty goal was to unlock China for Catholicism. It was a herculean task, given that few foreigners were even allowed into the massive kingdom within the Ming dynasty, where there was skepticism of foreign ideas. He knew he need more than his fervent faith, and he came well-prepared with mechanical clocks and musical instruments that were brought as gifts designed to impress and intrigue the Chinese with the technological sophistication of the West. Books on Euclidian geometry and Ptolemaic astronomy were meant to convince China's elites that they could understand the movements of the celestial sphere on which heaven rested. Most prominently he brought a map to convince the Chinese that there was a larger world beyond what they had imagined. A Chinese friend of Ricci's commented on the map's impact: "Their [Chinese] conception of the greatness of their country and of the insignificance of all other lands made them so proud that . . . it was scarcely to be expected that they, while entertaining this idea, would heed foreign masters. . . . From that time on [when they accepted the accuracy of the map], they had a much higher opinion of the European system of education." Strategically the map made clear links between China and Europe and hopefully Catholicism and Asia.

Besides convincing the Chinese of the value of interactions with foreigners, Ricci knew he also needed to understand their culture and their values if he was going to have success. As he made his way north from the Portuguese enclave of Macao to Beijing, a journey close to twenty years and fraught with challenges, he came to understand that the key to connecting with Chinese elite was Confucianism. It was the basis of the bureaucracy, and it was the foundation of intellectual life for much of the country. Ricci would not only study Confucianism, but he translated its seminal texts into Latin and brought them back to Europe, where they would strongly influence ideas and perceptions about the Chinese for centuries. This was clearly one of the most significant of many cultural exchanges credited to Jesuit missionaries.

As he studied Confucianism, Ricci concluded that central principles such as veneration of ancestors were not religious but rather cultural, and therefore, it was possible to follow Confucian practices and still embrace Catholicism. Some Catholics bridled at this conclusion and accused the Jesuits of preaching heresy. By the late 1600s, the Jesuit influence in China grew while other missionary orders, such as the Franciscans and the Dominicans, called on the pope to levy sanctions. Their attacks on the Jesuits coincided with a growing unease in the Chinese court regarding their own accommodation of Jesuit teachings.

By 1644 the Ming dynasty had been overthrown by peoples from the north, the Qing. Early on, the Qing rulers relied on foreign advisors like Jesuit missionaries because they did not trust the Confucian officials who had been so influential in the late Ming era. Emperor Kangxi (1661–1722) was receptive to these European advisors and the innovations they introduced. Several Jesuits, for example, took on the all-important tasks of running the royal observatory and of regulating the imperial almanac, which stipulated auspicious days for imperial celebrations and decisions.

There were others within the Kangxi's court, however, who rankled at this foreign influence. Eventually, Kangxi came to realize that if he were to govern China he needed to reconcile himself with the Confucian bureaucracy he needed to manage his realm. By 1721, Kangxi expelled the Jesuits from China. For the next 120 years, European access to and interaction with China was very limited. Europeans who were allowed to trade with China were confined to the port of Canton in the distant south, thousands of miles away from the inner halls and influence of the Forbidden City. They were no longer allowed to learn Chinese, and the Chinese merchants were barred from learning European languages. This system of confining Europeans, known as the Canton System, dominated Manchu relations with the western world until the 1840s, when European gunboats arrived to literally blow China's isolationism away.

Jesuit Missions in South America: The Reductions

During the sixteenth, seventeenth and eighteenth centuries, Jesuits traveled to the Americas also. In the Americas their missionary style was very different than it had been in East Asia. In Asia, they focused on the conversion of imperial leaders with the hopes of winning empires. In South America, arrival of European diseases and the conquistadors had already annihilated the great empires of the Incas and Aztecs. As a result, the missionaries became more focused on converting smaller tribes of indigenous peoples.

One of the most famous and infamous Jesuit missions in the Americas was in Paraguay. The Guarani Indians, whose population numbered in the 100,000s, lived by both slash-and-burn agriculture and hunting and gathering amidst the tropical jungles and rivers of modern Paraguay and southern Brazil. Prior to the coming of the Jesuits in the early seventeenth century, they had had limited connections with Europeans. There was limited trade for axes and hoes, and Spanish settlers occasionally raided Guarani encampments for labor on their plantations. Such raids were justified by the Spanish *encomienda* system, in which Spaniards were permitted to collect tribute from Indians and use them as labor in return for providing for their material needs and giving them religious instruction. In reality, these Indians received little material or spiritual sustenance in return for their brutal exploitation.

In 1610, the king of Spain endorsed a Jesuit plan to allow the Jesuits to replace the *encomienda* system with a mission system, the *reductions* or townships. The Jesuit strategy was to both 'civilize' and convert the Guarani by settling them in towns, where they could practice settled agriculture and receive religious instruction. In some ways these missions were a great success. Catholic historians note that during this period over twenty reductions were established and at their peak over 100,000 Guarani lived in them and were baptized. These historians argue that the townships indeed succeeded in providing not only spiritual liberation but also material succor and that at their height they were exporting significant amounts of cotton, hides and tobacco and reaping immense profits for the Guarani. Such wealth provided good housing, hospitals, schools and eldercare facilities.

Other historians, however, argue that even by the standard of religious conversion the reductions were not as bountiful as Catholic historians want to remember them to be. Moreover many Guarani who did convert failed to follow the Jesuit demands to give up their traditional marriage practices of multiple wives and simply lied to the priests when challenged on the issue. Even economically, they point out, the Jesuits controlled the reduction's trade, often to the detriment of the Guarani. In short, the missions benefited the Europeans far more than they did the Guarani.

While historians still debate the historical importance of the reductions, it is clear that their existence angered Spanish settlers mightily. Robbed of their labor for their plantations, slave-trading adventurers living in the lawless region of Sao Paulo, Brazil, began to raid the Jesuit missions. As these conflicts grew more violent, some Jesuits argued that they needed to defend the Guarani from these Europeans and, in order to do so, they must take up the sword. Antonio Ruiz de Montoya, S.J., was one of those Jesuits who made this decision. In his early life, Montoya was similar to Ignatius of Loyola. He grew up the bastard son of a Spanish officer in the rough colonial town of Lima, Peru. He was intent on enlisting in the army to join a Spanish brigade headed to fight Indians in Chile when he had a religious conversion. Instead of taking up the sword against the Indians, he took up the Bible. By the early 1600s, he left the Spanish colonial world and traveled to the world of the indigenous Guarani.

At first, as the raids increased, Montoya tried to lead led a band of 15,000 Guarani inland on a dangerous plight through the jungles. Hunger and raiding parties exacted a heavy toll. After months on the run, those who survived found a new home, however that was short-lived as European raiders found them and renewed their assaults. It became clear that the only way the Jesuits could civilize and evangelize the Guarani was by first protecting them. Montoya and his fellow Jesuits began to train the Guarani for war, which was an extremely controversial decision. After all, Jesuits were priests of the word, not the sword. In 1637 Montoya left the jungle and went to Madrid to convince the Spanish crown of the righteousness of their actions. Armed with adequate weapons the Guarani proved to be more than capable of defeating the raiders and settlers, and for the next one hundred years the Jesuit mission thrived.

The Jesuits, it turned out, had only won a battle, not the war. Imperial powers back in Europe grew increasingly concerned about rising political and economic issues in the colonies. By 1750 the Portuguese and Spanish crowns were split, and many of the Jesuit reductions were ceded to the new Portuguese king, who was strongly influenced by his anti-Jesuit advisor Plombal. The king soon ordered their immediate dissolution. Some Guarani decided to fight rather than leave, and over the next eleven years guerilla war raged. As the new Spanish king, Charles III, watched from afar, he too became convinced the Jesuits were becoming too powerful and independent, and by 1767 he ordered all Jesuits expelled from the new world.

The great experiment of the reductions was over. Some Guarani ventured into the colonial towns and sought what livelihood they could; others returned to the jungle or were captured by raiders. The reductions themselves eventually returned to the jungle; today only a few bricks and dilapidated walls attest to their former presence and vibrancy.

The Jesuits on the Pacific Island of Guam

Not all Jesuit missions practiced accommodation. Accommodation worked best when the European presence was light and the local control strong, like in Asia. In contrast, the approach used in the Pacific Islands and in South America was more strong-handed. Missionaries compelled locals to accept Catholicism by destroying their symbols of indigenous beliefs, statues, temples and the like, and even physically threatening those who failed to convert. Such practices had been widely used by other missionaries across the Americas. In the Yucatan Peninsula of Mexico, for example, the Franciscan friar Diego De Landa, in an effort to convert Mayans to Christianity, destroyed some five hundred idols and rolls of hieroglyphic Mayan texts that he felt contained "nothing but superstitions and falsehoods of the devil." Of the thousands of texts of poetry, history and religion that historians believe the Mayans produced, only four major collections of Mayan glyphs remain in the wake of de Landa's rampage.

In Guam, a Pacific island and key Spanish colony for the Manilla fleets, the Jesuits followed similar practices. As in Paraguay they set up reductions, but on Guam they made no pretense of empowering the local Chamorro people. Those who did not fulfill labor quotas were punished. Old symbols of venera- tion, the skulls of their ancestors, for example, were ordered buried; failure to do so was punished. Even the island's Spanish overlords complained that some Jesuits were too aggressive and abusive of their subjects. When the Jesuits were ordered to leave by orders of the Spanish crown in 1767, they carted all the livestock and farm implements they could load on their ships, leaving the Chamorro with little.

Conclusion

For over two centuries, from their establishment as a religious order in 1540 until their suppression in the late eighteenth century, the Jesuits were some of the most prolific and influential travelers. Their ambitions to be a global, Catholic missionary order meshed well with the expanding colonial ambitions of the Catholic empires of Spain, France and Portugal, and they ventured to almost every corner of the globe in hopes of achieving their goals. As they did so, the Jesuits became perhaps the most important and controversial organiza- tion of the age. Their encounters transformed the West's understanding of the world and exposed peoples to European ideas and values for the first time. They promoted cultural understanding and precipitated conflict; they chal- lenged European's colonial project in some places and helped build them in others. In short, they were central to the world history of the early modern period.

End Materials Chapter 2

Works Quoted

Brockey, Liam Matthew, *Journey to the East: The Jesuit Mission to China, 1579–1724* (Cambridge, MA: Harvard University Press, 2007).

Clossey, Luke, *Salvation and Globalization in the Early Jesuit Missions* (New York: Cambridge University Press, 2008).

Costelloe, M. Joseph, ed. and trans., *The Letters and Instructions of Francis Xavier* (St. Louis, MO: The Institute of Jesuit Sources, 1992).

de Landa, Friar Diego, *Yucatan Before and After the Conquest*, William Gates, trans. (New York: Dover Publications, 1978).

de Montoya, Antonio Ruiz and C.J. McNaspy, trans., *The Spiritual Conquest: A Per- sonal Account of the Founding and Early Years of the Jesuit Paraguay Reductions* (St. Louis, MO: The Institute of Jesuit Sources, 1993).

Donnelly, John Patrick, *Jesuit Writings of the Early Modern World, 1540–1640* (New York: Hackett Publishing, 2006).

Salvadore, Matteo, "Gaining the Heart of Prester John: Loyola's Blueprint for Ethio- pia in Three Key Documents," *World History Connected* (October 2013). https:// worldhistoryconnected.press.uillinois.edu/10.3/forum_salvadore.html (Accessed October 5, 2021).

Further Reading

Donnelly, John Patrick, *Ignatius of Loyola: The Founder of the Jesuits* (New York: Pearson, 2004).

Fontanta, Michela, *Matteo Ricci: A Jesuit in the Ming Court* (Lantham, MD: Rowman & Littlefield, 2011).

Gallagher, Louis J., trans., *China in the Sixteenth Century: The Journals of Matteo Ricci, 1583–1610* (New York: Random House, 1953).

Greer, Allan, ed., *The Jesuit Relations: Natives and Missionaries in Seventeenth-Century North America* (New York: Bedford St. Martin's 2000).

Stephen Neill, F.B.A., *A History of Christianity in India: The Beginnings to AD 1707* (Cambridge: Cambridge University Press, 1984).

Taylor, Tom, "Introduction to the Forum on Jesuits in World History: Scholarly Approaches and Classroom Resources," *World History Connected* (October 2013). https://worldhistoryconnected.press.uillinois.edu/10.3/forum_taylor.html (Accessed September 23, 2021).

Wiecko, Cynthia Ross, "Jesuit Missionaries as Agents of Empire: The Spanish-Chamorro War and Ecological Effects of Conversion on Guam, 1668–1769," *World History Connected* (October 2013). https://worldhistoryconnected.press.uillinois.edu/10.3/forum_wiecko.html (Accessed September 23, 2021).

3   Travelers and Travel in the Islamic World

Introduction

The early modern era represented a time when three Islamic empires—the Ottoman, Safavid and Mughal—dominated much of the Afro-Eurasian World. They were preeminent military powers whose armies controlled vast diverse lands. They were also centers of religious influence, not only for those within the empire but outside religious communities as well. They defined relationships across the region. Their economies and artisans produced goods that attracted buyers from around the world. Architecture from these empires, whether the mosques on the hills of Istanbul, the palace gardens of Isfahan or the majesty of the Taj Mahal, is some of the most widely admired in the world.

The powerful and prestigious Islamic empires encouraged envoys to travel to distant lands, conquering territories and negotiating treaties. The story of the Mughal Empire is defined by the exploits of its founder Babur, who, from his roots in Central Asia, came to establish a massive empire that dominated Northern India. Evliya Çelebi was an envoy for the Ottoman Empire during the height of its power in the seventeenth century. He traveled across the empire and into its neighboring territories to shape transregional affairs. His final sojourns during the late seventeenth century provided a glimpse into the beginning of the empire's fading glory that manifested in the centuries to come. Mustapha Effendi, another Ottoman, toured Europe in the 1830s looking for new technological and social innovations to revive the empire's fortunes, as decline was imminent.

The Ottoman Empire's conquest of the Arabian Peninsula gave them control of Mecca and Medina, the most sacred cities in Islam, and thus made the Ottoman Sultan the protector of the annual pilgrimages to these sites, the Hajj. Over the centuries hundreds of thousands of Muslim faithful from across the Islamic world traveled to join caravans partaking in this sacred journey.

These powerful empires entertained foreigners who came to curry their favor and shop for their wares. Lady Wortley Montague accompanied her husband, a British diplomat to the Ottoman capital of Istanbul. European artists flocked to the Safavid capital of Isfahan (Persia) to learn the secrets of their exquisite arts. Foreign merchants bartered for coveted carpets and paintings. Travelers

DOI: 10.4324/9781003168690-4

to these empires provided significant insight but also reflect the Orientalist prejudices of the Westerner. These contrasts shaped perceptions of the Islamic world well into the future.

Babur and the Founding of the Mughal Empire

Zahiruddin Muhammed Babur, the founder of the Mughal Empire, was a typical Central Asian raider and fiefdom builder. In many ways his story parallels the founders of the Ottoman (Osman I) and Safavid (Safi al-Din) Empires. All grew up in nomadic tribes in Central Asia, where clan relations were critical. They used those clan loyalties and their strategic knowledge of cavalry to survive and ultimately carve empires to the south. Those empires dominated the Islamic world during the sixteenth to nineteenth centuries and played a central role in shaping the modern world.

Babur had an impressive pedigree. He was the great-great-great grandson of Timur, perhaps the second-most famous Central Asian Emperor ever. His mother descended from Genghis Khan, the most famous one. He lived in Samarkand (Uzbekistan), one of the great cities of the early modern world. As royalty, he was educated in the finest schools the city had to offer and prepared from birth to assume the mantle of power. Such upbringing and pedigree, however, mattered little in the violent endemic succession struggles for territory. He took control of the crown of his kingdom at age seventeen in 1501. After a brief year in power, however, Babur, along with his mother and a handful of others, was forced to flee his city.

After wandering for a time, Babur's small clan of refugees finally found shelter in a sheepherder's village in the mountains. Much like Genghis Khan, he considered heading toward China to try his luck there but ultimately headed southeast to seek other fortunes. By 1504 he had managed to capture Kabul. Although pleased by his success it was not the capital of his imperial ambitions. "From the year Kabul was conquered," he later reported, "I had craved Hindustan," the rich and vast plains of the Ganges River in India.

Babur was not only an accomplished leader and horseman, he was also an accomplished writer. His memoirs mingle romantic couplets (some quite bawdy) with poetic descriptions of the lands he traveled, describing blunt details about the grisly world of early modern warfare. These matter-of-fact reports of the decapitations of enemy soldiers are interspersed with rhapsodic images of lush fields and raging torrents. Tales of bacchanalian excess and gambling dominate the extensive time spent on military campaigns. Once, he confessed, "We drank on the boat until late that night, left the boat roaring drunk, and got on our horses. . . . The next morning they told me that I had come galloping into camp holding a torch. I didn't remember a thing, except when I got to my tent and vomited." (Later in life Babur publicly renounced drinking spirits. His son and heir, Humayun, who frequently joined his drinking binges, continued and his indulgences played a major role in the fate of Babur's empire.)

Babur's literary talents are displayed when he describes his final decision to invade India. "We placed our feet in the stirrup of resolve," he wrote, "grabbed the reins of trust in God" and directed ourselves against Sultan Ibrahim . . . who controlled the realm of Hindustan at the time." It was a mismatch, one that became even more epic in the retelling. Babur had a force of only 12,000, including a contingent of Afghan cavalry who were "quite rustic and insensitive." Ibrahim fielded an army ten times that size, with over one thousand elephants. Babur was disadvantaged by numbers but strengthened in other ways. First, Babur's forces were cohesive and fiercely loyal to their leader and to the call to spread Allah's word into the land of the infidels. By contrast, there was dissension in Ibrahim's large army. Most of the sultan's forces were mercenaries whose loyalties were only as strong as their paychecks, and given the fact that Ibrahim was, according to Babur, "miserly," loyalty proved ephemeral in the heat of battle. Many of Ibrahim's troops either fled or joined Babur when he attacked. Babur also enjoyed a technological advantage using muskets and siege cannons, which allowed him to attack the Sultan's strongholds and destroy his elephant cavalry. In a matter of days, Babur captured Delhi and Agra to the south.

His memoirs show that while Babur had longed dreamed of conquering Delhi, his heart remained in Kabul. Hindustan was "a place of little charm. There is no beauty in its people, no graceful social intercourse, no poetic talent or understanding, no etiquette, nobility, or manliness." What India did have, however, was wealth. "The one nice aspect of Hindustan," he conceded, "[was] that it is a large country with lots of gold and money." It was for that reason that he stayed.

By the time Babur died in 1530, he had managed to carve a massive but fragile empire that stretched throughout Afghanistan, across modern Pakistan, and covered much of northern and central India. It was almost immediately lost by his son Humayan, who was forced to flee west and live under the protection of the Safavid Shah, Tahmasp I. While there, he gained a great appreciation for Persian art and architecture, an appreciation that would significantly shape Mughal buildings like the famous Taj Mahal. Eventually, with support from the shah, he was able to take back Hindustan in 1555. Sadly, his rule was not long-lasting. "As he was leaving his castle of pleasure," according to a Persian official who was visiting him at court, he fell down the stairs and broke his neck. Many believe that his indulgence in liquor and opium caused his demise.

Humayun's death once again put the fate of the young empire in mortal danger as rivals made claim to the throne. Eventually, his eldest son Akbar (r. 1556–1605) secured power and laid the foundation for one of the most powerful empires of the early modern age. By his death in the early seventeenth century, the Mughals controlled northern India from Kabul to Calcutta and into the central Deccan plains of South Asia. They ruled an empire of incredible wealth that fostered significant interest in India.

The Ottoman Empire and the Hajj

By the early sixteenth century, the dynastic empire founded by Osman I [r. ~ 1280–1324]) in the northwest corner of the Anatolian Plateau had expanded to include large swaths of the Balkans, much of the Near East and Egypt. In 1517, the Ottoman Empire conquered key regions of the Arabian Peninsula and took control of Islam's most sacred cities of Mecca and Medina. Those military victories gave the sultan of the empire the power to oversee holy sites and promote one of the Pillars of Islam: the Hajj pilgrimage to Mecca.

The Hajj is one of the central and unifying rituals of Islam. It is a pilgrimage to Mecca, the birthplace of the Prophet Muhammad, the founder of the religion. It takes place as a collective procession in which the faithful journey together to reflect on their religion and their community. All who can afford it are expected to do it at least once in their lifetime, and doing so confers special honors on its participants, including the honorific title of being a *Hajji*. When the Ottoman Empire took control of Mecca, they insured peace and unity. For those of modest means, the sultanate offered support so they too could participate.

Muhammad's Hajj had been a relatively short journey following the established trade routes between Medina and Mecca. As the Ottoman Empire came to control the travel routes to Mecca and continued to expand across the Arabian Peninsula, North Africa, the Near East and much of Southeastern Europe, the faithful they protected and supported were able to come from near and far. Most still traveled by land because it was the route taken by their revered founder. It was also the safest and most practical route, until developments in steamships and the opening of the Suez Canal came about in 1869.

Caravans often started in Cairo or Damascus and headed east across the arid land. Journeys could take anywhere from thirty-five to forty-five days. It was a time to reflect and learn about the global community of which the pilgrims were a part. It was also a time to do some business, as the massive undertaking of as many as 40,000 travelers in a caravan was like a city on the move. It was a city, however, that had to be set up and torn down on a daily basis. One historian noted that "the basic concerns facing any traveler, such as transportation, food, and lodging, were undertaken by a vast corps of specialized workers— cooks, firewood collectors, and water porters, carpenters and blacksmiths, donkey and camel drivers, veterinarians, guides, and grooms. Finally, pickpockets and thieves worked among the pilgrims, however impious their craft."

Raiding and plunder had often been a source of income for the tribes spread across the dessert regions traveled by the pilgrims. Although soldiers accompanied the caravans, it was often more expeditious to turn local thieves into local protection, and tribesmen were usually more than happy to not attack their religious brethren for a price.

The Hajj was, and still is, a time for peaceful interaction. Muslim empires may be at war, but Muslims from different sects and empires were all part of the global Islamic community. While most Muslims in the Ottoman Empire were Sunni, Shia Muslims from the Safavid Empire and those of other sects were also encouraged to go on the pilgrimage, and the sultan protected them when they were in his realm. It was an amazing display of toleration that was often not practiced in the political realms.

The annual Hajj that lasts for six days is determined by Islamic lunar calendar on the twelfth month, called Dhul-Hajjah, between the eighth and thirteenth days. It can be held in the searing hot winds of summer or the bitter colds of a desert winter. Day one starts with the pilgrims entering Mecca dressed in simple white robes as was the Prophet in 632 CE. All entering Mecca are to refrain from anger and sexual activity, as the focus is on peaceful reflection. On day two they go to the desert, an 8 kilometer walk outside the city to remember that Muhammad too went to the desert when he first began his faith journey. After an overnight stay, the pilgrims go to Mount Ararat, where the Prophet received his divine inspiration. After sunset they march again, stopping to pick up stones that they will use the next day in Mina, where they will throw them at columns. It is a symbolic stoning of the devil and a call for purification. Then, recalling the sacrifices of the first Prophet of the Islam, Abraham, they will sacrifice a sheep or goat. (These days a few will do it themselves; most hire a professional.) Having expelled the devil and made their sacrifice, they will then go to Mecca and walk around the Ka'ba, a sacred shrine, seven times before then walking seven times between the hills of Safa and Marwa. Almost certainly exhausted but ecstatic they return to Mina to rest.

By the second half of the nineteenth century, development of steam ships and the opening of the Suez Canal facilitated travel by sea to attend the Hajj. Muslims from Malaysia, Indonesia and South Asia had always traveled by ship, but their numbers increased as regular and reliable routes developed. Dutch records, for example, indicate that some 700,000 faithful traveled to Mecca by ship between 1879 and 1938. Pilgrims from southeastern Europe and North Africa, who had traveled by land, now took advantage of quicker routes available by traveling through the Suez Canal.

These maritime developments also strengthened the commercial aspects of this annual pilgrimage. As steamships were designed to increase carrying capacity, established routes encouraged more travel. Agents would cram pilgrims and cargo on ships. Passengers would haul whatever they could to help pay their fares, and according to estimates, between one-quarter and one-half of all passengers from South Asia sailing on a Hajj ship worked as crew members to help defray expenses.

The Hajj Railway launched by the Ottoman Sultan in 1900 did not have nearly the same impact as maritime access. The sultan, Abdul Hamid II, imagined that the railway would be a symbol of the technical sophistication of his empire and reflect continued efforts at modernization, replicating what had been done in the West. He also thought it would solidify his role as the protector of the Holy Places, allowing pilgrims to avoid the Bedouin raids that besieged caravans. However, it was never finished, and when the sultan was overthrown by a military revolt led by the Young Turks in 1909, the construction of the railroad ended. When the Ottoman Empire was dissolved after World War One, the role of the protector of the Hajj would eventually become the privilege of the House of Saud. It is a role they still play today.

The Greatest Ottoman Traveler: Evliya Çelebi

For many Muslim travelers, the Hajj was the impetus for even more ambitious sojourns across the vast expanse of the early modern Islamic world. Ibn Battuta, often considered the greatest traveler in world history, left Morocco as a young man in 1325 to fulfill his religious obligation to visit Mecca. After accomplishing this goal he kept going, for close to three decades traveling over 70,000 miles. Evliya Çelebi (1611–1684), widely considered the greatest traveler of the Ottoman world, began his life's adventures in a similar way. In 1631 the pious twenty-year-old Çelebi, son of a minor Ottoman court official, decided to go on a Hajj. He later recounted in his memoirs that the Prophet Mohammed appeared to him in a dream. He beseeched the Prophet, "*Shifá'at at yá ressúl-allah* [Intercession, O envoy of God]" in the hopes that the Prophet would help him fulfill his desire. Or so he thought. What he indeed uttered in his groggy, semi-sleep state was, "*Siyáhat at yá ressúl-allah* [Travel, O envoy of God.]. . . . And he [Allah], graciously smiling, granted my wish." For the next forty-one years, until he stopped to write his memoirs in 1671, he traveled the entire length and breadth of the Ottoman Empire.

While Çelebi eventually fulfilled his religious sojourn, much of his life was spent traveling as an Ottoman soldier and diplomat. In the 1640s, he fought in Ottoman attacks on the Mediterranean islands of Crete and Malta. (By then the Ottoman navy was the strongest in the eastern Mediterranean and a key part of its imperial policy.) He then traveled to Ottoman-controlled territories in North Africa. Later, he was part of the empire's continued efforts to expand control across the Arabian Peninsula into Georgia and across the Caucasus Mountains. En route to the Crimean Peninsula, his ship sank in the Black Sea, and he was forced to survive for three days at sea before he was finally rescued. Once ashore he joined the army's efforts to expand Ottoman reach beyond the Sea of Azov, into the river valleys of the Volga and Dnieper Rivers, which were controlled the Cossacks.

In his later life, Çelebi abandoned his military uniform and became an Ottoman diplomat, traveling to Tabriz, where he carried out negotiations with the Safavid Empire around a tenuous peace achieved after long periods of conflict. He also traveled to Vienna to negotiate the end to the Ottoman siege of the Habsburg capital. When those negotiations stalled he went to France, Holland and Sweden, where he discussed prospective alliances against their common foe, the Habsburgs. During this time he also made a side trip to London, where the English government hoped to elicit support from the sultan to supplant the Portuguese dominance of Indian Ocean trade. His extensive travels demonstrate the significant role the Ottomans played in the history of early modern Europe and Western Asia.

Çelebi reported victories and, increasingly over time, losses suffered by Ottoman forces. Those losses increased exponentially as the expansive reach of borders grew. In the Crimea, Cossacks forced the Ottomans to commit even greater numbers of soldiers to defend their garrisons. Renewed attacks against Vienna equally drained resources. Ottoman galleys and frigates succumbed to European powers who worked to gain footholds in the Indian Ocean and western Mediterranean. As Çelebi retired to write his memoirs in the 1680s, he recorded the greatness of an empire that would soon be in decline.

Çelebi's massive ten-volume chronicle of his travels traversing the empire remains one of the great intellectual accomplishments of the time. "It reflects," one historian noted, "the mentality of the Ottomans of the seventeenth century and also provides an acute insight into the inner dynamics of the Ottoman Empire and its organization."

Mustapha Effendi and the Ottoman Empire's Search for Models of Reform

By the nineteenth century, Ottoman imperial glories were fading. Its navy had lost control of the Eastern Mediterranean, and nationalist movements in Greece and the Balkans sliced off significant chunks of its holdings in Europe. Egypt was effectively independent. Russia was pushing into the Black Sea and beyond. Faced with a growing sense of stagnation and decline, Ottoman travelers began to venture abroad to seek out new models for reform and to identify allies who may help protect their increasingly fragile borders. One of those travelers was Mustafa Sami Effendi, an advisor to the sultan who went to Europe in the 1830s to better understand the rising power of its military forces and economic systems.

Traveling across the continent and throughout Great Britain, Effendi witnessed Europe at the dawn of an industrial age. He concluded that clockwork organization, expanding educational opportunities for all and increased focus on science, health and technology were spurring Europe's rapid economic and military advance. Reporting back, he noted that "all the industry and organization, which the Europeans found using a lot of time and work, could be spread among our people in very little time. The situation," he affirmed, "would be advantageous in every aspect."

Effendi's views were largely echoed by the manifesto written by Ahmed Midhat in *Mehmed Emin's From Istanbul to Central Asia* (1879). This work was written during the implementation of what were collectively known as the *Tanzimat* (Reorganization) Reforms of the 1840s to 1870s that aimed to modernize the army and state according to western models. He argued that travel served an essential purpose for the empire, expanding knowledge and access to new ideas: "When the range of travel increases, man's ideas will also widen. . . . Thus emerges the desire to see the state of affairs of other nations which are truly different than ours. . . . When the range of ideas and knowledge of a man with a very strong predisposition to investigation increases, the extraordinary things he is curious to see, in fact multiply accordingly." Both of these examples highlight a shift in Ottoman travel and travel literature from largely descriptive of their religious experiences and wonders of beauty to a pragmatic tool presenting comparative models of reform pointing to the future.

A Woman's View of the Islamic World: Lady Wortley Montagu in Istanbul

By far the vast majority of foreigners traveling to the Islamic world during this period were men. It was the men who were the missionaries, the merchants and diplomats who proselytized, bought, sold and negotiated. The accounts of their travels, while valuable, are limited in perspective. They tell us about certain aspects of the empires but often little about the lives of ordinary people and most importantly the women who were parts of these societies.

One of the women who traveled to and wrote about the Ottoman society was Lady Mary Wortley Montagu, the wife of a British ambassador was assigned to Istanbul in 1717. She accompanied him on this assignment and lived in Istanbul for three years. During this time she wrote numerous letters back to family and friends describing her experiences. They were saved and later published in a book after her death.

One of the most important letters was one she wrote after visiting a number of older women who gathered in the autumn after "the great heat had abated." Gathering children around them, these women would open a vein and then place a dab of goo in it. The goo was a weakened strain of small pox, and Lady Wortley Montagu was witnessing inoculations that were common in the empire. Having watched her brother die of the disease when she was young and having been scarred by its lasting effects herself, she was very impressed. When she later returned to England, she had herself inoculated in the presence of King George I to prove its safety and value.

Several of her letters describe visits with elite women in their private quarters. Despite the fact that they wore veils and some lived in seclusion inside the harem, Montagu concluded that they controlled their own resources and "upon the whole I look upon Turkish women as the only free people in the empire."

Some praised Lady Montagu for not "romanticizing or demeaning Turkey," however, it also important to note that many of her letters focused on the harem and perpetuated the idea that this phenomenon was the central to Ottoman life when, in reality, most women did not live in seclusion as concubines for the elite. As Edward Said has famously noted in his groundbreaking work, *Orientalism*, "The Orient was almost a European invention, and had been since antiquity 'a place of romance, exotic beings, haunting memories and landscapes, remarkable experiences. A place of beauty a place of sensuality, a place of history but a place stuck in the past. A land of idolatry and lassitude, a place of corruption and ignorance, a place of the past and not of the future."

For many European travelers, the harem, the inner sanctum of the house or palace where the women resided, became the place that symbolized the Orient. Images of scantily clad women feeding grapes to their husbands or lords, who lulled in overstuffed chairs, became a prevailing symbol of what westerners took to depict sensuality and the lassitude of the East. While Montagu's writing dispels some of those images, she does perpetuate the illusion. As a source, Lady Montagu's writings are interesting and valued; however, they reflect the experiences and perspective of one person.

European Travelers to the Safavid Empire in Persia

While Said cautions against taking the reports of European travelers in the Islamic world at face value, Rudi Matthee, in looking at European travelers to the Safavid Empire, is clear to argue that these travelers did often report what they saw accurately. Yes, he says, there were some who were pejorative and dismissive of the people they met, but most were careful and detailed empathetic observers, not judgmental critics. He also notes that because some of the central cities of the empire, especially the capital of Isfahan, were located so far inland, travelers often spent more time there than in other areas, thus making their observations richer and more detailed.

Many travelers to the Safavid Empire came in the early 1600s when the economic, artistic and military achievements of the empire attracted outside interest. Under the leadership of Abbas I (r. 1588–1629), the empire developed its export economy and expanded its influence in the Persian Gulf. Both initiatives attracted European and other merchants. A German traveling through Isfahan, the Safavid capital, noted:

> There is not any nation in all Asia, not indeed almost of Europe, who sends not its merchants of Isfahan. . . . There are ordinarily about twelve thousand Indians in the city. . . . Besides these Indians, there is at Isfahan a great number of Tartars from the provinces of Khurasan, Chattai, and Bukhar; Turks, Jews, Armenians, Georgians, English, Dutch, French, Italians and Spaniards.

Abbas also encouraged outsiders to come and explore military and diplomatic relations with their common enemy to the west, the Ottoman Empire. The Safavids, who were Shia' Muslim, had both religious and territorial differences with the Ottomans. As Europeans increasingly tried to cleave into Ottoman power in the eastern Mediterranean, they saw the Safavids as willing allies, and as a result foreign diplomats and military attachés often visited the Abbas' court.

These travelers, Matthee notes, often wrote straightforward accounts of the places they went and the people they met. They portrayed the people, cultures and societies by praising the efficiency of the courts, honesty and graciousness of the rulers and the integrity of the transactional economy. They also often gushed over the beauty of the art and poetry.

Perhaps the most important of these travelers was Sir John Chardin, a French jeweler and merchant who spent several years in Persia during the glory days of the empire, between 1673 and 1677. He was critical at times. For instance his travel account begins by saying that the Persians are "the most lavish men in the world and the most careless on the 'morrow." Yet he immediately says they are the most hospitable people in the world. He makes it clear that he does not see these Persians as the equal of Europeans in terms of science and engineering but notes that they had strong interests in education; "they are very well brought up." They are, he concludes, reflecting this critical but appreciative tone, "the most civilized people of the East."

Conclusion

For over three centuries the Ottoman, Mughal and Safavid empires dominated much of the Afro-Eurasian world. Behind powerful armies and navies they controlled vast swaths of land and diverse populations. Those forces, in turn, dictated political affairs far beyond their borders, shaping the fate of Europe and North Africa and the future of the Indian Ocean and Persian Gulf worlds. Led by Islamic leaders, they also played critical roles in supporting and protecting the religious lives of the millions of their Muslim subjects. The Islamic nature of these empires also defined the experiences of the many non-Muslim peoples who lived within their borders. The economic power and artistic sophistication of these empires' subjects drew merchants and artisans from many places to purchase their goods and learn their crafts.

By the early eighteenth century, however, the dominance and glories of these empires had begun to fade. In the early 1700s, Russian forces and Afghan tribes brought mounting pressure to the borders of the Safavid Empire, and in 1722 Isfahan fell to foreigners; the Empire was no more. By then the Ottoman and Mughal Empires had also passed their apogee. The Ottoman attempt to conquer Vienna had been foiled, and European forces were beginning to push into the Balkans. The Russians were moving into the Black Sea region and charting plans to move further south. In South Asia, Europeans—long confined to trading forts along the coasts of India—moved inland, threatening Mughal strongholds. Dissident princes who reluctantly accepted Mughal suzerainty began to plot for more independence.

The changing fortunes of these Islamic empires were reflected in the nature of travel to and from the empires as the nineteenth century unfolded. Ottoman travelers like Mustapha Effendi now ventured to the West, not to demonstrate dominant power as Evliya Celebi had, but rather to seek means and understanding to adapt and survive. Travelers to Istanbul, Isfahan and Delhi came demanding concessions not begging for access. They came to admire the glories of the past rather than the possibilities of their futures. They increasingly came to conquer, not learn. The Ottoman, Safavid and Mughals empires' fortunes would wane as Europe's imperial ambitions grew in the nineteenth century.

End Materials Chapter 3

Works Quoted

Celebi, Evilya, *An Ottoman Traveller: Selections from the Book of Travels of Evliya Celebi*, Robert Dankoff and Sooyong Kim, trans. (London: Eland Press, 2012).

Chardin, Sir John, *Travels in Persia, 1673–1677* (New York: Dover Publications, 1988).

Claude Brower, Benjamin, "Travel by Land," in Eric Tagliacozzo and Shawakat M. Toorawa, eds., *The Haj: Pilgrimage in Islam* (Cambridge: Cambridge University Press, 2016).

Effendi, Mustafa Sami, "One the General Conditions of Europe," in David Damrosch, ed., *The Longman Anthology of World Literature, vol. E, the Nineteenth Century* (New York: Longman, Pearson, 2004).

Herzog, Christoph and Raoul Motika, "Orintalism 'alla turca': Late 19th/ Early 20th Century Ottoman Voyages to the Muslim 'Outback'," *Der Welt des Islams*, new series, vol. 40, no. 2, *Ottoman Travels and Travel Accounts from an Earlier Age of Globalization* (June 2000): 139–195.

Olearius, Adam, *The Voyages and Travells of the Ambassadors Sent by Frederick, Duke of Holstein, to the Great Duke of Muscovy and the King of Persia* (London: Printed for John Starkey and Thomas Basset, 1669).

Said, Edward, *Orientalism* (London: Routledge, 1978).

Tagliacozzo, Eric and Shawakat M. Toorawa, eds., *The Haj: Pilgrimage in Islam* (Cambridge: Cambridge University Press, 2016).

Thackston, Wheeler, trans., *The Baburnama: Memoirs of Babur, Prince and Emperor* (New York: The Modern Library, 2002).

Wortley Montagu, Lady Mary, *The Complete Letters, 1708–1720*, Robert Halsband, ed., vol. I (Oxford: Claredon Press, 1965).

Further Reading

Adas, Michael, ed., *Islamic & European Expansion* (Philadelphia, PA: Temple University Press, 1993).

Dalrymple, William, *The Last Mughal: The Fall of a Dynasty: Delhi, 1857* (New York: Random House, 2008).

Davidann, Jon Thares and Marc Jason Gilbert, *Cross-Cultural Encounters in the Modern World* (New York: Pearson, 2013).

Imber, Colin, *The Ottoman Empire, 1300–1650: The Structures of Power* (London: Red Globe Press, 2015).

Newman, Andrew, *Safavid Iran: Rebirth of a Persian Empire* (London: Bloomsbury Press, 2008).

Richards, John, *The Mughal Empire* (Cambridge: Cambridge University Press, 1995).

4 The Atlantic Slave Trade

Introduction

For over four hundred years, from the late fifteenth century until the middle of the nineteenth century, African men, women and children were forcibly taken from their homes in West and Central Africa, thrown into forts where they were poked, prodded and sold, then crammed into the fetid holds of ships to be carried across the Atlantic to the plantations of the Americas and Caribbean. Over time, some 12 to 13 million people experienced this nightmarish journey. The journey was so precarious that it is estimated that over two million of these people never disembarked; they died of disease, violence or despair en route. Those who survived found a strange, harsh world working in the fields and homes of their white masters. Almost no one ever returned home.

The Atlantic Slave Trade, as this infamous enterprise has become known, was the largest forced migration in human history. Yet, despite its magnitude and scope, historians are challenged to understand the feelings and thoughts of the millions involved. Of the millions of Africans who were enslaved, we have written accounts of the experiences from precious few. One narrative, short in its length but long in value, is that of Venture Smith, a young boy captured in West Africa, sold into slavery at a slave fort in modern Ghana and then carried across the Atlantic in 1739. His autobiography offers important insights of how one person experienced this life-shattering journey.

We also lack insight into the mindset of those who practiced this trade, the slavers. Slavers often did not leave detailed narrations of their trips, not simply out of guilt for their actions but more likely to hide their trade secrets. Fortunately, we do have one such record, the journals of a young lieutenant, Robert Durand, who traveled aboard a French slave ship, the *Diligent*, in 1739. It provides perspective into the calculus of those who bought, shipped and sold slaves.

By far the most valuable resource to better understand the Atlantic Slave Trade is the Trans-Atlantic Slave Trade Database, which contains logs and manifests of some 36,000 slaving expeditions. This incredible work offers insights into many aspects of slave trade; the nature and size of the ships; the demographics around who was enslaved; dates, numbers and destinations from

DOI: 10.4324/9781003168690-5

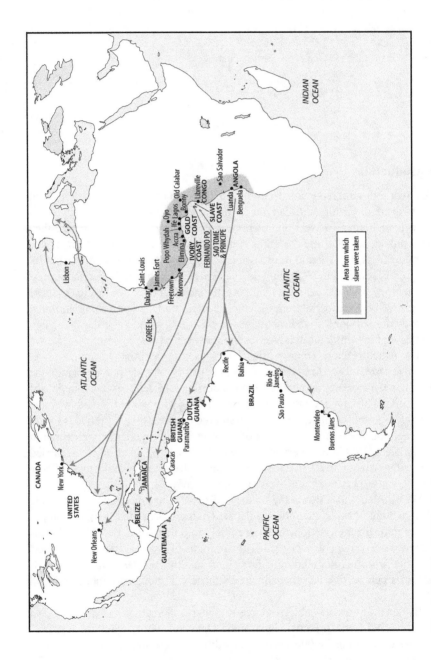

Map 3 The Atlantic Slave Trade

manifests over the four centuries. More and more historians are also using these numbers to fill in the gaps of personal narratives of slaves and slavers we often do not have.

Although the scale and magnitude of the Atlantic Slave Trade makes it a transformative singular experience in human history, it was only part of the global system of enforced labor and transoceanic slavery. Similar yet smaller systems of servitude existed across the Indian Ocean. Understanding the similarities and differences can provide important comparative perspectives on what transpired during this time.

The Atlantic Slave Trade: An Overview

Europeans made their way to the New World by the tens of thousands. Many who sailed across the Atlantic often did so with the dream of becoming a landed gentleman, not a lowly paid laborer. As the encomienda system of labor and disease ravaged the peoples of the New World, colonists looked for new sources of cheap labor; working the plantations and mines required millions of hands. They found it on the west coast of Africa; they found it in the millions of African men and women who became slaves in the New World.

Slavery was the system of forced labor in which captured human beings became the property of another to be used and disposed of at the will of a master; it was nothing new. In fact slavery had been part of most large economic systems since the dawn of mankind. Slaves from Africa had long been part of expansive trade systems across the Sahara, throughout the Red Sea and Indian Ocean. The Atlantic Slave Trade was different in part because of the sheer numbers of people involved. Over the course of four centuries, tens of thousands of European colonists and Africans bought and sold approximately 12 to 13 million African men, women and children. Slavery became one of the largest and most profitable enterprises during the early modern world. For those sold into slavery, however, the system was brutal. Taken prisoner in war or raids, these men and women (and often boys and girls) were herded miles across Africa to slave forts that dotted the West African coast. There they were poked, prodded, bought and sold. They were then crammed on ships to cross the Atlantic only to be dehumanized again as they were bought, sold and for many forever separated from their families and homeland. Their labor was critical to how the New World evolved. They also shaped the New World through their religion, their culture and their gene pool. The tectonic effect of the Atlantic Slave Trade destroyed old continents and created new worlds.

The Atlantic Slave Trade began even before Europeans crossed the Atlantic Ocean to establish colonies and plantations in the Americas. As Portuguese venturers sailed along the West African coast during the fifteenth century, they colonized island archipelagoes—including the Azores, Madeiras and Canaries. The islands were used as supply stations and as plantations to support the emerging sugar industry. As the indigenous populations were decimated by resistance and disease, they quickly sought African labor to work the fields.

The first known slave ship crossed the Atlantic in 1525, sailing from San Tome to New Spain (the Americas). At first, the number of ships was minimal. Until the middle of the seventeenth century most sailed under the Portuguese flag, but as more plantations were established across the Caribbean and the Americas and profits from the trade increased, the numbers began to swell. Almost every European power was engaged, and soon the competition for slaves grew incessantly. During its peak in the late eighteenth century close to 80,000 were captured, sold and transported across the ocean every decade. Almost eighty percent of all those traveling across the Atlantic during this period were slaves.

Denmark, albeit a relatively small player, was the first to abolish the slave trade in 1803. Great Britain and the United States followed a few years later, and by the mid-nineteenth century every nation had outlawed the massive system of forced migration. That said, while the Transatlantic Slave Trade was outlawed, slavery and forced labor continued to be legal in many countries for decades to follow. The United States is one example, as slavery was not officially abolished until after the end of the Civil War in 1865.

Sources on the Atlantic Slave Trade

Many historians struggle to find sources to understand the magnitude and human experience of the largest forced migration in human history. The European and African slavers left few records. In some cases, this was likely done with intent, so as not to risk having evidence of their nefarious actions for which they may become liable should these records come to light. More often it was because as merchants carrying out what they saw as a legitimate trade, they did not want to give away their trade secrets.

Even more challenging are the accounts from slaves. Of the some 12 million sold into slavery, we have only perhaps a dozen accounts written by slaves. Most of these are sparse; some with unclear provenance and legitimacy. This is not surprising because slavers and owners intentionally kept slaves from learning to write, as this skill could be used for organizing resistance in their communities.

Despite these challenges, remarkable work, carried out on many fronts, has allowed many to understand the extent of the enterprise and to try get some understanding the personal experiences of those involved. Archival research has unearthed the journal of a young French officer who sailed on the slave ship *Diligent* in 1739 that offers insight into the mentality of a merchant slaver. A few more accounts by slaves have also surfaced and, perhaps most importantly, painstaking work to amass records of slave ships has yielded an enormous trove of data that has changed and deepened our understanding of the Atlantic Slave Trade.

The database is comprised of records for some 36,000 slave ship voyages across the Atlantic, close to ninety percent of all the voyages on record. It is the culmination of at least a half a century of intensive labor by scholars from across the globe. Chronologically, it contains information from the first ships involved with slave trade in the early sixteenth century to the last ships that sailed in the mid-nineteenth century. These records, based on ships logs, contain a wide range of information on the ships, their voyages and their slave cargo. It includes dates of when they sailed, which ports they visited and where they sold their cargo as well as demographics on age and gender of those aboard. As much as possible, this information offers insights into changing demographics and even rates of mortality. Some records note slave mutinies or major disease outbreaks, which allow us to glean some ideas on the frequency of these issues. Also noteworthy, there is sparse data available about ship crewmembers.

Given the wide range of records collected, it is understandable that the type and quality of data varies. Some ships, for example, only list the total number of slaves bought in Africa and say nothing about their destiny and fate in the Americas. Others provide detailed records on the gender and age breakdown of people aboard (ref. cargo) and information about the crew. As the database summarizes it: "The details . . . facilitate the study of cultural, demographic, and economic change in the Atlantic world from the late sixteenth to the mid-nineteenth centuries."

It is equally important to note what sources do not tell us. As the authors of the database note: "The data set contains thousands of names of ship owners and ship captains, but it contains almost no names of the millions of slaves carried to the Americas." The voices of those who suffered are largely silent. Researchers have found the names of close to 100,000 slaves, giving identity to some, but overall, many remain nameless victims.

Despite inconsistent records, we can extrapolate data to frame a story; even if it is fragmented. Records can also be used to verify the accounts made by the French slaver Robert Durand on his voyages on the *Diligent*. Using similar methodology, the account of Venture Smith can be verified and coupled with additional information to expand on his sparse account.

Triangular Trade in the Atlantic World: The Voyage of the *Diligent*

The *Diligent* sailed out of the port of Vannes along the French coast of Brittany on May 31, 1731. It was not a large ship, having originally been built to haul grain around the Atlantic coast, but this day it was loaded with a variety of desirable goods: bolts of cotton and silk, flintlocks, shot and powder, large quantities of brandy and other sundry goods that could be had for a good price. This ship was headed south to the West African Slave Coast, where it hoped to trade its wares for humans who would be crammed below deck, shipped across the Atlantic and sold for tremendous profit to the sugar, coffee and tobacco plantations in the French Caribbean. This area of western Africa, once the site of intense trade for gold and ivory, was now sought out for its human wealth.

During the eighteenth century, slavery was the largest form of commerce in the world, and thousands of ships like the *Diligent* hoped to cash in on the lucrative trade. African men and women purchased or captured were sent to slave forts along the coasts of West Africa (notably modern-day Ghana). Upon delivery, slaves were sold to the plantation owners for up to five hundred percent profit. Full circle, prosperous plantations then sold sugar, tobacco and cotton that was shipped back to Europe. Profits were immense. The Triangular Trade, as this commercial system was called, was a supply chain profitable to everyone—everyone except the millions of slaves who fueled it.

It appears that few slave traders had ethical qualms about such a business. Robert Durand never expressed reservations about his job. His journals are full of navigation records, technical analyses of ship and merchant strategies, but no moralizing about his career. Working as a slaver was a job and, if we can infer from the care he took to record its particulars, one in which he hoped to have a long career.

Like most slave ships, the *Diligent* initially steered toward the Canary and Cape Verde Islands off the west coast of Africa. Both sets of islands were critical ports of call to resupply food and water and to gather information about pirate activity, among other things. Traveling along the three-hundred-mile coast had become increasingly dangerous. Skirmishes for control and rapid shifts in political and economic fortune meant that coastal territories were often changing allegiances. African kingdoms, now supplied with European firearms, fought to control the key trading harbors and procure slaves for sale. An independent slave ship like the *Diligent* needed to move cautiously to gain as much knowledge as possible about the current state of affairs and then to choose its port of call carefully.

After several stops, the *Diligent* made its way to the thriving port of Savi, the capital city of the kingdom of Whydah (in modern Benin), the largest and most vibrant slave-trading kingdom of the early eighteenth century. However, since it was also at war the ship's captain, Pierre Marie, decided to move on. Getting embroiled in local conflicts was not worth the risk, and there were always other choices of ports not far away to purchase slaves. Eventually it dropped anchor at Jakin, a short distance down the coast.

At the time, Jakin's harbor was packed with fifteen European vessels, and Captain Marie quickly realized that trading at favorable rates was going to be difficult. Competition raised prices, and the king was a skilled diplomat and businessman. Bribes were required; fees for food and moorage paid. Slaves had to be inspected for value. Plantation labor in the New World was brutally hard, and owners wanted strong, physically capable young men to handle the job. Some 'how-to' slaver manuals recommended purchasing slaves in a three to one male-to-female ratio for maximum profit. "Buy as few females as is in your power," advised another slaver, "for females are a tedious business." Early on, women had been more desired in the slave trade to be used as domestic servants. Then, again later, in the nineteenth century, when calls for the abolition of slavery began to curtail the trade, women became more desired as breeding stock in case the trade was shut down.

There were some regions such as Bight of Biafra that did sell more women into slavery. Some speculate this was because this region did not have connections to other systems, such as the Trans Saharan Slave Trade, where women were more highly desired. Paul Lovejoy, in his study of the Trans Saharan system says that women were sold in a three-to-one ratio, likely because in this system more slaves were used as domestic servants and women were preferred.

After three months of hard bargaining, Captain Marie had selected two hundred fifty-six slaves. Once the bargaining was complete, they were shackled together and herded to canoes that would take them across the roiling coastal surf to the *Diligent*. According to ship records available on the Slave Trade Database, about fifty-seven percent were men, thirty-two percent women, slightly over seven percent boys and the rest girls. The records do not indicate where the slaves came from, but Durand's records say that they were from many regions, linked not by family or custom or language, but simply by chains of servitude.

The Middle Passage

As they climbed aboard the *Diligent*, the men were driven into the hold of the ship, where they spent the majority of the next two months. Each male slave existed in a space approximately one foot wide by 5 feet long. There was no room to sit up or lie down. The few women on board were forced into a special area at the rear of the top deck. Sailors shouted at both groups in what was likely heard as unintelligible gibberish. Cat o' nine tails ripped the skin of those who resisted. About one-fourth of those subjected to these brutalities were children; and there was little or no consideration of their age.

The voyage across the Atlantic was known as the Middle Passage. Slaves were allowed above deck just enough to keep them alive. Slavers constantly feared that slaves on deck may either try to rebel or jump overboard to end their misery. When storms battered the ship, slaves were left below even though many became violently ill. Only as the ship entered the Caribbean did the routine change. Then slaves, in small numbers, were carefully allowed above deck. They were showered with salt water to clean off the grime and then fattened up for sale. After two months at sea, the *Diligent* slipped into port at Martinique, an island in the Caribbean. (Until the advent of steam ships in the final stages of the slave trade in the mid-1800s, this was a fairly typical crossing time.)

According to Durand's records, nine slaves and four crew members did not survive. By the standards of the slaver's calculus, it had been a remarkably successful trip. Two to three million Africans did not survive the crossing, estimated at twelve to fifteen percent of all those embarked from Africa. Numbers varied considerably depending on the length of the voyage, whether there were attempted escapes and uprisings, disease, weather and many other factors. As the slave data base concludes, "The eighteenth-century world was violent and life-expectancy was short everywhere given that the global mortality revolution was still over the horizon, but the human misery quotient generated by the forced movement of millions of people in slave ships cannot have been matched by any other human activity."

Loss of cargo was part of the business calculus of trade, and Captain Marie was hopeful he would turn a profit. Before that could be determined, the remaining two hundred forty-seven slaves were readied for sale. Males were shaved raw to look younger; purchasers hoped that younger slaves would be easier to control and would work longer. Initially they were asking a high price and bidding was slow, but as the days dragged on and slaves died in holding, he grew worried that news would spread, so he dropped the prices. In the end, Captain Marie did not get the price for the slaves he expected, and by the time his ship returned to France with his payments of sugar, coffee and other com-modities, the voyage had lost a considerable sum for its investors. Marie was sued for negligence, and the *Diligent* never sailed for Africa again.

The Middle Passage: A Slave's Perspective

Despite the fact that millions of Africans experienced the Middle Passage, sources describing the ordeal from a slave's perspective are minimal. Few slaves were literate, and so few left written records. Slave owners deliber-ately kept slaves from learning to read and write, fearing that communication could lead to emancipation. For a long time, historians relied on one of the most detailed testimonials of the Middle Passage, *The Interesting Narrative of the Life of Olaudah Equiano* (1789). It details an agonizing voyage, but it has also come to be challenged for its veracity as baptismal records found in South Carolina may suggest Equiano was born in the Americas. If so, he did not experience the Middle Passage and may have constructed his narrative by talking with others who did. He worked for the abolitionist movement after he was able to buy his freedom, and some think that work led him to overdrama-tize or exaggerate his descriptions of the Middle Passage. Still others contend that, even given these concerns, his story rings true and should not be ignored or dismissed.

One account that has been corroborated with evidence from slave ship records is that of Venture Smith. His account details where he embarked; the name of the ship, the *Charming Susanna*; the name of the captain of the ship and the owner who bought him once he got to the United States. Records of the Slave Trade Database confirm details and lend credence to the veracity of Smith's autobiography, *A Narrative of the Life and Adventures of Venture, a Native of Africa: But Resident above Sixty Years in the United States of Amer-ica. Related by Himself*, which he wrote in his later life after he was able to buy his freedom.

Smith's description of his passage across the Atlantic Ocean comprises a scant paragraph in his autobiography. After a lengthy recounting of the cir-cumstances that led to his capture as a young boy in West Africa, he was taken to Anamaboo, a slave fort in modern Ghana. Like so many, he was held in the castle fort until he was sold to a slaver out of Rhode Island and put on a ship captained by Collingwood. "I was bought on board by one Robertson Mumford, steward of said vessel, for four gallons of rum, and a piece of calico, and called VENTURE, on account of his having purchased me with his own private venture. Thus I came by my name. All the slaves that were bought for that vessel's cargo, were two hundred and sixty."

Ship records place the number of slaves on board at eighty-four. Smith, only six or seven at the time, was in his seventies when he finally committed his story to paper. It is not surprising, therefore, the numbers did not match. Things often seem bigger when we are young. A wave of small pox, certainly not uncommon on these crowded ships ravaged the slaves, and he notes that only two hundred of the slaves disembarked in Barbados. Slave ship records indicate that seventy-four slaves made it to Barbados, a twelve percent mortality rate. Smith did not get off to work the plantations of the Caribbean Island but continued on to become one of three slaves destined for Rhode Island, where he became a house servant.

One advantage of Smith's account versus others is that it does not appear to have been created with any particular purpose in mind except to keep his story alive. By the time that Olaudah Equiano wrote his narrative, he was deeply involved in the abolitionist movement, and that may have shaped his autobiography. Even so, there are a couple of caveats to consider as we examine the veracity of his account. Smith never learned to read or write, so he would have needed help to get his story down on paper. When it was first published, it appeared in a "very politically active newspaper," making some wonder whether there was an agenda. Despite these cautions, most historians think Smith's narrative is an incredibly important if terse window into the experience of slaves as they suffered the Middle Passage.

The Indian Ocean Slave Trade

While the Atlantic Slave Trade has been the focus of much of the scholarship on the early modern slave trades, it was not the only transoceanic movement of enslaved peoples during this period. As European colonists extended the reach of their empire into the Indian Ocean and Southeast Asia, they too established plantation economies that needed labor to thrive. Slavery had been part of the fabric of this world for centuries, but the expanding plantation systems of the colonizers required even more labor and, as a result, the Indian Ocean Slave Trade grew exponentially.

The Indian Ocean Slave Trade focused on three regional sources of captive labor: East Africa and Madagascar; Southern India and Sri Lanka; and Southeast Asia. For the most part Europeans did not directly seize slaves for their plantations but rather relied on indigenous raiders for their purchases. Markets were long established and ready and willing to trade. Most of the captured slaves came from rural villages and small, weak or stateless regions that could not oppose aggressive raiders. Sometimes raiders required local leaders to provided indentured labor in return for sparing others. While these individuals were therefore not technically slaves, in reality there was little difference.

The scope and magnitude of the Indian Ocean Slave Trade is hard to calculate. Efforts to gather data are still underway. To date, the information has not yielded anything close to what the Atlantic Slave Trade Database has made available. The Dutch East India Company maintained records that indicate that perhaps 5,000 to 6,000 slaves were brought to their plantations in Indonesia every year during the late seventeenth century. This would indicate that perhaps 65,000 to 70,000 slaves were laboring in that empire at any point in time. Some records indicate that mortality rates of slaves during passage were roughly twenty percent; a figure higher than in the Atlantic world. These records also indicate that the number of humans enslaved for this region was about twenty to twenty-five percent of the numbers forced into slavery in the Atlantic Ocean system. That said, the human toll and cost of suffering was significant. Thousands of people were displaced against their will for the benefit of an elite class.

Conclusion

In May of 2019, the *Clotilda*, the last slave ship to arrive in the United States was found lying in the mud in the harbor of Mobile, Alabama. Records indicate that it had landed there with a cargo of some one hundred ten slaves in July 1860, long after the United States had outlawed slavery in 1807. The owner knew that this voyage was illegal, but apparently he had no problem with enslaving Africans. He was driven by the notion of enormous profits. He had purchased the slaves in West Africa for $9,000 in gold and sold them for twenty times that amount in Alabama. To hide his crime, he ordered the shipped burned and scuttled. The story of the *Clotilda* is a stark reminder that the history of the Atlantic Slave Trade continues to be written. This new history continues to raise debates about the legacies of the insidious trade and calls for justice and reparations for its victims.

Although slavery has been abolished, sadly it has continued under illegal and illicit terms. According to experts, some 20 to 40 million people around the world, many of them children, are held in some form of forced labor. Some are trafficked for sex, others for work in brutal and marginalized conditions. Similar to the slave trades centuries ago, their stories remain unheard.

End Materials: Chapter 4

Works Quoted

Harms, Robert, *The Diligent: A Voyage Through the Worlds of the Slave Trade* (New York: Basic Books, 2002).

Slave Voyages Consortium, *Slave Voyages* (2021). https://www.slavevoyages.org/ (Accessed April 10, 2021).

Smith, Venture, *A Narrative of the Life and Adventures of Venture, a Native of Africa: But Resident Above Sixty Years in the United States of America. Related by Himself* (New Haven and London: Yale University Press, 1798).

Williams, Karen, "An Introduction to the Indian Ocean Slave Trade," *An Introduction to the Indian Ocean Slave Trade—Media Diversified.* https://mediadiversified. org/2016/05/04/an-introduction-to-the-indian-ocean-slave-trade/.

Further Reading

Black, Eric, *The Atlantic Slave Trade in World History* (London: Routledge, 2015).

Equiano, Olaudah, *The Interesting Narrative of Olaudah Equiano, or Gustavus Vassa, Written by Himself* (1789).

Keyes, Allison, "The 'Clotilda,' the Last Known Slave Ship to Arrive in the U.S., Is Found," *Smithsonian Magazine* (May 22, 2019). www.smithsonianmag.com/ smithsonian-institution/clotilda-last-known-slave-ship-arrive-us-found-180972177/ (Accessed May 12, 2021).

Nellis, Eric, *Shaping the New World: African Slavery in the Americas, 1500–1888* (Toronto: University of Toronto Press, 2013).

Northrup, David, ed., *The Atlantic Slave Trade* (Lexington, MA: D.C. Heath & Co., 1994).

Salvadore, Matteo, "Between the Red Sea Slave Trade and the Goa Inquisition: The Odyssey of Gabriel, a Sixteenth-Century Ethiopian Jew," *Journal of World History*, vol. 31, no. 2 (June 2020): 327–360.

5 Enlightened Travelers and the Search for the Laws of Nature

Introduction

As a wider circle of Europeans traveled the world during the 1600s, they discovered new lands, full of unknown plants and animals, and new people of which they had no prior knowledge. These discoveries precipitated an intellectual revolution as scientists, philosophers and thinkers tried to comprehend the meaning of new worlds. The voyages themselves stimulated a greater interest in astronomy, as they used an understanding of the heavens to refine navigational calculations and techniques to rethink the place of humans in the cosmos. New plants and animals stimulated curiosity into the structure and order of the natural world. Encounters with humans who looked different, with cultures and belief systems, led many to reflect on the essence of human nature.

Three very different travel expeditions played a role in this movement. The story of pirate, adventurer and scientist William Dampier; the three monumental voyages of Captain James Cook, who traveled the Pacific between 1768 and 1779; and the South Pacific voyages of the French Admiral Bougainville each strengthened beliefs in the value of science and the ability of humans to understand the natural world.

As observations of the natural world were disseminated, writers and reformers began to ask how this new knowledge may help us better understand social and political systems. Some argued that these discoveries showed that all humans, whatever their race or ethnicity, were fundamentally the same and all deserved equal treatment before the law. Others concluded that racial and social difference were indeed natural and felt that these discoveries justified imperialism and the continuation of the slave trade. Enlightened answers to these questions varied widely to say the least.

In addition to actual global voyages, fictional journeys played a key role in shaping Enlightenment-era ideas about social and political reform. Writers like the satirist Jonathan Swift or the French philosopher Voltaire created elaborate tales of sojourns to mystical lands or distant empires and, in so doing, cast a light on the governments and societies of their homeland. By using fictional travels, writers escaped the wrath and censorship of governments and were

DOI: 10.4324/9781003168690-6

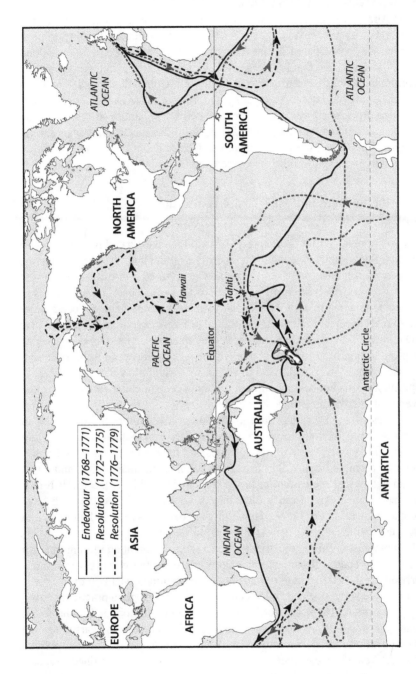

Map 4 The Voyages of Captain Cook and Enlightened Era Travelers

able to take creative liberty to spice up their stories (and increase readership). They were widely read and highly influential.

The Age of Enlightenment was a European intellectual and cultural phenomena, but its impact was global. Intellectuals in North American European colonies also participated in the dialogue. Reformers in Latin America and the Caribbean argued that European calls for more freedom and representative government should be afforded to them as well. Colonial subjects and slaves argued that they too deserved equality and liberty, as the Declaration of Independence proclaimed that they were "created equal" and also "endowed by their creator with certain inalienable rights." Enlightenment-era voyages, both real and fictional, set the global stage for debates about the human condition that remain part of our public discourse today.

Scientific Voyages and New Insights into the Natural World

As a young man, William Dampier (1651–1715) investigated tides and ocean currents. Such knowledge was valuable for a pirate, and, by many accounts, Dampier used it effectively. This expertise also served him well when he was invited to join British scientific explorations along the coasts of Australia and the Pacific Islands. In addition to helping chart the waters, he collected plant and animals species, something that would bring modest fame in his later life.

Dampier's transformation from pirate to scientist and explorer highlights the proliferation of voyages that marked the Age of European Enlightenment. His rise from a lowly deck hand to author of seven books demonstrates how opportunities for intellectual and cultural engagement came about during the seventeenth and eighteenth centuries.

Voyages like those undertaken by Dampier gave Europeans new faith in the power of technology to overcome seemingly impossible obstacles. More importantly, the discovery of new peoples and fresh encounters with old civilizations prompted many Europeans to rethink both their understanding of human nature and their relationship to the larger world. As the English philosopher, Francis Bacon put it, "By distant voyages and travels which have become frequent in our times, many things in nature have been laid open and discovered which may let in new light on philosophy."

Dampier began sailing on British ships as a pirate intent on raiding Spanish galleons and coastal forts. He made his way around the world several times. Early on, he started keeping journals of his observations. Many of these observations were about tides and ocean currents, which was good practical knowledge for a pirate. He also recorded information on the flora and fauna found around the world. When he returned to England after a dozen years at sea, he was broke. Fortunately, his notes proved fortuitous and he was able to publish a book, *A New Voyage Round the World* (1697). As a result, he gained a reputation as a keen observer of nature. In the late 1600s he was invited by the British Royal Society to accompany some of their voyages as a scientist, traveling to the Pacific to gather plant and animal specimens; the pirate had become a legitimate explorer.

From 1766 to 1779 the British Royal Society also sponsored several expeditions to the Pacific led by Captain James Cook. The first expedition was undertaken to help calculate the distance of the earth from the sun by making observations on the orbit of Venus as it passed in front of the sun. Cook's measurements of this phenomenon were then triangulated with other observations from two other parts of the globe to determine distance. Such feats demonstrated the lengths to which eighteenth-century Europe was willing to go in pursuit of scientific knowledge. There was, however, another side to this voyage of discovery. Cook also had secret orders, to look "for the southern continent and with the consent of the Natives to take possession of Convenient Situations in the Country in the name of the King of Great Britain" or if uninhabited to "take possession for his Majesty." This secret agenda suggests how scientific exploration and colonial expansion worked in tandem. After all, Royal Societies were supported by the government, and governments were sometimes motivated by more than just pursuit of truth.

Cook's voyage accomplished half of its goal. Astronomers were able to make the celestial calculations while in Tahiti, however they were unable to locate the fabled 'southern continent.' Cook later became the first European to discover New Zealand and Australia. His report on Botany Bay (the future site of Sydney) along the eastern coast of Australia was noted to be of great value for future settlement. The bay itself was described as "capacious, safe and commodious" with abundant sources of water and fuel. Its shoals rich in fish and its shores teeming with birds earned it its name—Botany Bay. The "natives," he noted, "did not seem to be numerous, nor do they seem to live in large bodies."

Although Cook's visit was a brief two-day stay, he was there long enough to convince the British government that it would be feasible to establish a colony in Australia. Eighteen years later, in 1788 a small fleet of British colonists disembarked on the shores of Botany Bay. Most of the seven hundred seventeen colonists (five hundred twenty of whom were men) were convicts. They were sent their by the British government to establish villages and farms in return for the promise of obtaining land at the end of their sentences. As more convicts arrived, they pushed the indigenous aborigines back from the coast. Many aborigines were hunted and killed, and over time their numbers fell from about 650,000 at the time of the arrival to less than 100,000 a century later. Most who remained survived on the margins of Australia in the vast and largely inhospitable interior. The story of colonial decimation of indigenous populations told in so many parts of the world was again repeated in the Pacific.

Years later Cook returned to look for the southern continent. His third and final voyage sailed in 1776 with a commission to explore the Pacific to find the Northwest Passage. He sailed along the Pacific Northwest coast looking for safe harbor but grew frustrated and eventually set off to sea. In April 1779, he made his way back to the "Sandwich Islands" (i.e. Hawaii). He had landed there previously on his way east and, at that time, found the locals to be generally friendly. This time was another matter, as a confrontation and skirmish over a stolen skiff led him to take hostages. The Hawaiians retaliated. Cook was hit with rocks and left dead on the beach of the Big Island. His crew continued on returning to search for the Northwest Passage before making their way through the South China Sea, the Indian Ocean and around the Cape of Good Hope before sailing home. All totaled, the three expeditions sailed more than 150,000 miles and added countless details to large sections of the world map that had been largely left blank.

The voyages of Dampier and Cook are two examples of many that furthered scientific discovery, exploration and colonization,—efforts that would continue to revolutionize western scientific paradigms and further imperial control and influence around the world. Cook's expeditions made such significant contributions that one writer has likened his voyages to "a laboratory to test the latest theories and technologies, much as spaceships are today." Ever since the work of Nicolas Copernicus, postulating a heliocentric, sun-centered, solar system some two centuries before, scientists had been trying to both prove this and to ascertain its implications. While the heliocentric model had been accepted by the time of Cook's voyages, his astronomical observations of Venus in front of the sun on June 3, 1769, changed our understanding of the solar system. It was a rare event, but the timing was critical to measure the planet's distance from Earth. (It was one of seventy-six observations taken around the world that day.) That data was ultimately used to calculate distances of the other four known planets that orbit the Sun and, therefore, the size of the solar system. Technology (the limited power of telescopes) and other issues limited the accuracy of the measurements but should not diminish the magnitude of his accomplishment.

On the first voyage, Cook sought to solve what plagued many at sea, the scourge of scurvy. The human body can only store Vitamin C for about six weeks. Without it, the body begins to break down, gums rot, hemorrhaging increases and sailors literally begin to go crazy. Magellan's earlier expeditions across the Pacific had been decimated by scurvy. Getting fresh fruit, a common source of Vitamin C, when ships were at sea for weeks and months proved impossible, so Cook's crew experimented with "pickled foods" to improvise. Sailors were ordered to regularly consume sauerkraut and were flogged if they refused. It worked, and by the time the expedition reached Tahiti, he could report that the crew "had, in general, been quite healthy." (Later the British navy would rely more on limes, a citrus that preserved reasonably well in the tropical heat. British sailors thus earned the nickname 'limeys.')

Many of the flora and fauna samples Dampier collected on his voyages were used by the English botanist John Ray, who compiled the massive three-volume *General History of Plants* (1668), which presented a systematic account of the structure, physiology and distribution of plants. Ray's work, in turn, was expanded upon by the Swedish naturalist Carolus Linnaeus who, in his magnum opus, *Natural Systems* (1735), developed the classifications of plants and animals used today. Nature, once capricious and mysterious, was, at least according to Linnaeus and many who accepted his ideas, rational and ordered; each plant and animal served a specific purpose within a grand scheme. In the true spirit of the Enlightenment, individuals could use reason to discern that purpose. As with Newton's physics, Linnaeus thought that the grand pattern of a rationally constructed natural world would reveal the mind of God at work.

The Search for 'Natural Man'

The discovery of new plants and animals paled in comparison to discoveries of new peoples in distant, unknown and undeveloped lands. This fueled interest in finding peoples who lived in what Europeans considered a "natural state" in harmony with Linnaeus' ordered and structured natural world. Many argued that because these peoples lived close to nature, they were 'noble savages'— savages in the sense that they lived in a state of pre-civilization without government and laws, and noble because in that state they lived in virtuous harmony with nature's laws, which made them free of shame or sin, much like Adam and Eve in the biblical garden of Eden. This image of the noble savage was a far cry from the image proposed by the Englishman Thomas Hobbes in *The Leviathan* (1651), written during the English Civil War; according to Hobbes, a state of nature was a "condition of war against everyone . . . in which the life of man [was] solitary, poor, nasty, brutish and short."

The first person to coin the term *noble savage* was John Dryden in his play, *The Conquest of Granada* (1670). In a crucial part of the play, he has a Caribbean Indian (before being conquered by Europeans) proclaim, "I am as free as Nature first made man, eyre the base laws of servitude began, when wild in the woods the noble savage ran." Dryden proposed that men in a state of nature were happiest, and those who were stuck in civilized society, with its artificial laws and proscriptive customs, were the ones who suffered. It was government censorship that stifled natural creativity; it was religious commandments that called natural human instincts sinful.

For many Enlightenment-era thinkers, the quintessential state of nature was 'discovered' by the French expedition that sailed in 1766 under the direction of Louis-Antoine de Bougainville to circumnavigate the globe. The ship made its way around Africa, across the Indian Ocean, skirted past New Guinea and in May landed on Tahiti. It was to his European eyes, heaven on Earth.

> Having an elementary knowledge of those crafts that are adequate for men who still live in a state close to nature, working little, enjoying all the pleasures of society, of dance, music conversation, indeed of love, the only God to which I believe these people offer any sacrifices. . . . Each moment of enjoyment is a festive occasion for this nation.

Philibert Commerson, the naturalist on board and a strong believer in Rousseau's ideas, perhaps best described Tahiti: "We have come upon the state of natural man, born without remorse, the gentle impulse of an instinct always sure because it has not yet degenerated into reason." (Interestingly, it seems that Commerson snuck his mistress aboard the ship, disguised as a man. Jeanne Baret was the ship surgeon and consequently the first woman to circumnavigate the world.)

While many writers extolled the state of nature that Commerson had observed in Tahiti, others emphasized that true human progress came from mankind's use of reason to challenge thoughtless traditions and superstitions. The German philosopher Immanuel Kant in his seminal pamphlet *What is the Enlightenment?* (1784) wrote, "Man, solely, through the use of reason, is capable of perfecting the good life on earth." For intellectuals there was an inherent tension in the quest for social improvement. While many extolled the innocence of the noble savage, there was also a lingering sense that the noble savage was instinctive rather than reflective, intuitive rather than rational. The noble savage was considered, in a sense, stuck in the past, and it was rational society that pointed the way to Kant's good life. In his work titled *The Social Contract* (1762), one of the most well-known thinkers of the day, Jean-Jacques Rousseau, explained that whatever the benefits of living in a natural state, humans were now part of societies and thus could "no longer subsist on plants or acorns or live without laws and magistrates." Immediately after Bougainville referred to Tahiti as utopia in his journal, he declared possession on behalf of the French crown. Like Columbus almost two centuries before, European 'discovery' often went hand-in-hand with European colonialism.

The French writer Denis Diderot wrote a fictional account of Bougainville's journey, *The Supplement to the Journal of Bougainville* (1772). In it he argued that Tahiti was no longer paradise precisely because it was controlled by France. "We are a free people," he has his Tahitian character say, "and now you have planted in our country the title deeds of our future slavery." Diderot was even more savage in his critique of the influence of the western world's religiously moralistic prudery. "Our enjoyments once so sweet, are now accompanied by remorse and terror. That man in black [a priest] who stands near you listening to me, has spoken to our lads. I do not know what he has said to our girls. But our lads are hesitant; our girls blush."

Writers reflected on and responded to the discovery of places such as Tahiti mostly through the lens of how such information could better inform high-minded institutions and societies of Europe, of the West. Very little regard was given to the fate of the indigenous peoples they met; many were decimated by the diseases carried by the European travelers and stripped of their culture by colonial overlords.

Imagined Travel and Reform in the Enlightened Age

Writers embraced travel as inspiration for 'new ideas.' Discovery through science and reason prompted creative fictional journeys. Francoise de Graffigny's account of the travails of an Incan princess stranded in France, Jonathan Swift's tale of wondrous adventures had by a marooned ship's surgeon in a land of diminutive humanoids, or Baron de Montesquieu's fictional letters from the Persian court all represent stories in exotic settings that could make inference to the problems of European society while artfully advocating for reform.

Travel-inspired literature added a sense of exoticism (and eroticism) that fueled readership. Many enlightened writers, after all, while committed to their reformist agendas, also needed people to buy their books. One study of the book trade in France found, for example, that "clients did not want abstract or theoretical works . . . instead they favored the popularizers and vulgarizers of the Enlightenment." (Diderot, for example, also wrote a work of soft-core pornography.) Using fictional settings also served a less materialistic and prurient goal; namely, placing these critiques of Europe in foreign or imaginative lands helped authors get their work past the government and religious censors who scoured the publishing houses for offensive material. Preaching the gospel of social and political reform served little purpose if people were not in the pews to listen.

A fascinating example of this imagined travel genre is Bernard de Fontenelle's *Conversation on the Plurality of Worlds* (1686). The story takes place in a chateau's garden where the young male narrator, the Marquis, strolls for several nights in the moonlight trying to convince his companion, the enchanting Marquise, that the universe is not what she imagined and that, perhaps one day, they would be able to travel and explore it together. The Marquis offers that Earth may not be the only inhabited planet and imagined "a plurality of worlds." At first the female protagonist is skeptical, but the Marquis uses the analogy of the worlds that Columbus' voyages opened up for the European mind to convince her that what we think of as impossible may not be. Just like Columbus bridged once separate worlds with his ships, the Marquis argues, so may the people on Earth may one day figure out how to travel the seemingly inseparable distance between Earth and the moon. "True, it will be necessary to cross the great expanse of air and sky between the Earth and the Moon. But did the great seas seem to the Americans more likely to be crossed?"

Fontenelle's book *Conversations* is noted for its inclusion and promotion of women in the new science. The Marquise, beautiful and charming, is also smart. At first she seems overwhelmed by the narrator's speculations, but by the end of the conversations she is leading the discussion. For Fontenelle the point was simple: Women were capable of being part of the new intellectual developments in Europe, and men should let them do so. His work became a model for similar works published throughout Europe. Although women did indeed read and discuss these works, few became true partners in scientific work; access to the community of intellectual discourse was slow.

The new astronomy of the seventeenth century intrigued Fontenelle. He embraced Copernicanism and the ideas of leading French thinker of the time, Rene Descartes. However, he was well aware that censorship by

French Catholic officials would likely squelch any overt support for these ideas, so he couched the views of the new science in a fictional stroll. He also wanted to reach broader audiences and knew that a drab scientific treatise would not attract a wide audience. Espousing his ideas through a witty banter laced with romantic tensions enhanced his readership; *The Conversations on the Plurality of Worlds* was one of the most popular books of the time.

Persian Letters: Political Lessons from the Harem

Fontenelle's use of exotic, imaginary travel and romantic dialogue was a model adapted by one of the most well-known political and social critics of the Enlightenment era, Baron de Montesquieu. His most famous work in this genre was *Persian Letters* (1721). According to one critic, it is "the book [that] inaugurated the eighteenth-century phenomenon known as the Enlightenment." The story is told through a collection of letters between two Persian men forced to leave their homes and wander through the Near East and most importantly, Europe. One of the two men, Usbek, corresponded with his wives who remained confined to his harem and to the eunuchs whom he ordered to watch over them in his absence. They become, in Montesquieu's telling, proxies for the French monarchy of Louis XIV.

Usbek thought that even though he was away from home he retained complete control over those he left behind. He is, Montesquieu wants us to know, much like Louis XVI sitting in the Halls of Versailles thinking he had the loyalty of, and control over, all his subjects. Usbek's power is far from absolute; without his presence to run roughshod over his wives, they begin to betray him, as did his deceitful and disobedient eunuchs. Even his (supposedly) loyal wife Roxanna betrayed him in the end. "Yes, I deceived you," Roxana wrote in the work's last letter, her suicide note. "I suborned your eunuchs, outwitted your jealousy and managed to turn your terrible harem into a place of delightful pleasures." Usbek's power was hollow, clearly only one of coercion. Montesquieu insinuated that Usbek's power would also have been ethereal even had he stayed, because power is not achieved by coercion but must be based on mutual respect and loyalty. He is, in a sense, the eunuch he so derisively threatened.

For Montesquieu, Usbek was a fictional version of the French King Louis XIV and the absolute authority he tried to hold over his kingdom. By 1721, when the book was published, Louis XIV had died, but Montesquieu hoped that the new king, Louis XV (r. 1715–1774) who was only five years old, would be amenable to a reformed state. That vision, eventually presented in *The Spirit of the Laws* (1748), argued that the best sate was one where there was a separation of powers and the rule of law. These ideas were embraced by reformers across the Atlantic world who pushed for the end of absolute monarchy and the establishment of representative government during the eighteenth and nineteenth centuries.

Other Imagined Journeys and Enlightenment Reformers

Without a doubt, the literary and financial success of Montesquieu's *Persian Letters* inspired more tales of foreign adventures that were not-so-veiled attacks on the social, political, cultural and religious values of Europe. One of the clearest imitators was Francoise de Graffigny's *Letters from a Peruvian Woman* (1747), the story of an Incan princess, Zilia, who was kidnapped and eventually brought to France. From there she wrote letters back to her beloved that explained the situation of women in France. She noted that they are held in contempt by almost everyone because of the "appalling lack of educational opportunity for females who from their earliest years find their natural state of virtue and spirit crushed by controlling and indifferent parents." The end result of this upbringing, Zilia sadly concludes, is that French women "participate in this entire little universe only though appearance. She is a decorative figure to amuse the curious."

De Graffigny was a relatively rare eighteenth-century European woman who found success in defying the social strictures she wrote about in her work. After she left a husband so debauched that the Church granted her an unusual legal separation, she moved to Paris and made her living writing plays for the *Comédie Francaise*, France's national theater, and published popular works such as *The Peruvian Letters*. By the end of the eighteenth century, women were beginning to demand access not only to education but to more active roles in public affairs. While such goals were only superficially and temporarily realized during the height of the French Revolution, they set the stage for the emergence of women's suffrage movements in Europe and the Americas that followed a century later.

In Jonathan Swift's *Gulliver's Travels* (1726), a ship surgeon finds himself stranded on different islands each populated with fantastic caricatures. The first is a land of Lilliputians—diminutive humanoids whose initial beauty and charms belie a pettiness and narrow-mindedness. They are just the opposite of the monstrous Brobdingnagians whose grotesque bodies conceal honest hearts and insightful minds. Later he encounters a land where horses are rational and humans are brutish beasts. Through imagined travels, Swift challenged his reader to question everything, not to accept superficial judgments and simplified explanations. English life and political institutions were held up to scrutiny and ridicule. At one point, for example, the leaders of the Houyhnhnms, horses who are "the ideal of rational conduct," asked Gulliver to explain law in England. Having previously been told that laws were designed for the protection of everyman how could it be, the Houyhnhnm leader asked, that some of those who Gulliver traveled with had been forced to leave England because they had been ruined by the law? Gulliver replied with an answer often heard today, "It is the lawyers." They "are bred from their youth," the doctor explains, "in the art of proving by words . . . that white is black and black is white."

One other example of imaginary travel literature is *Candide* (1759) by Voltaire. He was arguably the most recognized figure of the Enlightenment. His fame came about because of his scathing critiques of the Catholic Church (for which he spent much of his life in exile from his native France) as well as his acerbic indictments of hereditary monarchy. Voltaire voraciously scoured the growing flood of travel accounts to find models of reforms needed in Europe, although his own travels were confined to Western and Central Europe. Among the many works he read were the Jesuit writings on China, and based on those writings he came to admire the empire's political and educational achievements. China's Confucian system of education, he felt, was an ideal basis for a government bureaucracy based on reason rather than religion. Such a system, he reasoned, allowed for equality of opportunity for all, something that hardly existed in Europe's rigid social system. (In reality, China's educational and bureaucratic system was not as egalitarian as Voltaire interpreted it to be.)

It is ironic and yet also perfectly sensible that the Enlightenment's most celebrated proponent, Voltaire, was also its most celebrated critic, questioning everything. Just as he bellowed that we should "crush the infamy" of the absolutist pretensions of religion and the state, we should also question the absolutist pretensions of those who believed that reason was some secret elixir of universal insight. This skepticism of the Enlightenment became the central theme of *Candide*, which told the story of a young man, Candide (so named because he was "quite sound in his judgment and he had the most straightforward of minds"). He was educated by the "greatest philosopher in the province and thus the whole world," who could prove that Candide lived in the "best of all possible worlds." Candide's life is shattered when he is caught in an embrace with his step-sister Cunégorde (who initiated the encounter after witnessing Pangloss "giving a lesson in applied physiology to her mother's maid"), and he is "expelled from paradise on earth." Like Adam after eating the apple, he was forced to wander the world. Wars of rape and brutality, earthquakes followed by tortures of religious recompense, shipwrecks all become the grim reality for Candide, who, despite these natural and man-made savageries, continued to optimistically believe in the ideals of his tutor. Swept across the world in this swirl of events, at the end of the book he found himself on a small farm in Turkey still searching for meaning. He found it in the simple words of a farmer who (rather than worrying about great events) simply cultivated his garden. "Let's get down to work and stop all this philosophizing," a friend of Candide thinking about the wisdom of the simple farmer says. "It is the only way to make life bearable." "That is well put," replied Candide. ". . . We must tend our garden."

Conclusion

The new knowledge of the natural world brought back to Europe by voyagers like Dampier, Cook and Bougainville radically transformed thinking about everything from the structures of plants and the characteristics of animals to the nature of the human person and the divine. Dampier's detailed description of the flora and fauna he observed while sailing around Australia and into the

Pacific played an important role in prompting others to rethink the very nature of the natural world. Once capricious and idiosyncratic, the natural world was now increasingly seen as rational and ordered. Cooks' observations on the movements of Venus confirmed ideas on the solar system and the earth's place in the cosmos that had been evolving for centuries. Bougainville's encounters with the Pacific Island people in Tahiti provoked questions about human nature and the meaning and purpose of our lives.

Writers like Fontenelle brought these new discoveries to popular audiences and encouraged a generation of thinkers to translate these new insights into practical use for social and political change. They held to the belief that the natural world provided models for how humans should organize themselves and that the best societies were those structured on the laws of nature.

The problem was that there was little consensus on what were these laws of nature. Did new understandings of plants and animals reveal the mind of God directing the world or a world separate from the creative spark of a divine? Should people continue to believe in the central role of God in their lives or adopt a secular view of society and politics? Where the peoples of Tahiti, living close to nature, truly more advanced than Europeans who had regulated systems of government, society and economics?

Debates about these questions roiled across the Atlantic world. Buoyed by the ideals of the Enlightenment, revolutionaries in the American colonies, France, Europe and the Caribbean as well as throughout South America sought to "release man from the bonds of arbitrary authority," as Kant suggested. Many succeeded, but few found the promised land that enlightened thinkers argued was possible. Kings were deposed, but social inequalities persisted. Women remained relegated to inferior status, and ideas on equality were often only applied to certain classes and races. The Enlightenment movement of the eighteenth century, in short, raised fundamental questions that we are still trying to answer today.

End Materials Chapter 5

Works Quoted

Bacon, Francis, *The Philosophical Works of Francis Bacon* (New York: George Routledge and Sons, 1905).

de Bougainville, Louis-Antoine, *The Pacific Journal of Louis-Antoine Bougainville, 1767–1768*, John Dunmore, ed. and trans. (London: Hakylut Society, 2002).

de Fontenelle, Bernard le Bovier, *Conversations on the Plurality of Worlds*, H.A. Hargreaeves, trans. (Berkeley: University of California Press, 1990).

de Graffigny, Francoise, *Letters of Peruvian Woman*, Jonathan Mallison, trans. (Oxford: Oxford University Press, 2004).

Diderot, Denis, "Supplement to the Voyage of Bougainville," in April Alliston, ed., *The Longman Anthology of World Literature*, vol. D (New York: Longman Press, 2004).

Dryden, John, *The Conquest of Granada* (1670).

Edwards, Philip, ed., *The Journals of Captain Cook* (New York: Penguin Books, 1999).

Kant, Immanuel, *What Is the Enlightenment?* (Konigsberg, Germany, 1784).

Montesquieu, *The Persian Letters*, C.J. Betts, trans. (New York: Penguin Books, 2004).

Rousseau, Jean Jacques, *On the Social Contract*, Donald Cress, trans. (Indianapolis, IN: Hackett Publishing, 2019).

The Secret Instructions to Lieutenant Cook. www.foundingdocs.gov.au/resources/transcripts/nsw1_doc_1768.pdf.

Tony, Horowitz, "Blue Latitudes: Boldly Going Where Captain Cook Has Gone Before," cited in "James Cook and the Transit of Venus," *NASA Science*. https://science.nasa.gov/science-news/science-at-nasa/2004/28may_cook.

Voltaire, Nicholas Cronk, *Candide*, 3rd ed. (New York: WW Norton, 2016).

Further Reading

Dampier, William, *A New Voyage Round the World* (1697).

Liebersohn, Harry, *The Traveler's World: Europe to the Pacific* (Cambridge, MA: Harvard University Press, 2006).

Pagden, Anthony, *The Enlightenment: And Why It Still Matters* (Oxford: Oxford University Press, 2015).

Paine, Lincoln, *The Sea & Civilization: A Maritime History of the World* (New York: Vintage Books, 2013).

6 The Industrial Revolution and the Global Transportation Revolution

Introduction

The development of the steam engine in the eighteenth century led to a revolution in global travel in the nineteenth century. Originally developed to help pump water out of coal mines in England, the steam engine was gradually adopted for use in transportation. The technology continued to be refined, and by the 1830s it was used on railroads and steamships. The results were truly revolutionary, and over the course of the century railways and steamships became dominant modes of transport. They allowed the movement of people and goods without the constraints of animals (that may get sick or lame) or weather (winds that may blow only seasonally). They moved people faster and farther and stimulated a new age of global integration. As one historian noted, "The triumph of trains and their general acceptance meant that technological innovations, once regarded as toys or nuisances, were recognized as powerful levers for manipulating both the physical world and life itself."

This revolution also imposed new structures of social and economic organization. Steam engines required fuel, mostly coal, and this prompted the need for depots and fueling stations. Trains routes impacted where people lived; they defined what parts of the economy would be tied into transregional trade and isolated others. They also facilitated the continued expansion of western control across parts of the globe and became key developments of the imperial age.

By all accounts the steam engine changed both the speed of travel as well as the culture of travel. As travel now became reliant on fixed schedules, people measured the days in minutes and hours; the clock in some ways became the symbol of this new age of movement. Railroads and steamships opened the possibilities of long distance, affordable travel for more people. Tourism, an industry devoted to leisure vacations, emerged in tandem with new modes of travel available. What was once viable for an elite few was now more common, at least for those of the emerging middle class of professionals and businessmen who had time and resources.

The nineteenth century also witnessed the invention of the bicycle, "the feedless horse," as one writer called it. It promised the opportunity for people

DOI: 10.4324/9781003168690-7

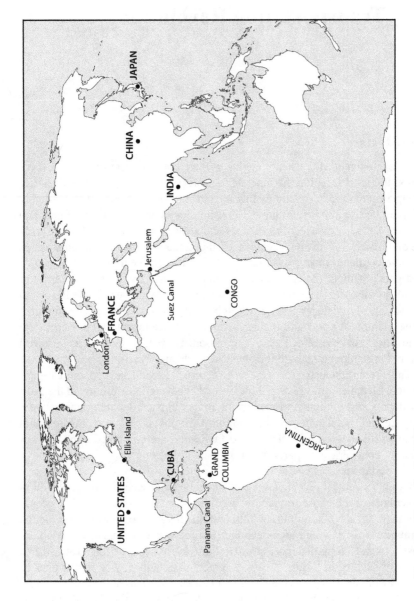

Map 5 Key Places for the 1800s

to move faster and farther under their own power. When Thomas Stevens completed his trip bicycling around the world, some portended a world that would be open to travelers, simply, under their own power. Add to that, a world in which women were finally free to move about as they wished.

For some, these new modes of travel promised liberation and freedom. For others they foreshadowed a world in which humans would be beholden to the machine. Poets and philosophers bemoaned a world controlled by the ticking of a clock rather than the rhythms of nature. Environmentalists were concerned about the damaging effects of acrid smoke billowing from steamships and trains. The steam engine and the bicycle ushered in a revolution in transportation; it remained to be seen whether it would be beneficial or not.

The Development of Railroads in Great Britain

Steam engines were initially used to pump water out of mines and run spinning jennys in textile factories of Great Britain. Gradually they became adapted for use in transportation, and in 1831 the first steam-powered passenger train, or iron horse, carried passengers between Manchester and Liverpool. Thousands lined the tracks to witness the inaugural run. Dignitaries, including members of the royal family, were among the first passengers. One of those dignitaries, William Huskisson, also became the first official rail passenger fatality when he stumbled and was crushed while trying to board the train as it pulled out of the station.

The Manchester-to-Liverpool train traveled at 16 miles per hour, not at all impressive by today's standards but a wonder in a world that moved at the speed of horse and foot. Over the next two decades, a network of rail lines was built to link every major city in England, and speed of train travel increased to 50 miles per hour.

Turning technological innovations into practical application took time. The railroads in Great Britain are a prime example. Although some 6,800 miles of track crisscrossed the British Isles by the mid-nineteenth century, there was little standardization in either track size or scheduling. This was because the train lines were privately built and operated and each owner could decide what worked for him or her. A train that traveled for 30 miles on one company's track would have to transfer to a track designed for different-sized trains to travel the next 30 miles. This changed over time, and soon train travel became a common, almost trivial event. By the mid-1850s, over 100 million passengers annually rode on the iron horses of Great Britain.

Railroad construction rapidly expanded across Europe. By the 1880s, France and the new German Empire surpassed tracks built in Great Britain. These rail lines were critical to strategic developments that led into World War One, they were especially important for Russian's imperial ambitions. As the Tsar's forces ventured into the Black Sea region and Siberia, rail lines moved troops to secure Russian outposts and provided access to the immense natural wealth found in different regions. By the early 1900s, Russia completed the main lines of the

Trans-Siberian Railway that connected St. Petersburg to the Pacific terminus at Vladivostok. Travel by rail was vital to movement during World War One and the Russian Revolution that followed.

Railroads in the Americas

The combination of westward expansion, brought about by significant immigration and cheap labor, and together with ready capital from British and American investors, spurred the growth of the railroad industry in the United States throughout the 1840s and 1850s. By the eve of the Civil War the United States had almost as many miles of rail lines as the whole of Europe. In the decades after the war, rail lines were laid even faster. In 1869, a golden spike was driven into the train track on Promontory Summit, Utah, to mark the completion of a transcontinental railroad. Canada completed its own transcontinental railroad in 1885. As one historian noted, "Instantly the world got smaller." Prior to the transcontinental railroad, travelers going between San Francisco and New York would have had to venture by ship down to Panama and across the rugged Isthmus by horse or some wagon contraption before once again getting on a ship, sailing across the Caribbean and up the East Coast. The other alternative was traveling by horse or wagon train, trips that were measured in seasons not weeks. After 1869, people could board a train and be on the East Coast in six to seven days.

To grasp the magnitude of the transportation revolution in the United States, some comparative statistics are helpful. By the beginning of the twentieth century, the US had a network of close to 200,000 miles of railroad; Canada's was only a tenth that size. Argentina, which enjoyed its own impressive network of railways, went from 470 miles of line in 1870 to over 10,000 by 1900; Mexico claimed about 12,000 miles of track. By the beginning of the twentieth century, distinct patterns of economic development were beginning to emerge between North and South America. Areas with rail lines saw increased settlement and the development of industrial manufacturing. Areas that did not get rail lines remained mainly rural and self-sufficient.

Steam Ships and Globalization

Steam engines also transformed the transoceanic shipping industry by the mid-nineteenth century. At first steamships were not practical as long-distance ocean vessels because they require constant refueling, but gradually, as better engines were developed and as re-coaling stations were established along key shipping routes, steamships dominated the waterways. Wood hulls were replaced by iron and then steel, making ships more reliable and able to carry heavier loads. By the end of the nineteenth century, given the combination of the speed at which they could travel and the volume they could carry, steamships had revolutionized global commerce. By the 1870s, with the opening of the Suez Canal that linked the Mediterranean and Red Seas, shipments that had typically taken five to six months could now move from Liverpool to Bombay in a month.

Between mid-century and the start of World War One, the tonnage of the global merchant marine fleet quadrupled in size. Moreover the development of refrigerated ships in the 1870s allowed ranching economies like Argentina to become part of this global system. The export of hides and tallow to Europe increased by nine hundred percent in the last quarter of the century. Steam shipping dramatically increased Argentina's wheat exports. Overall, the total value of its exports went from roughly $15 million in 1855 to close to $80 million by 1880.

Railroads, Steamships and Colonialism

Steam-powered, ironclad ships allowed western forces to travel up rivers and attack local forces more easily than before. They allowed colonial powers to move beyond the coasts to control vast tracts of foreign land. Once they had established footholds along these rivers, railroads were used to further control the interior. Building railroads in colonial territory was enormously profitable for the colonizers. The transportation revolution of the nineteenth century played a central role in the age of imperialism that followed.

Europeans had long desired to expand their influence throughout Africa, but diseases and the difficulties of moving inland off the coasts kept ambitions at bay. The development of quinine, a prophylactic against malaria, helped with the medical issues, and soon steamships opened up Africa's rivers to European travel. Able to travel against the strong currents of the Nile, Niger, the Congo and other key arteries, and able to carry significant weaponry to use against native populations, steamships were a game changer in the imperial enterprise. As the Scottish merchant Macgregor Laird put it after using steamships to travel up the Niger: "[With the steam engine] every river is open to us, time and distance are shortened . . . carrying the glad tidings of 'peace on earth and good will toward men' into the dark places of the earth."

In India and other colonies, railroads were also critical tools of empire. The development of India's plantation economy benefited from railways that could transport bulk goods like cotton and wheat economically, reaping substantial profit. By the end of the nineteenth century India had the fourth-largest rail network in the world (only surpassed by the United States, Canada and Russia). Many still claim that India's railroad system was one of the greatest achievements of British colonialism. They point to its continued importance in postcolonial India as firm evidence of the benefits of imperial rule. Others are not so sure. Historians skeptical of the benefits point out that the materials to build the railroads were produced overwhelmingly in Britain to the benefit of British, not Indian industrialists.

Railroads also accelerated the British takeover of much of India's artisanal and commercial economy. Since plantations were mostly controlled by British overlords, cottons and household goods produced in England could, using these newly built railroads, now penetrate Indian markets. This economic reality, combined with a colonial policy that aggressively restricted the export of Indian cloth and other goods, decimated many sectors of India's society. Lord Bentinck, the English governor of India, reported in 1834 that "the bones of the cotton weavers are bleaching the plains of India."

Railroads: On the Clock

In 1838 an emissary of the Ottoman Empire, Mustapha Sami Effendi, toured Europe, investigating the reasons for the continent's technical and economic surge and wondered what lessons he could bring back to his sultan. One of the things that most impressed him was how society was organized: "Indeed everything is organized like the machinery of a clock."

The factory systems, synced with the rail systems, defined the era. As one historian observed, "Train timetables imposed a precision nobody had bothered about before." Where pre-industrial society had largely lived by the rhythms of day and night, where localities defined the patterns of life, the expansion of railways necessitated that everyone be on the same schedule. People no longer traveled by their own clock but rather by timetables set by engineers and bureaucrats. By 1847 Greenwich Mean Time was adopted as the standard time for almost all British railways, and by 1880 it was standard in the western world.

Advocates argued that learning to live according to train schedules was a necessary step on the road to civilization and modernization. Mary Carpenter, a British woman traveling through India in the 1860s, for example, argued that "habits of punctuality and attention to duty are also taught, both directly and indirectly, by the railway. . . . The Indian railways are very wonderful and show the possibility of improving even the inferior portions of the native races, under judicious government and proper training."

Of course, Carpenter's admonition reflects her views, prejudiced by colonial position, and ignores the devastating impact that railways had on the livelihoods of many colonized people. Train travel brought about even more colonial control over the lives of the colonized. It reshaped cultures to fit western norms of time and order and facilitated the movement of colonial troops and traders in country to take greater control of the land and its resources.

Canals and Cables

The globalization and acceleration of travel during the nineteenth century ushered in by the development of the steam engine was further enhanced by the development of new technology that would speed communication in unprecedented ways through the development of transoceanic cables and transit canals, especially the building of the Suez and Panama Canals.

An American inventor, Samuel Morse, fascinated by the emerging science of electromagnetic energy designed a system in the 1830s whereby an electric signal of dots and dashes could pass down a wire. Those dots and dashes, in turn, corresponded to an alphabet he designed and named on his behalf. It was simple, effective, allowing information to be carried long distances; and the world was never the same.

By the 1850s, Morse's designs were being parred with rubber casings and put underwater. Cables were not only carrying information over land but now over oceans. The first transatlantic cable was successfully laid, after many failed attempts, in 1865. Great Britain enthusiastically embraced the new technology to help tie their global empire together, and by the 1870s cables connected London to key outposts all the way to Australia. By the early 1900s, cables crossed the vast Pacific, linking Asia and the Americas with direct communication.

Although long-distance telegraphy was relatively simple, it was by all accounts a very significant move toward globalization. Prior to these cables, for example, a letter from London to Bombay took at least a month. (This in and of itself was incredibly fast compared to prior centuries, when it could take over a year.) In 1870 the first cable message was sent between Queen Victoria of England and US President James Buchanan; the reply came back in five minutes!

In a similar but different context, the dream of connecting the Mediterranean and Red Seas had been around since ancient Egypt, but the technological engineering and compelling need did not coalesce until the mid-nineteenth century. Given the growing European presence in Egypt and beyond, ambitions to bring the dream of the Suez Canal to fruition were realized.

It was a French consortium, under the leadership of Ferdinand Lesseps, that launched the project. He negotiated with the Egyptian and Ottoman powers of the region for the rights to build the project under a ninety-nine year lease in return for a minority slice of the profit. Construction began in 1859 and lasted for ten long, backbreaking years of labor. Over one million men, mostly using shovels, dug the canal. Almost all were peasants, more slaves than wage laborers, and given the grueling effort, an estimated 120,000 became sick and died. It was only near the end of the project that steam-powered shovels were able to take on the bulk of the grinding work.

The Suez Canal opened with great international fanfare in 1869. The 120-mile canal saved travelers going between Europe and Asia some 9,000 kilometers of distance and ten to twelve days on ship by not going around the southern tip of Africa and across the Indian Ocean. Like the undersea cables that crossed the oceans, the canal further connected Europe's growing colonial presence in Asia and the Pacific. For Islamic travelers participating in the Hajj, it presented a much-preferred option compared to the lengthy overland routes that were typically used.

The Panama Canal, linking the Pacific Ocean and Caribbean Sea, was an even more arduous engineering and construction endeavor. The idea of a canal spanning the 50-mile Isthmus of Panama had been contemplated since the early days of Spanish colonialism, but the geography and work conditions in disease-infested jungles seemed insurmountable. By the 1880s, Lesseps (sponsored by the French government) took on the project, but his efforts were stymied after a few years. In 1902, the US President Theodore Roosevelt negotiated the purchase of the failed enterprise as a way to boast his global ambitions. Twelve long very brutal years of digging (and dying) ensued, and finally the Panama Canal opened in August of 1914, just as the cannons of World War One erupted across Europe.

Travel for the Sake of Travel: The Emergence of Tourism

Up to this point travel, particularly in the Western world, was largely afforded to the upper class. Aristocratic families traveled across Europe, maintaining extended family ties and enjoying a lifestyle afforded by wealth. Sons of the wealthy and aristocracy were expected to travel as a rite of passage before adult responsibilities demanded otherwise. They were expected to go on a 'Grand Tour,' visiting the major capitals of Europe, natural wonders and museums. Grand Tours were also times when these young men could 'sow their oats' before settling down to marital and family duties.

As the Industrial Revolution progressed, new sectors of the economy—businessmen, lawyers, bankers and financiers—imitated aspects of the well-to-do lifestyle. This emerging middle class had the resources to think about vacations, and some of these professional jobs now offered paid vacations as part of the compensation package. Their children were expected to spend more time studying and preparing for future careers, and, as a result, desired to emulate 'Grand Tours' of the aristocracy. As one Parisian said in 1877, "Until recently no one left his native town. . . . Today no one stays put."

The tourist industry in England began in the 1830s with Thomas Cook organizing tours for meetings of a temperance society to which he belonged. He mostly managed travel logistics so more people could attend meetings. He did a good job, and more people asked for his help to manage the increasingly complex travel schedules associated with the railroads. Rail lines were privately owned, and getting anywhere involved figuring out schedule and prices for several companies. Because railways were privately owned, they often had little coordination, and there were often long waits in between connections. Cook decided he could expedite the process by making it more efficient and negotiating with the rail companies for cheaper fares. Over the next decade he expanded to include leisure excursions, first to the British Isles and then later to continental Europe. Thomas Cook Travel became the first travel agency, and tourism as an industry was born.

Cook, whose roots were of common background, envisioned that his company could make travel available to everyone. "Travel for millions" was his slogan. Like the British aristocracy on their Grand Tours half a century before, commoners, farmers and industrial laborers were able to now enjoy the beauty of the Swiss Alps and the culture of cities like Florence and Paris. In 1880 Cook's agency secured the rights to run tours in Egypt, opening up the broader world to the British public. Moreover, he preached, peaceful relations between countries would be enhanced as travelers shared their commonalities with those who seemed so different from afar. (Unfortunately, the catastrophic wars of the twentieth century shattered his hopes.)

Actual data on the tourist industry during this period was limited. It seems as though most of Cook's clients were white-collar professional males, although it also seems that, over time, middle-class women were also beginning to go on his excursions. Perhaps this reflected greater freedom for women. It may also have been an opportunity for women to see the world while protected by a guided tour. By the end of the nineteenth century, and the fiftieth anniversary of the founding of his company, over three million people had booked vacations.

Although Cook primarily served the British, travel increased around the world. For example, statistics indicate that in 1827, four hundred twenty-two Americans visited Paris; of those few hundred travelers, about half were land-owners, about a quarter were men, another sixth were students or professionals and only a few were "men of modest means." After the steam ship was introduced in the 1860s, numbers grew exponentially and many more people of "modest means" traveled abroad. The American oceanographer Matthew Fontiane noted in 1861 that the Atlantic was crossed by steamers on a daily basis. Frederick Douglass proclaimed that the "oceans no longer divide, but link nations together. Travel from Boston to London was now a holiday excursion. Space is comparatively annihilated. Thoughts expressed on one side of the Atlantic, are distinctly heard on the other."

The Not-So-Innocent Abroad: Mark Twain

As travel and tourism were commonplace in the second half of the nineteenth century, writers and journalists found lucrative careers bringing distant places to audiences who had to stay at home. Perhaps the most famous tourist-turned-travel-writer of the nineteenth century, certainly in the United States, was Mark Twain. While today his novels about Huck Finn and Tom Sawyer are standard in many literature courses, it was his travel writing and lectures that made him famous in his lifetime and, from his perspective, paid the bills.

Samuel Clemens, aka Mark Twain, grew up in the pre-Civil War United States. At one point he dreamed of becoming a river boat captain on the Mississippi River. During the Civil War, now in his thirties he made his way, like many men, west to seek his fortune. By then, he thought his fortune could come through writing and journalism. While in California he managed to get a short story published: *The Celebrated Jumping Frog of Calaveras County* (1865). It was a success, and shortly after that the regional newspaper, *The Sacramento Union*, hired him to go to Hawaii and write about the growing US presence. That launched his career as a travel writer and lecturer.

Twain spent four months in Hawaii (known as the Sandwich Islands at the time) writing stories for the *Union* about "roughing it," lolling on the beaches and sauntering in the tropical forests. When he returned he embarked on a wildly successful lecture tour focused on "Our Fellow Savages in the Sand-wich Islands." The lectures highlighted his (often exaggerated) skills at story-telling, coupled with a style of using humor and sarcasm that made insightful and often biting commentaries on the people he met on his trips. He used this style throughout much of his subsequent work. In his lectures, the growing number of American tourists to Hawaii were none too sophisticated and often came off as country bumpkins or worse, as rapacious colonists. The indigenous Hawaiians were little better, often uncouth and uncivilized. In short, there was a common humanity in the failings and foibles of us all.

Buoyed by the financial success and personal acclaim of this lecture circuit, Twain immediately set his travel ambitions higher, heading off on one of the first steamship crossings between the US and Europe in 1867. "I am wild with impatience to move—move—*Move!*" Twain wrote to his mother in 1867, "My mind gives me peace only in excitement and restless moving from place to place. I wish I never had to stop *anywhere*." This trip took him across the Atlantic, to Iberia and through the Mediterranean, culminating with a trip through the Holy Land on horseback. That journey became the fodder of one of his most successful travelogues, *Innocents Abroad* (1869). "It was to be a picnic on a gigantic scale," he wrote in the introduction. We were to "take a royal holiday beyond the broad ocean in many a strange clime and in many a land renowned in history!"

Unlike other writers, Twain promised to "tell is like it is," to be the eyes, ears and voice of the common man. He cast his acerbic wit on all he met. He described Europeans as either dilettantes, with excessively haughty views of their traditions, or rubes, "no better than the donkeys they sleep with," as he derisively referred to the Portuguese. Everyone came off badly as he reported on his travels in the Holy Land. Americans were "vandals" plundering ancient artifacts. The peoples of the Near East were stuck in the past, living the same dull life their great-great-great grandparents had. Twain clearly adopted the Orientalist tropes that others had perpetuated.

Twain became a global phenomenon and his books, notably *A Tramp Abroad* (1880) and *Following the Equator* (1897) bestsellers. As much as anyone, he launched travel writing as a major genre.

The Bicycle: A Human-Powered Transportation Revolution

In October 1885, the *New York Times* ran a story about Thomas Stevens, a young Brit attempting to become the first person to "circumcyle," i.e. ride a bicycle around the world. When the article came out Stevens was in Teheran, Persia, waiting out the winter. By then he had made his way across the United States from San Francisco to Boston. He had pedaled across Western Europe and the Ottoman Empire and had wintered in Persia. For all of it he had largely traveled alone and unsupported, "an ordinary cowboy" as he called himself astride his "feedless horse." His feedless horse was a penny farthing, an early bicycle with a massive 50-inch front wheel and a tiny back wheel (which gave it the name of a "penny farthing," a small English coin). It did not have any gears and barely had any brakes. There was no room to carry much of anything but a change of underwear, a poncho and a gun.

Admiring his grit and fortitude the *New York Times* hailed his trip as "the most splendid personal journey of this century" and prognosticated that "who knows but that before the next century dawns it will be recognized that the inventor of the bicycle has done more to revolutionize the religious, moral, and social ideas of mankind than all the philosophers of our time." Steven's journey represented the global coming of age when the bicycle became a symbol of the individual freedom that could be had by anyone. "What corner of the world will be left unvisited by the silent riders of the iron steed?" the *Times* asked. "We shall have tricycling parties to Tibet and bicycling tours to Peking."

First introduced in the 1860s in France, the bicycle rapidly transformed from amusement toy to transportation vehicle. By the early 1880s, thousands were being made annually in the United States, and many people were beginning to speculate on their revolutionary potential. Bicycles offered individuals the possibility of going anywhere they wanted. Conservative moralists rued the possibility of married women using bicycles to ride to trysts. Women suffragettes like Susan B. Anthony praised the bicycle for giving a "woman a feeling of freedom and self-reliance. It makes her feel as if she were independent."

Eugene Weber, in his social and cultural history of turn-of-the-century France, notes that during this era the bicycle was considered "an emblem of Progress." While Stevens himself never said so, at least directly, an editorial in *Outing* magazine in July 1886 professed that Stevens had undertaken his quest "mainly for the purpose of displaying the powers of the modern bicycle." That he could ride around the world on his own power was for him a testament of Western technological superiority. It promised a new age of individualism in which one person, powered by his or her own legs, could go anywhere he or she wanted. It was for him, "[a] graceful triumph of Western ingenuity and mechanical skill."

Stevens completed his trip in 1886 having successfully negotiated his final legs across India, and then through China and Japan. He was a global hero, feted everywhere he went. By the time he returned to San Francisco, factory manufacturing replaced the artisanal style production of the penny-farthing he had ridden, and the new 'safety' (a bike with wheels of equal size and rubber brakes) was the standard ride. By the end of the decade, the bicycle industry was one of the largest in the country. Almost one million bikes were now being produced a year in the US. Author Stephen Crane announced that "everything is the bicycle."

Stevens' trip, while it heralded the advent of the bicycles, also represented the apogee of the bicycle industry. By the beginning of the twentieth century, his fame and the bicycle craze were fading. By 1900, bicycle production was a quarter of what it had been only a few years before. With much less effort, motorcycles and cars promised the freedom of movement first offered by the bicycle.

Reactions to the Transportation Revolution: Romanticism

Not everyone preached the liberating gospel of travel for the masses as Thomas Cook did. Already by the middle of the nineteenth century, literary figures of the Romantic Movement were decrying the impact of industrialization and railroads on the natural world. One of the best-known examples of this reaction was the life and work of the English poet William Wordsworth (1770–1850). Wordsworth lived most of his life in the area of the Lake District of England, north of Manchester. It is an area of lakes and tarns, slate hills and pastures, and Wordsworth hiked there endlessly. He became a well-known poet, extolling the beauty of the lands.

In the 1850s, however, he saw the evils of industrialization descending on his romantic refuge: a rail line was proposed to bring the Lancashire masses to the pastures and hills of his beloved country. "Is there no nook of English ground secure from this rash assault?" he despaired in one of his many poems on the subject. His friend, the artist John Ruskin, argued that industrialization was desacralizing nature with its crowds and smoke. It was turning the land into a commodity to be exploited not a place to be nurtured. In the United States one of the leading figures in the nineteenth century naturalist movement, Henry David Thoreau, bemoaned that "we do not ride upon the railroad but the railroad rides upon us."

Reactions to the Transportation Revolution: Science Fiction of Jules Verne

The downside of the nineteenth century transportation revolution was also reflected in the growing industry of science fiction writing in the later part of the century. These novels became widely read by the masses, especially the work of the most famous writer of his day, Jules Verne (1828–1905). Through his fantastical voyages to the moon or under the sea, he opened up a world of new possibilities and potentially catastrophic conflicts.

It is likely that Verne ventured further than anyone in the nineteenth century, at least in his mind and his writings. Through his literary imagination, Verne took trips to a *Mysterious Island* (1875), voyages *Twenty Thousands Leagues Under the Sea* (1869), *Journeys to the Center of the Earth* (1864), adventures *Around the World in Eighty Days* (1872) and even *Around the Moon* (1869). In all he wrote over fifty books, most of them about fantastical journeys. Through these immensely popular works, which were quickly translated from French into every major European language (and Turkish), he took millions of eager readers along with him. Long after his death he continues to do so. His adventures have become staples of popular films, and he is one of the top five most-translated authors of all time.

Verne's works extolled the power of technology to overcome the limits of nature. Planes that could fly around the world nonstop, spaceships that could go to the moon, "telegraphic" communication networks that linked the globe with instantaneous contact—these were only some of his imaginative inventions. (Many of these inventions came to be in the twentieth century, albeit not in the exact way he described.) His works also revealed deep anxieties about the dangers for mankind that these advances may hold in the wrong hands. While science could overcome nature, science could ultimately not overcome human nature, which remained flawed by greed, ambition and avarice. The immense popularity of Verne's works reflected a public interested in, and worried about, the prospects and perils of the new technology.

The dark side of science's power to be used as an instrument of oppression is the theme of one of Verne's last works, *Master of the World* (1904). It is the story of Robur, a brilliant scientist who creates an airplane powered by electricity that can sail around the world nonstop. Rather than using this invention to master the world, however, the machine masters him, turning him into a megalomaniac. In the end Robur is killed by his science, and the earth is barely spared a disastrous fate. The ominous forebodings of Verne's science fiction became much less fiction and no longer forebodings as the technologies of movement were translated into weapons of war in the twentieth century. During World War One, trains would move millions of soldiers across Europe to feed the insatiable demands of trench warfare. The world would witness the use of tanks, planes and submarines to expand the theaters and deadliness of war in unfathomable ways. And World War Two would see the development of air warfare that would level cities in a night and carry atomic weapons to drop on the cities of Japan.

Conclusion

The nineteenth century saw the development of new technologies of transportation that changed the world forever. They accelerated and regularized global connections. They opened opportunities for many to experience a world far beyond their homes as never before. Proponents preached the gospel of freedom and liberation for all. For some, however, this revolution in transportation had a darker side. It was a future structured by the ticking of a clock. It was a future of billowing clouds of coal ash blackening the skies. It was a future in which the machine controlled mankind rather than the other way around.

The story of the transportation revolution of the nineteenth century is the story of many revolutions. It was a revolution that opened new avenues and left many behind. It facilitated change and forced changes on many who did not want them. It made life easier and more enjoyable for those able to take advantage of it and brought hardships to others who could not. It gave people more opportunities to see the wider world and distant lands than ever before and, at the same time, threatened to ruin the very world that was now accessible. Revolutions are usually two-way streets; the transportation revolution of the nineteenth century certainly was.

End Materials Chapter 6

Works Quoted

Effendi, Mustafa Sami, "One the General Conditions of Europe," in David Damrosch, ed., *The Longman Anthology of World Literature, vol. E, the Nineteenth Century* (New York: Longman, Pearson, 2004).

Ghose, Indira, ed., *Memsahibs Abroad: Writings by Women Travellers in Nineteenth Century India* (New Delhi: Oxford University Press, 1998).

Stevens, Thomas, *Around the World on a Bicycle* (Mechanicsburg, PA: Stackpoole Books, 2001).

Verne, Jules, *The Best of Jules Verne* (Knoxville, TN: Wordsworth Classics, 2016).

Weber, Eugen, *France: Fin d'Siecle* (Cambridge, MA: The Belknap Press of the Harvard University Press, 1986).

Further Reading

Gordon, John Steele, *Threads Across the Ocean: The Historic Story of the Transatlantic Cable* (New York: Harper Collins, 2003).

Headrick, Daniel, *The Tools of Empire: Technology and European Imperialism in the Nineteenth Century* (Oxford: Oxford University Press, 1981).

Herlihy, David, *Bicycle: The History* (Hartford, CT: Yale University Press, 2004).

Pacey, Arnold, *Technology in World Civilization* (Cambridge, MA: MIT Press, 2001).

Porter, Gabrielle and Tom Taylor, "The Impractical Scheme of a Visionary: Thomas Stevens and the Quest to Travel Round the World on a Bicycle," *World History Connected* (June 2013). https://worldhistoryconnected.press.uillinois.edu/10.2/forum_porter.html (Accessed September 22, 2021).

7 Global Migration in the Nineteenth Century

Introduction

The nineteenth century witnessed global migration on an unprecedented scale. During the first part of the century, the global slave trade, and especially the Atlantic Slave Trade, reached a peak. By the second half of the century the slave trade was largely abolished, but the demands for labor around the world continued to rise. Industrial factories in Great Britain, Europe and the United States needed millions to fill jobs. Industrial production also required insatiable amounts of raw materials to feed the machines. Plantations and mines demanded more men, more women and more children to grow and extract resources. New transportation technologies allowed people to move further, faster and more reliably than ever before. As Adam Mckeown in his seminal study of global migration said, "The rise of a global economy centered on European, North American, and Japanese industrialization was the context for increased long distance migration of settlers and workers."

Migration patterns correlated with significant population growth and reflected the needs of many to find livelihoods. The world's population almost doubled over the course of the nineteenth century. Europe's population surged from approximately 100 million to 400 million. Farming communities in Ireland, Scandinavia and Central Europe found more and more people trying to live on smaller and smaller plots of land. China witnessed horrific wars, revolutions and famines for much of the mid-century and yet still saw its population increase by fifty percent to about 450 million. India, despite disastrously negligent famine relief policies under their British overlords, saw its numbers grow from 170 million to over 240 million over the course of the century. Japan's population surged by thirty percent by in the second half of the century. In each of these regions many decided to leave in order to survive.

Labor migrated to where there was work. Chinese laborers built the rail lines that linked the eastern seaboards of Canada and United States to the expanding frontiers of the West. Indian coolies performed the same for the British Empire across India and Africa. The expanded rail networks even carried workers to the less-developed regions of Siberia and Manchuria. These networks became so organized and affordable that, by the end of the century, farm workers were

DOI: 10.4324/9781003168690-8

picking crops in Argentina in March and returning to Italy in time for spring planting.

Global migration shaped almost every part of the world during the nineteenth and early twentieth centuries. Population movements affected the social and economic trajectories of countries that both lost and gained people. Governments were forced to address the issues raised by migration and to deal with issues of assimilation created by the flood of foreigners. The global movement of people accelerated and initiated circumstances that still shape the world well over a century later, such as prosperity and poverty, prejudice and inequality, oppression and opportunity. The history of global migration was the story of the push of peoples out of their often desperate circumstances and the pull of hope the new places offered.

Who Were the Migrants?: Defining the Term

In order to better understand the history of migration during the nineteenth century, it is important to define what we mean by a migration. In their seminal study of gender and migration, Donato and Gabaccia define a migrant as any person "who crosses an international border (or, in the past, an ocean)." Others add that migrants move across borders with the intention of moving permanently or staying for a period of time. In short, migrants are not tourists or short-term travelers. Adam Mckeown expands this definition, noting that "transoceanic migration accounts for only a portion of global migration. Some migration was temporary or permanent movement to nearby cities, towns, factories, mines, and plantations." Most migrants moved of their own volition, although, as we shall see in the case of conscripted labor from China, contracts clearly constrained choices and freedom of movement.

Donato and Gabaccia added another caveat to their definition of a migrant, namely the immigrants they study are found in four major data bases: the Atlantic Slave Trade Data base; the records of the International Labor Organization (ILO), which examined patterns of male immigration in Europe; the League of Nations study, which largely looked at interwar movements; and finally census data that examined who lived in any given country along with ethnicity and country of origin at given points in time. The census data represented sixty-six nations. Their caveat is a reminder that historians are dependent on the available source data to study. In the case of migration, information is predicated by the records of was actually tracked; informal crossings of borders or those who Mckeown notes traveled internally from rural to areas to cities were usually not captured in official statistics. His work, he explains, focuses on "three main circuits of long-distance migration from 1846 to 1940:" the Americas; Southeast Asia, the Indian Ocean and the Pacific Rim; and Northern and Central Asia and Japan." While there was likely significant transregional movement in Africa, he notes, the lack of data makes any analysis of migration patterns on the continent difficult.

Beyond sources used by researchers like Mckeown, Donato and Gabaccia, others have studied migration patterns by analyzing commission reports (produced by countries examining the fates of people as they left and ventured abroad), manifests from passenger ships (collected and collated from many archives, similar to the Atlantic Slave Trade data base but not on the same scale and consistency) and records from immigration offices (such as those available from Ellis Island in New York). In addition, newspaper articles and personal accounts can also be valuable in order to understand migration through a more personal lens.

For most of this period, the vast majority of migrants were single men. Over time, women migrated and traveled more but for different reasons. Many found work in the Americas as the demand grew after the slave trade ended; others traveled to join their families. Toward the end of the century, Jewish women fled religious persecution, making their way to the Americas. In the British colonial empires, especially in the Indian Ocean basin there were attempts to encourage women to migrate so that they could "civilize the men" and make the areas "more governable." Overall, women remained a smaller segment of the global immigration story until after World War One, when migration "became more gender balanced and female predominant."

European Immigration to North America

The nineteenth century saw massive numbers of Europeans migrating to the Americas and the Caribbean. Of the millions who left their homelands for a future across the Atlantic, close to two-thirds went to the United States. Smaller numbers ventured to Canada, Brazil, Argentina and, to a lesser extent, Cuba. Up until the 1870s, most emigrants came from the British Isles, particularly Ireland, followed by Northern and Central Europe. By the end of the century, as transportation networks improved and cost of passage was cheaper, more came from southern Europe, Russia and the Near East.

Immigration to the Americas was a classic case of push and pull. The push was prompted by overpopulation coupled with devastating famines that decimated many parts of the British Isles and Northern Europe. This was especially acute in the 1840s, when a blight struck the potato crop that sustained many of the poorer farming families of this region (the Irish Potato Famine), killing hundreds of thousands and impoverishing scores more. Ireland—with a population of about 8.8 million—saw one million people die and another two million leave in order to survive. During that decade almost half of all immigrants coming into the United States were from Ireland.

While the vast majority of these immigrants settled in the United States, many traveled to Canada first because transatlantic fares were cheaper. They traveled on ships that carried timber to Europe and returned with human ballast. The passage was brutal; ships became known as 'coffin ships' because so many died. Some estimate that thirty percent died on the sea or as they were quarantined in port. One witness described the scene as "hundreds of poor people, men, women and children of all ages . . . huddled together without air, wallowing in filth and breathing a fetid atmosphere, sick in body, dispirited in heart."

The pull factor was the promise of land and better jobs. In 1862, during the darkest days of the Civil War, the United States passed the Homestead Act, promising one hundred sixty acres out west for anyone willing to settle and improve the land. Canada passed a nearly identical bill a decade later. For millions of land-starved Europeans, it was the equivalent of winning a lottery: their own land, not simply land that they worked for their landlord, and plenty of it. As the Wisconsin Congressman John Potter noted during the legislation's debates:

> Immigration has almost ceased, and the present unsettled condition of Europe, tending to a general war on that continent, should invite, on our part, the adoption of the most liberal policy, which will induce the immigrant to seek a home here, and invest his capital and direct his labor to the development of the now unproductive resources of the country. . . . We shall do all in our power to invite immigration and capital to our unoccupied public lands.

But the Homestead Act was more than a land law. Immigrants had to agree to stay on the land five years, thus anchoring themselves to their parcels and in turn declaring intention to become US citizens.

White settlers had been making their way west ever since the founding of colonies on the Atlantic seaboard. However, the "public lands" that they were allowed to claim were home to Native Americans. US and Canadian government-sponsored land grabs sparked violent wars to remove the Native American people who had long lived in these areas. Across the Southeast, Native Americans from the so-called Five Tribes of the Cherokee, Choctaw, Chickasaw, the Creek and Seminoles—where close to 80,000 people who had lived there forever—were marched from their homes to the barren, arid lands of Oklahoma. As many as 10,000 never made it. Forced relocation of countless Native American tribes to reservations became the long-standing legacy of the Homestead Act.

Around the same time as the natives peoples of the southeast were being marched west, religious groups such as the Mormons, who had faced hostilities in the eastern and central United States, made their way across the Great Plains and into what at that time was part of Mexico and later became the Utah territory. Settlers hoping to find land to farm also headed to Mexican territory in present-day Texas. Wars between the United States and Mexico ensued, and after the United States won, Mexico ceded much of the southwest, including the future states of New Mexico, Arizona, Utah and much of California.

The new territories won by the United States from Mexico further accelerated the movements of peoples to the West. Traveling by wagon along the Santa Fe and Oregon Trails, thousands made an arduous journey across the

Great Plains and Rocky Mountains to the Pacific coast. Adam Mckeown estimates that as many as 10 million people migrated across the United States and Canada from the East to the West during the nineteenth and early twentieth centuries. Perhaps another 2.5 million laborers moved north from Mexico to work in the expanding agricultural economies of California and the American Southwest. Similar numbers of Canadians made their way south, looking for jobs in the burgeoning factories of the US northeast.

Ellis Island and the Establishment of Formal Immigration Policy in the United States

Prior to 1890 the United States had no federal immigration policy; states set quotas and determined who was eligible for entry. However, faced with growing numbers of immigrants, as well as issues of racism against migrants from certain regions (particularly Asia), the federal government established a federal bureau of immigration. Ellis Island was constructed in New York Harbor to handle the surge. Europeans arrived by steamship on a regular basis. Those in first and second class were allowed to walk through; those in steerage were inspected more closely for any potential diseases, criminal history or (after 1903) a connection with anarchist politics.

Annie Moore, a teenage girl from Cork County, Ireland, was the first of 12 million immigrants who passed through its gates. She was headed to meet her parents and two younger brothers, who immigrated four years earlier. This pattern was fairly typical. Some family members made the trip and then brought over the rest of their family once conditions warranted. Irish immigrants, in part because they were mostly Catholic and who often faced strong prejudice, tended to move to communities that offered them support and sanctuary.

Annie's arrival typified immigration legends—the young, 'rosy-cheeked' lass makes her way to America and finds the American dream. Immigration officials gave her a ten-dollar coin. Newspapers scrambled to get pictures of her as she was reunited with her parents. That grand entrance, however, was followed by a more typical, and mundane, immigrant story. She lived her whole life in Lower Manhattan in a modest flat, married a German-American fishmonger, had ten children, five of whom died before the age of three. She died at age fifty, in 1924, of heart failure.

European Immigration to Latin America

In Latin America, there was perhaps no country more transformed by the mass migrations of the nineteenth century than Argentina. Although fewer total immigrants went to Argentina than the United States (around 6 million versus 32 million) the proportional impact was significant. "If one measures the numbers of arrivals against the preexisting population of the respective receiving countries it turns out that in Argentina and Uruguay the ratio of newcomers to residents surpassed that of the United States and Canada during much of the second half of the 19th century." Brazil was the only other Latin American country that was close. The Argentine constitution of 1853 encouraged immigration and made citizenship attainable. More Spaniards immigrated to Buenos Aires, the capital of Argentina, in 1910, for example, than in the previous three centuries.

Unlike in North America, where there were waves of immigration first from the British Isles, then from northern Europe and finally southern Europe and the Near East, Argentina's immigrants were overwhelmingly from Spain and Italy. Italians also made up the majority of immigrants into Brazil. They came to work the coffee plantations after the country outlawed slavery in 1853. By the early twentieth century, Japanese and Portuguese arrived, albeit in smaller numbers.

Michael Goebel, in his study of immigration patterns in Latin America, argues that most immigrants who came to Latin America did not intend to stay; they hoped to cash in on the seasonal work available and return home. By this point, frequent and less expensive transportation options opened the possibilities of travel for seasonal work as temporary laborers. Because Argentina was in the southern hemisphere, workers could harvest crops in Europe and then work the harvest season in Latin America. Called *golondrinas* (Spanish for "swallows") they only needed to work two weeks to pay for a round-trip ticket. Estimates are that half of those who immigrated to Argentina during this time did indeed return home. As was the case in North America, most immigrants migrated to cities like Buenos Areas and San Paulo, where they had points of contact from family and friends who were already there.

Asian Migration to the Americas and the Caribbean

As slavery was abolished in the Americas and Caribbean, landowners looked to find new ways to secure plantation labor. One plan was to bring indentured workers from Asia, especially India and China, and later Japan. They came from areas that were highly populated, and many were poor and desperate for work. Governments wanted to lessen the burden of support required by too many people, so they were eager to help them move abroad. The labor contracts that were brokered enriched the businessmen and government officials who arranged them. And host countries often saw diplomatic advantages to making these deals. China and Japan, for example, were anxious to curry favor with the Western powers, and they saw these laborers as a way to establish good will abroad.

Indian labor was imported into British controlled areas like Jamaica and the West Indies. They officially came as free workers on labor contracts that stipulated a period of work abroad, usually at least five years. Workers were given a small wage; some were promised a plot of land when their contract was completed. Others were given return passage. Given the increasingly desperate conditions of many of India's rural poor under British colonial rule, it seemed like a good deal; the reality was often different. Workers could not read the contracts and often did not know where they were going. They were largely dependent on the good will of the overseer who signed them on, however there was not much good will forthcoming. Some attempted to escape only to be recaptured and then had their time of indentured labor doubled to ten years.

China's role in building the Americas came after the defeat of the Chinese by the British in the Opium War of 1839–1842 had opened China to western interventions. From approximately 1842 until early in the twentieth century approximately three million southern Chinese left their homes for work around the world. Over a third of them went to the Americas; around 150,000 to work the sugar fields of Cuba. Like Indian laborers they signed contracts that promised wages and work conditions. Those contracts were often ignored, and their experiences were, in many ways similar to those of the African slaves who had worked under similar conditions. Mortality rates on the vessels that carried them were also similar to what had been reported on slave ships. Once in port laborers, much like slaves, were often paraded naked around the central city's labor markets. Contracts that stipulated that they work only twelve hours per day and be given a certain amount of meat along with their staples were routinely dismissed.

One notable difference between the Atlantic Slave Trade and the Asian contract labor system was that international pressure brought about change more quickly. In the case of Chinese labor to Cuba, tens of thousands of Chinese who went to Cuba to work the sugar cane plantations returned home and reported that terms of agreements were not honored. As a result, in a fairly extraordinary move, the Chinese government sent a commission to Cuba to interview Chinese laborers and to see the conditions firsthand. They interviewed 1,176 workers and published findings in the *Cuba Commission Report* (1876), "one of the most unusual sources for the study of labor migration ever assembled."

The report concluded that "it thus appears that of the Chinese laborers who have proceeded to Cuba, 8 or 9 out of every 10 have been conveyed against their will." And, once in Havana "they are at once confined in barracks from which they can only go forth to labor under guard, being unable to move a single step with freedom." Because they could not speak Spanish, any attempts to report their ill treatments to local authorities were literally not heard. Once word got back to China and the report was completed, the Chinese government to voided many of the labor contracts. After they left Cuba the workers were redirected to Japan, where they were treated just as poorly.

Chinese labor brigades came to North America and Australia by the tens of thousands to work in the mines and later building railroads across the United States, Canada and Western Australia. Again, they told stories of harsh treatment, dangerous work and agents who refused to pay earned wages, and many did not have enough money after they finished their contract to return home. Forced to stay, many Chinese laborers were victims of increasing prejudice and violence by Americans, who worried they would take their jobs and corrupt their culture.

By 1882, tensions escalated. The number of Asian migrants living in the US had gone up, and the need for labor had gone down. In order to deal with the situation, the United States passed the Chinese Exclusion Act banning Chinese immigration into the US for ten years (it was renewed for another ten years in 1892), and this made life for many Chinese even more difficult. In 1885 the Canadian Parliament approved a tax on all Chinese in the country with the hope that this tax would deter more workers from coming. Anti-Asian prejudices also emerged in what would become Australia. In 1855 the provincial government of Sydney imposed taxes on all Chinese immigrants. Anti-Chinese riots erupted in the gold fields. By the 1900s the Australian government passed a "prescribed language test" that made it far easier for Europeans than Asians to immigrate. In essence Australia wanted to be a 'white' colony.

Early in the twentieth century, Asian migration to North America and Australia had slowed significantly. Japanese and Chinese workers looked to South America for work, however Argentina and Uruguay had also passed Anti-Asian legislation similar to laws in the US and Canada, so many headed to Peru and Chile, where there were no exclusionary laws.

Migration Patterns in East Asia

China's ongoing struggles with overpopulation and famine over the second half of the nineteenth century also encouraged the Qing government to promote migration into Northern Asia, Manchuria and Korea. These were regions were underdeveloped and presented agricultural and industrial opportunity and wealth to whomever controlled them. Perhaps it also supported national security geopolitics, as Mckeown notes: "The opening and encouragement of migration into Siberia and Manchuria were both partially impelled by the perceptions of the Russian and Chinese governments that these borderlands must be claimed and fortified."

Migration into Northern Asia was facilitated by the construction of railroads into these regions. Once Europeans secured control of many of China's ports after the Opium Wars (1830s–1860s), they began to build railways. Business was very lucrative, the labor cheap (and often coerced) and profits were driven by the desire to get access to valuable minerals. Many Chinese laborers who moved north to build the railroads worked on these European concessions. When their contracts were over, many stayed and worked the mines and factories that were springing up across the region. While exact numbers are hard to access, it is safe to say that millions of Chinese migrated from the south to the north during the late nineteenth and early twentieth centuries.

Russia invested heavily in construction of railways across Siberia and into Manchuria. Clearly they too were aware of the vast mineral wealth available in Northern China. Cities like Harbin, a frontier outpost in the mid-nineteenth century (its name is *Manchu* for place for 'drying nets'—an indication of its size and function), became a major metropolis and a center of Russian culture on the east end of the Siberian Railway. By World War One it had a population of close to 70,000, most of whom came from other places. Census records indicate that there were fifty-six resident nationalities, a clear indication of the dynamic migration patterns that shaped the city.

Buoyed by successful wars against China in 1894 and Russia a decade later, Japan eyed expansion and migration into northern Asia. It was a clear step toward larger goals of dominating Asia. By the early 1900s Japan colonized Korea, once under the protectorate of China. Shortly thereafter, Japan was sending its military and settlers into the area. By World War One they were also sending troops, engineers and managers into Manchuria.

In many cases, migrations provoked national confrontations. Key battles in the Russian civil wars of the 1920s were fought in the streets of Harbin and surrounding regions. Japan and China were locked in an undeclared war over Manchuria during the interwar period. In many ways it was these clashes that set the stage for the cataclysmic battles that would decimate all of Asia during World War Two.

Conclusion

The United States established an Immigration Bureau in 1891, and other countries followed. Laws were enacted to formalize processes for immigration in many countries around the world during the late nineteenth and early twentieth centuries. Many of these processes, like the Chinese Exclusion Acts, defined who would be allowed to come into the country. While countries like the United States proclaimed on the plaque found at the base of the Statue of Liberty: "Give me your tired, your poor, your huddled masses yearning to breathe free," Ellis Island was not a gateway for everyone, and over time nations began to define who 'fit' their national character along racial and ethnic lines. Diego Sarmiento, the one-time pro-immigration president of Argentina later decried the Italian 'invasion' of his country. Brazil and other countries promoted immigration that facilitated the whitening of their country. (Some politicians in the country accepted Japanese immigration because their productivity proved they were 'whiter' than Portuguese.)

The experience of migration varied widely; some immigrants found leaving their homeland for a foreign land exceedingly challenging and frustrating, but for others it opened the door to new dreams and prosperity. While the oppressive issues of overpopulation, war and famine drove many away from home, the allure of land, jobs and freedom from persecution pulled many to leave home and seek a new life abroad.

World War One largely ended this era of global migration. Countries in Europe closed their doors to foreigners, who they increasingly worried could be spies or provocateurs. The risks of travel, as ships crossing the Atlantic were now military targets, made immigration too dangerous to contemplate.

End Materials Chapter 7

Works Quoted

Bakich, Olga Mikhailovna, "Emigre Identity: The Case of Harbin," *The South Atlantic Quarterly*, vol. 99, no. 1 (2000).

Bell, Blake, *America's Invitation to the World Was the Homestead Act the First Accommodating Immigration Legislation in the United States?* www.nps.gov/home/learn/historyculture/americas-invitation-to-the-world.html.

Donato, Katherine and Donna Gabaccia, *Gender and International Migration* (New York: Russel Sage Foundation, 2015).

Helly, Denise, "Introduction," in Stanley Mintz, trans., *The Cuba Commission Report: A Hidden History of the Chinese in Cuba* (Baltimore, MD: The Johns Hopkins Press, 1993).

The Irish Potato Famine and American Immigration, *The Constitutional Rights Foundation* (Winter 2010). Constitutional Rights Foundation. www.crf-usa.org.

Jachimowicz, Maia, "Argentina: A New Era of Migration and Migration Policy," *Migration Policy Institute* (February 1, 2006). www.migrationpolicy.org/article/argentina-new-era-migration-and-migration-policy.

McKeown, Adam, "Global Migration, 1846–1940," *Journal of World History*, vol. 15, no. 2 (June 2004): 155–192.

Pruitt, Ida, *A Daughter of Han: The Autobiography of a Chinese Working Woman* (Stanford: Stanford University Press, 1967).

Wejsa, Shari and Jeffrey Lesser, "Migration in Brazil: The Making of a Multicultural Society," *Migration Policy Institute* (March 29, 2018). www.migrationpolicy.org/article/migration-brazil-making-multicultural-society.

Further Reading

Anitha, Sundari and Ruth Pearson, "Striking Women: An Educational Site About Migration, Women and Work," *Striking Women*. www.striking-women.org/.

Goebel, Michael, "Immigration and National Identity in Latin America, 1870–1930," *Latin American History* (May 9, 2016). https://doi.org/10.1093/acrefore/9780199366439.013.288.

Manning, Patrick and Tiffany Trimmer, *Migration in World History* (London: Routledge, 2020).

Mintz, Steven, trans., *The Cuba Commission Report: A Hidden History of the Chinese in Cuba* (Baltimore, MD: The Johns Hopkins University Press, 1993).

Northrup, David, *Indentured Labor in the Age of Imperialism, 1834–1922* (Cambridge: Cambridge University Press, 1995).

8 Political and Social Reformers in the Nineteenth Century

Introduction

As revolutions overturned old regimes around the world, in the later eighteenth and nineteenth centuries, reformers traveled widely looking for social and political models to bring back to their home countries. Some were inspired by the overthrow of monarchies in France and the American colonies and hoped they could learn how to end monarchical rule in their homelands. They studied the constitutions of France and the United States for ideas on rights and citizenship they could use once their own revolutions succeeded. They studied military power structures to stave off incursions. They also looked for allies to help them with their cause. Sometimes they looked abroad for sanctuary to escape the prejudices and mistreatments they faced at home.

Simón Bolívar was the architect of many South American revolutions. In the early 1800s he went to Europe to study the events unfolding in France. There was a great deal to be learned from the French Revolution led by Napoleon that he thought could benefit his own political ambitions.

Domingo Sarmiento, an Argentine politician and writer, often criticized the authoritarian nature of his country's political and social culture. His thoughts and critiques were influenced by what he learned while in exile, traveling in the United States and Europe. Later in life, he later became the president of Argentina.

While revolutions in Europe and the United States proclaimed freedom and equality for all, they fell far short of implementing those ideals. In Europe national movements often denied rights to those not deemed part of the new state. This was especially the case with Jews when Anti-Semitism exploded across Europe in the nineteenth century. This growing prejudice compelled Theodor Herzl, a Jewish journalist, to travel the ancient Jewish homeland in the Near East with the hope of finding a safe and secure place to live, free of persecution against their religious beliefs and traditions.

During the nineteenth century, both China and Japan faced growing incursions by Western powers. While government leaders fretted over how to keep out foreigners, some Chinese and Japanese reformers welcomed the 'new thinking' that came from travelers to their lands. In Japan, a low-level samurai

DOI: 10.4324/9781003168690-9

Fukuzawa Yukichi became an outspoken advocate for engagement with the West and adoption of Western cultures. His writings provided important insights into imperialism that defined the history of East Asia during the twentieth century. In China, Sun Yat-Sen, trained in western medicine, turned to Western political models looking for ways to end China's long slide into poverty and political collapse.

Simón Bolívar and Movements of Independence in South America

Well into the eighteenth century, the Spanish crown still had a powerful hold over much of Central and South America; but the winds of change were coming. As revolutionary fervor roiled across the Atlantic world and the United States became independent from British control and France overthrew their king, many in Latin America began to dream that they too could carve a new political destiny. One of those dreamers was Simón Bolívar.

Born into a well-to-do family in modern Venezuela, Bolívar initially followed a typical path of a colonial elite by going to Europe to study; he wanted to become a military officer. Naturally, he was drawn to the most powerful and charismatic military leader of the time, Napoleon Bonaparte. According to one biographer, Bolívar was "captivated by, and frankly admired, the cult of glory that was so important a trait of the French leader." Napoleon had started his career as an artillery officer and had risen through the ranks, eventually becoming the head of the French military. By the time Bolívar arrived in Europe, Napoleon was the leader of France. He seemed committed to preserving the gains of the French Revolution, such as civil liberties and the Declaration of the Rights of Man, and not allowing a monarchy to be reestablished.

Bolívar spent two years in Europe. During that time Napoleon crowned himself emperor of France and abandoned any commitments to representative government. Bolívar still admired Napoleon's military success but began to question his politics. He imagined himself as a leader of Latin America's liberation from Spain, and he wanted that to be a liberation from the tyranny of monarchy as well. On August 15, 1805, while in Rome, Bolívar later wrote, his dream became crystalized and he vowed to liberate the Americas from Spanish imperial control. "[Rome] has examples for everything," he later reported he said that day, "except the cause of humanity." For humanity's freedom, man must look to the New World. "I swear before you . . . that I will not rest body and soul until I have broken the chains binding us to the will of Spanish might."

After traveling through Europe and stopping briefly in the United States, Bolívar returned to Venezuela. He anxiously awaited for the opportunity to turn what he had learned abroad into action. His chance came in 1808, when Napoleon invaded Spain and overthrew the Spanish king, Ferdinand VII, and installed his own brother Joseph on the throne. Spain erupted in civil war, and revolutionaries like Bolívar seized the opportunity to end Spanish control over their homelands.

Bolívar's dream was to unite all of Latin America under one flag. For eight years he led forces across the northwest part of South America, fighting against the Spanish crown. Some estimate he covered 75,000 miles on horseback during this time. In the end, he did not succeed in liberating the continent, but he did pry an area known as Gran Columbia (Venezuela, Columbia and Ecuador) from Spanish control. The question now was what sort of government would these newly liberated lands have? And what role would he play in the future of Gran Columbia? Shortly after this successful war of independence, he noted that "the [newly liberated South] American states need the care of paternal governments to heal the sores and wounds of despotism and war." He proclaimed himself supreme general and president for life, although he vehemently rejected any claims of megalomaniacal intentions. "I am not Napoleon, nor do I wish to be. . . . The title of Liberator [his chosen appellation] is superior to any ever granted to human pride."

Bolívar's model of strong, paternalistic government became the norm throughout Latin American. Rather than focusing on rights of the common person, they protected the interests of the elite land owners and the Catholic Church who, in turn, propped up their authoritarian regimes. Eventually, it was the elites who deposed Bolívar and forced him into exile. As he left, he reflected sadly on his life as 'liberator,' "I have derived . . . a few sure conclusions: 1) America is ungovernable for us; 2) Those who serve revolution plough the sea."

Diego Sarmiento: Social and Political Reform Movements in Latin America

Many in Latin America rankled against the dictatorial rule of Bolívar and the rural elites who had come to control most of the continent after the end of Spanish colonial rule. They thought the rights of commoners were to be hallmarks of their anti-colonial revolutions and felt that the new governments were, in reality, no better than those during Spanish rule. They thought the future called for immersion into the global economy and promoted urban development, not the continued dominance of the old landed elite.

One of the most important and vocal critics of these new governments was Argentinian Domingo Sarmiento. As a writer, educator and politician he spent his life fighting against the rule of Argentina's strongmen. It was work that almost got him killed and forced him into long periods of exile in the United States and Canada. Those travels profoundly shaped his political and social philosophy and become the foundation of his government when he later became the president of Argentina.

Sarmiento's trip to the United States in 1847 was a journey of both necessity and opportunity. He had published a novel, *Facundo: Civilization and Barbarism*, in 1845 that was a historical biography of Juan Facundo Quiroga, a "gaucho chieftain" who dominated Argentina during the 1820s and 1830s, "wanting in the ability to manage the machinery of civil government, he substituted terror for patriotism and self-sacrifice." The main character, Facundo, died in 1835 but everyone knew that Sarmiento's work was really a not-so-veiled attack on the Facundo's successor, General Rosas, the military dictator of Argentina from 1829 to 1852. Rosas put a bounty out for Sarmiento, and so his trip to the United States was one of survival.

While not wanted, it turned out that Sarmiento's exile in North America presented the opportunity to explore new models of governance. He was convinced that if Argentina, and by extension all of South America, was to overcome its frontier mentality it needed new direction. The United States, after all, had overcome colonial beginnings and had become a world symbol of promise and civility. He found that two key elements of success were representative government and the rule of law. In South America by contrast, he argued, governments were controlled by an oligarchic elite intent on strangling efforts to develop constitutional republicanism. He saw those same elites using their political and military power to siphon off the rich natural and land resources for their own interests rather than for the benefit of the populace as a whole.

Sarmiento firmly believed that the foundation of republicanism and civil government in the United States was a public education system. Only through education for all could the values of equality become realized, giving everyone a chance to develop their talents and interests. For Sarmiento, education for everyone, including girls, could end the regressive male-dominated culture that shaped Latin American society. His was view shared by many. Adele Toussiant-Samson, a Parisian woman who lived in Brazil for about a dozen years in the mid-nineteenth century, noted, for example, that Brazilian housewives were "the first slave of the house," although she went on to say that as more women were educated in European boarding schools, "very gradually they acquire their liberty."

Sarmiento believed that public education promoted secular civic values. Like many liberals, he also felt that Latin America's future required a separation of church and state. For too long, Sarmiento argued, the Church had propped up dictators like Rosas in the name of social stability and morality and that, in turn, dictators had allowed the Church to dominate education and social policy. The Church continued to own vast tracts of land, while the poor peasants had little. He felt equity for all was central to modernization.

Diego Sarmiento returned to Argentina in 1862 when his long-time nemesis, General Rosas, was finally overthrown. In 1868 he was elected the first president of Argentina's new republican government. One of his first political acts was to expand public education. During his term in office, enrollment in public schools grew from approximately 30,000 to over 100,000 students. He also promoted immigration from Europe to help grow cities and laid the foundations for what he hoped would become a modern industrial economy.

Theodor Herzl and the Foundation of the Zionist Movement

Revolutions in France, the United States and Latin America that overthrew monarchies and established representative governments reverberated through-out the nineteenth century. Nationalist movements swept across Europe, demanding an end to imperial rule and new governments based on the will of the people. Defining the will of the people, however, was not easy. Some people defined who was part of a nation by the language they spoke or the cultural values they held. In much of Europe, nationalism was defined by its exclusionary nature. If you did not speak a certain language or follow a certain religion, then you could not be part of the nation and enjoy its political rights. This vision was strengthened during the second half of the nineteenth century by linking nationalism and ethnicity. If a community was defined by its ethnic-ity, then those deemed foreigners could not become part of the nation. Neither linguistic fluency nor cultural assimilation could make a person a citizen of the nation; only race could.

The view of nationalism as excluding those of a different ethnicity was clearly manifested in terms of attitudes toward Jewish people. At the same time that some governments were beginning to recognize Jews as equal citi-zens, many nationalists argued that Jews, by their nature, could not be part of the polity. As Jews were gaining more rights than ever before, Anti-Semitism spread throughout Europe. Anti-Semitism not only shaped domestic politics, but it led to the creation of a new movement, Zionism, which called for a Jewish homeland in Ottoman-controlled Palestine. Theodor Herzl, a journalist from the Habsburg Empire, came to personify the struggle for equal rights for Jews in Europe and the Zionist search for a Jewish state.

Herzl was born into a liberal Jewish family in Budapest, then a provincial capital in the Habsburg Empire. Throughout much of his early adult years he had little sense of a Jewish identity; he believed, like many liberals at the time, that the future of for Jews was assimilation into European culture. Herzl embraced a career as a journalist and playwright in Vienna and felt he was truly part of the social fabric.

Just as opportunities for Jews to participate in Europe's political and cultural life began to open up, however, there was a growing backlash against them. In Russia the assassination of the Tsar Alexander II, which some, including the new Tsar Alexander III, blamed on Jews, let loose a wave of attacks against the empire's large Jewish community. Over the next three years, synagogues were burned and Jewish people were attacked. A new word, *pogrom*, from the Russian word 'to destroy' was coined to define the horror.

In Herzl's adopted home of Vienna, Karl Lueger campaigned for mayor on a platform that blamed Jews for any and all problems facing the city. In 1894 in Paris, where Herzl went to work as a reporter, a young French Jewish military officer was accused of perhaps the most despicable crime of the time, spy-ing for the German army. Although evidence against the young Jewish officer,

Alfred Dreyfus, was immediately contested, many in France were convinced that the case proved that Jews could never be trusted to be good citizens of the nation. ("Anti-Semitism," one historian of the period has written, "is as French as croissants.")

Herzl later claimed that it was the injustice of the Dreyfus affair in France that compelled him to devote his energy to the cause of Zionism. In 1896 he penned an essay, *The Jewish State*, which laid out his hopes for Jewish people to be free of the prejudices of Europe by having a place of their own. It was, as Herzl says at the beginning of his pamphlet, "a very old [idea]" but one given the "outcries against the Jews" that has "awakened the slumbering idea."

In 1898 Herzl traveled to Jerusalem when he heard German Emperor William II planned to visit. The emperor had indicated no interest in Zionism, but Herzl hoped that if he could meet with the him he could change his thinking and, in turn, use German influence with the Ottoman sultan to convince him to agree to the creation of a Jewish state there. He booked his own passage to Jerusalem and on November 2, 1898, was granted an audience with William II.

His diary entries for those days tell us a lot about Herzl's vision for his new nation. It makes clear that he was not an historical romantic. While he vowed to keep parts of Jerusalem's ancient treasures, he envisioned a new, modern capital for his state. "I would clear everything that is not sacred, set up workers' houses beyond the city, empty and tear down the filthy rat-holes, burn all the non-sacred ruins, and put the bazaars elsewhere. Then, retaining as much of the old architectural style as possible, I would build an airy, comfortable, properly sewered, brand new city around the Holy Places."

He also makes it clear that he reproached religious fanaticism from all groups. While touring the city he noted, "We have been to the Wailing Wall. Any deep emotion is rendered impossible by the hideous, miserable, scrambling beggary pervading the place." Later in the day he ambled down the *Via Dolorosa* (the path Jesus took when he was crucified). His Jewish friends admonished him from walking on this Christian route, but he retorted that he would have felt like a coward to not do so and walked to the Church of the Holy Sepulcher by himself. One biographer of Herzl has called him "a fierce Westerner" who envisioned Zionism as an extension of secular liberalism gaining strength in parts of Europe.

After all of the hope and anticipation he had put into the trip, it is revealing that Herzl left Jerusalem in the dark of night. Herzl did not want to draw attention to the mission's lack of success. His entreaties for a Jewish state were neither accepted nor rejected; they were, politely and diplomatically, ignored. Despite this setback Herzl continued to travel incessantly in order to convince European leaders and Ottoman officials to support his idea. Increasingly wracked by illness, he died of heart failure in 1904.

In 1908 a revolt by young military officers against what they saw to be the weakness of the Ottoman Empire ended any discussion of Zionism. The sultan survived, but discussion of yielding land to European Jews was off the table. Yet, even without official approval for a Zionist state, Jews began to immigrate to Palestine in greater numbers. On the eve of World War One there were some 63,000 Jewish settlers in the area, estimated at ten percent of the total population.

Herzl's ideas for a Jewish homeland would gain momentum in the period after World War One when the defeat of the Ottoman Empire led to its breakup. Jews hoped that they would get control of Palestine, but instead Great Britain began to oversee it. The horrific tragedy of the Holocaust during World War Two made the sanctuary of a Jewish state homeland an essential imperative for the Jews who did survive the conflagration, and the state of Israel was established in 1947.

Sun Yat Sen and Political Reform in China

Prior to the nineteenth century, China dictated the terms of their relationships with the outside world. When the British envoy Lord Macartney arrived as part of an elaborate retinue to pry the doors of China open to British trade in 1793, he was ceremoniously, and from his perspective ingloriously, rebuked. The Chinese government had little interest in what the British hoped to sell, and they were skeptical that any beneficial developments would come from contact with outsiders. For decades contact with Westerners was limited; foreigners could only reside in the very southern port of Canton, far from the capital of Beijing. They could only stay in Canton for part of the year, and they were not allowed to learn Chinese or have much contact with the local population.

China's relationship to the outside world changed dramatically when, in 1839, war erupted between China and Great Britain over the sale of opium. China considered the trade illegal and wanted it stopped; the British flaunted China's laws and sold huge quantities and reaped enormous profits from sales. When Chinese officials seized tons of opium stored in Canton warehouses, British merchants insisted their government declare war. British gunboats attacked Chinese ports. The war lasted three years, and when it was over China suffered a humiliating defeat.

The Opium War marked what is widely called China's 'century of humiliation' (which only ended with the rise of the Communist state under Mao in 1949). As a result of the treaty with Great Britain, foreigners were allowed in, and cities like Shanghai became controlled by overseas interests. Foreigners were not subject to Chinese laws and ran many of the important business and financial institutions in the empire. These humiliations, coupled with growing problems of poverty and corruption, spurred unrest. By the end of the nineteenth century foreign powers, including Japan, were carving away pieces of the empire at will. The Qing Dynasty was in its death throes, and it was becoming apparent that radical reform was needed to survive.

The Empress Dowager Cixi, who held the real power in the government, vehemently disagreed. When some of her advisors recommended reforms along western lines, including modernizing the army and making the bureaucracy more efficient, she had them arrested and sentenced them to death. Her actions convinced many reform-minded Chinese, as if they needed any more convincing, that there was little prospect of change from within. China's only hope was revolution from outside.

One revolutionary who shared this view was Dr. Sun-Yat Sun. His vision for the future was encapsulated in the Three People's Principles: nationalism, democracy, and equalization. Nationalism was a China controlled by neither western nor Asian foreigners. He argued that Qing rulers, who were Manchu—foreigners from the north, must be expelled. Government officials should be elected by the people—although not all the people. China would be a republic, Sun argued, but it was not ready for full-scale democracy. He also called for more equitable distribution of the nation's vast resources. Land should be nationalized, and the government could then give permission to work it.

Dr. Sun's revolutionary ideology was a blend of the experiences that shaped him growing up and a reflection of his multi-cultural background. Born into a village of farmers and fisherman, he grew up in a traditional southern Chinese lifestyle. Like many he received a rudimentary education in the village school, learning traditional Chinese subjects. In 1879, that world changed dramatically when his elder brother, Mei, invited him to Hawaii. Mei had gone to Hawaii as a contract laborer and began to make a living claiming and clearing unused land. He used the modest profits from his land to buy a grocery store and then a farm. Eventually he owned over 6,000 acres of land on Maui and employed a reported 1,000 workers. By the time he invited his younger brother to join him, he was one of the most powerful businessmen on all the islands.

Sun attended missionary schools in Hawaii and developed an appreciation of Western ways. After spending time in Hawaii, he made a short stop back in his native village, where he no longer felt at home. From there he went on to Hong Kong and earned a degree in Western medicine. In his spare time he steeped himself further in Chinese history and classics. By the time he graduated from medical school Sun Yat-Sen was very much a combination of his Chinese and Western identities. He was also committed to the revolutionary overthrow of the decrepit and corrupt government of the Empress Dowager Cixi.

Given the Empress Dowager's brutal crackdown on dissenters, Sun decided it was safer to work for change from abroad. Throughout the 1890s he led the life of a revolutionary in exile. He set up clandestine cells amongst overseas Chinese. He traveled the world trying to galvanize international interest in his cause and soliciting funds for guns and troops. At one point he was kidnapped while in London by Qing agents who tried to sneak him back to China. Fortunately, some of his friends heard of the plot, alerted British authorities and got him released.

While Dr. Sun courted foreign support for revolution, disgruntled Chinese began to rebel against increasingly brutal treatment by foreigners in China. Known as the Boxer Rebellion, violence against any and all foreigners exploded across Northern China for three years, between 1899 and 1902. (*Boxers* was the name of the rebellions, given to them by foreigners because they practiced certain boxing techniques when they prepared for battle.) The

Empress Dowager Cixi, while no friend of commoners, allied with the 'boxers' with hopes of benefiting from their success and strengthening her hold against outside interests.

Dr. Sun also hoped to use the unrest to further his goals. In 1900 he returned to China and helped orchestrate a revolt in the south that at one point had 20,000 fighters in the field. Unfortunately for him his forces ran out of supplies, and the revolt fizzled. The Boxer Rebellion in the north also ended, as foreigners ruthlessly suppressed efforts and captured the capital, Beijing. The Dowager Empress Cixi bargained her country's future for her own survival. The Qing Empire had survived, but its days were clearly numbered.

As fate would have it, the death of Cixi and the emperor on consecutive days in 1908 led to the final collapse of the dynasty. Throughout China, revolts against the new emperor broke out. The final decisive revolt that led to the collapse of the Qing dynasty erupted in Wuchang (central China) in December 1911. With virtually no one willing to come to the defense of the Qing leaders, this largely localized revolt spread rapidly across the country.

Dr. Sun read about the Wuchang uprising while in Denver, Colorado, and immediately returned to China. As he passed through London on his way back to China, he received a telegram from his revolutionary comrades asking him to assume the role of provisional president of China's new republic. It was a position he readily accepted even though he knew that it would be temporary. He was happy to play a role in bringing about the end of the hated Qing Empire and was willing to act as president until the country could decide what type of government it should adopt.

In the end, Sun's provisional government only lasted for a couple of years. Political fighting amongst the various revolutionary groups and war lords who carved regional fiefdoms ended any hope of a united, republican China. Over the following decades the country was largely run by war lords who used their subjects for personal gain rather than civic improvement. Foreign powers took advantage of the instability and lack of central government to further cement their control over China's ports. Sun fled south and eventually set up a provincial government in Canton. When he died in 1924, the old China he deplored was dead, but the new China he hoped to create was yet to rise.

Fukuzawa Yukichi and the Meiji Reforms in Japan

The Opium War not only sent shock waves through China but unsettled Japan as well. Like China, the Japanese government had long felt that the best way to deal with 'the foreign barbarians from the west' was to keep them at bay. In 1853, when a delegation of American ships led by Commodore Matthew Perry sailed into Tokyo harbor, the Japanese government was faced with making choices. Politely but sternly Perry insisted that Japan open its doors to the outside world. At first the Japanese government deployed delay tactics, but the next year Perry retuned with even more military power. Fearful that continued delay and resistance could result in Japan facing the same fate as China had during the Opium Wars, the shogun (the head of the Japanese government) relented to the American demands. Perry secured an agreement with the Japanese that allowed a US envoy permanent residence in Japan and more access to Japan by American citizens and goods.

Adding further insult, the US government insisted that in order to ratify the agreement a Japanese delegation needed to sign the treaties in Washington, DC. After much debate, a delegation finally made the transpacific voyage in 1860. This was the first time an official Japanese delegation had ever left Japan, and it represented an abrogation of the government proscriptions on travel, creating deep resentment from many in the delegation.

One delegate who did not share that sentiment Fukuzawa Yukichi, a translator among the group. He was ecstatic to be on board. Ever since he had been a young, low-level samurai growing up in southern Japan, he was fascinated with the Western world and believed strongly that opening up to the West would benefit Japan. Fukuzawa's voyage to the United States certainly played out to his benefit. He earned royalties from the bestseller he wrote about the trip titled *Conditions in the West* (1867) and wrote numerous other works to follow. He became a valued commentator on the West and a vocal advocate for radical reform in Japan.

In his writings about his trip to the United States, Fukuzawa downplayed the American industrial innovations he observed in San Francisco. He was, however, amazed by the social and cultural differences. As he later said, "It was rather in matters of life and social custom and ways of thinking that I found myself at a loss in America. . . . Before leaving Japan, I, the independent soul . . . feared nothing. But on arriving in America, I was suddenly turned into a shy, self-conscious, blushing 'bride.' The contrast was even funny to myself."

Much of what fascinated Fukuzawa about America was its sense of relaxed social norms. At official receptions it was hard to tell the high officials from the common attendees. He had grown up in a Japanese society where every social distinction was meticulously defined and choreographed; the lack of social cues befuddled him. He was also surprised by the casual interactions between men and women, which was completely different than in Japan, where women were out of the public eye and subservient to male heads of households. (This was most visibly displayed by the fact that wives walked several steps behind their husbands.)

Despite his initial unease, it is clear from his writings that Fukuzawa approved of the American ways. He had always struggled against the lack of opportunity his own lowly social position afforded him. His popular sequel to *The Conditions of the West, an Encouragement of Learning* (1872) strongly advocated for social equality and the possibilities of social mobility. "Heaven never created a man above another, nor a man below another. Therefore, when people are born, heaven's idea is that we should all be equal." And, as the title indicates, he believed strongly that education, based on Western models, was the key to the promotion of that social equality.

The young translator returned to Japan, now a very divided country. Factions supporting the military leader, the shogun who had been the de facto ruler in Japan for centuries, fought against those loyal to the emperor. The latter's supporters eventually won this civil war, and in 1868 a young emperor, Mutsuhito, whose reign became known as Meiji (r. 1868–1912), meaning 'enlightened rule,' set out to restore the position of emperor and reform the government and society. Meiji leaders recognized that if Japan was not to go the way of China, it needed to embrace reform based on the Western models suggested by Fukuzawa. Modernization required education both for the necessary technical expertise to guide state and industry, and to develop a sense of national identity among all. In 1872 universal elementary education, for both boys and girls, was instated. Fukuzawa came to play a key role in these reforms.

Government and education reforms were only part of the dramatic changes taking place in Meiji Japan, as many Japanese now began to eagerly adopt all things Western. Western dress and hairstyles were perhaps the most visible symbols of this new age. (Fukuzawa himself promoted these changes by growing out his hair in Western fashion and donning a Western suit.) Public dancing, once observed with consternation and disgust by Japanese travelers, became *de rigueur* for progressive Japanese.

As would be expected, changes took hold quicker in the cities than in many of the rural parts of the country. When he arrived in Japan in 1886, Thomas Stevens, who was completing the first bicycle trip around the world, observed that "for decades Japan will present an interesting study of mountaineer conservatism and ultra-liberal city life."

The social and cultural divides amongst the Japanese people in reaction to these rapid changes were stark. Conservatives castigated the willingness of so many in Japan to abandon their culture for the vulgar values of the West. Many of these conservatives argued for a return to Confucian teachings as the appropriate foundation for Japanese education. In 1890 they succeeded in convincing the emperor to issue the Imperial Rescript of Education, which shifted the emphasis in national education from training in Western technology and science to Japanese values and tradition.

At the same time the government reaffirmed Japanese values, it pushed for industrial modernization and a shift toward export economy. Railway and telegraph lines were built across the country. Silk production, the mainstay of Japan's export economy, grew significantly. Ocean-going ships that one time had been banned by the old Shogun government became a major focus of industrial production. By the 1920s Japanese exports dominated much of the Asian markets and were a major source of foreign capital.

The economic successes of the Meiji reforms stimulated a rethinking of the country's relations with the wider world. Long admired by many Japanese intellectuals and leaders for its culture, China was now disdained for its ignorance and weakness by many of those same leaders and thinkers. China's protégée Korea was reviled for its weakness and backwardness. Fukuzawa became a critic of China and a vocal advocate of Japanese imperialism in Korea. In an editorial published in 1885 he emphasized that while it may appear from the outside all Asians were alike, the reality was far different. Chinese and Koreans, he wrote, "were of another racial origin" and that a study of cultural customs revealed that they "resemble each other more closely than they do Japan." While Japan had already "shaken off the backwardness of Asia," China and Korea were wallowing in "servility and shamelessness," even "foolish, cruel and lawless" behavior. The conclusion of his analysis was that Japan should "break with our evil friends of Eastern Asia."

Japan not only broke with their "evil friends of Eastern Asia," but they helped break them. War with China in 1864 precipitated the political and social unrest that led to the collapse of the Qing Dynasty. Taiwan and Korea, once under the protection of China, became occupied and controlled by Japan. Fukuzawa, who died in 1901, did not live to see Japan's takeover of Korea, but he would have likely approved. He had come to see that embracing of Western reform meant that Japan needed and deserved to become a great power, a colonial power. It was a mentality that would shape the country's relations with East Asia for decades and lead to war with the United States in World War Two.

Conclusion

Revolutionaries and reformers went abroad in the nineteenth century seeking models and ideas that helped them bring about significant changes. They went abroad trying to find sanctuary from the prejudices and discrimination they faced at home. Often the ideas and models they found abroad did not translate into the outcome they imagined at home. They were important journeys, nonetheless. They did lead to sweeping changes in governments from South America to China. They diffused ideas on education, economic policy and social norms. Many of the changes elevated debates about the rights of women and minorities from Europe to Japan. They may not have achieved the goals they wanted, but they did, to paraphrase Simón Bolívar, set loose the waves of change in the modern world.

End Materials Chapter 8

Works Quoted

Bolivar, Simon, *El Liberator: The Writings of Simon Bolivar* (Oxford: Oxford University Press, 2003).

Duus, Peter, ed., *The Japanese Discovery of America: A Brief History in Documents* (Boston: Bedford, St. Martin's Press, 1997).

Herzl, Theodor, *The Diaries of Theodor Herzl*, Marvin Lowenthal, trans. and ed. (New York: The Universal Library, 1962).

Herzog, Christoph and Raoul Motika, "Orintalism 'alla turca': Late 19th/ Early 20th Century Ottoman Voyages to the Muslim 'Outback'," *Der Welt des Islams*, vol. 40, no. 2, *Ottoman Travels and Travel Accounts from an Earlier Age of Globalization* (June 2000): 139–195.

Hopper, Helen, *Fukuzawa Yukichi: From Samurai to Capitalist* (New York: Ablong-man, 2005).

Sarmiento, Domingo, *Facundo, or Civilization and Barbarism* (London: Penguin, 2002).

Stevens, Thomas, *Around the World on a Bicycle* (Mechanicsburg, PA: Stackpoole Books, 2001).

Further Reading

Arana, Marie, *Bolivar: American Liberator* (New York: Simon & Schuster, 2013).

Reid, Michael, *Lost Continent: The Battle for Latin America's Soul* (New Haven: Yale University Press, 2007).

Toussiant-Samson, Adéle, *A Parisian in Brazil*, Emma Toussiant, trans. (Boston: James H. Earle, 1891).

Wei, Julie, Ramon Meyers and Donald Gillin, eds., *Prescriptions for Saving China: Selected Writings of Sun Yat-Sen* (Stanford, CA: Hoover Institution Press, 1994).

9 Travel and Imperialism

Introduction

In 1800, a world map showed European powers controlling about one-third of the land area in the world. Great Britain had recently lost its colonies to the United States but still ruled Canada and many islands in the Caribbean. It had just started to send prisoners to Australia. Spanish and Portuguese flags flew over the capitals of much of Central and South America, but those flags were tattered and would soon be taken down by the coming winds of independence movements. Beyond the Americas, Europeans were mostly represented by small spots on the map, forts and trading posts clinging to the coast lines of Africa and Asia. Only in India had the British recently established something more than a foothold by taking control of the Bengal province at the delta of the Ganges River. A few missionaries and adventurous traders managed to venture inland, but they were by far the exceptions to the rule.

Fast forward to the dawn of the twentieth century and the world map is strikingly different. Most of Africa and Southern Asia are now controlled by Europeans. Indonesia and many of the islands of the Pacific are now under European influence. China's coast is riddled with foreign enclaves. Only Ethiopia in Africa, and Japan and Siam in Asia, remained independent kingdoms. The nineteenth century was the Age of Imperialism. Global economic and labor systems as well as cultural and social interactions changed. They were forced to adapt to new imperial relationships.

Travel and technology played key roles in the Age of Imperialism. Western powers (Europe and the United States) used new innovations in transportation and military weapons to impose their political and economic control. Travelers reported on the riches of Africa and Asia and encouraged Western powers to consider control of these lands. As the colonial powers established political and military control, travelers then were instrumental in shaping interactions between the colonizers and colonized. Travelers from the colonies to the metropole—the capitals of the colonial powers—in turn significantly defined how both sides saw the benefits and determents of imperial control. These encounters can best be understood when examined through different lenses

DOI: 10.4324/9781003168690-10

(men and women, the colonizer and colonized) and through different geographic and cultural perspectives.

The travels of British explorer Henry Stanley demonstrated how journeys of 'discovery' turned into enterprises of conquest. Stanley became famous for 'finding' Dr. Livingstone in East Africa and later infamous both for his travels Africa and then as the director of the King of Belgium's so-called humanitarian project in the Congo. He was not only an explorer but a collaborator in one of the most violent, exploitive systems of imperialism anywhere.

Women travelers in India offer another perspective, even though colonialism was overwhelmingly a male enterprise. It was women who often had contact with local servants and laborers and who saw the realities of how ordinary people experienced colonialism.

Colonialism was largely a one-way street, with the colonizer setting the parameters of engagement. Most of the sources and the records we have represent the viewpoint of the colonizer, however in a few rare but important cases, we have accounts from the colonized (Indians) who traveled to the land of the colonizer (England). Two such travelers, Behramji Malabari and Cornelia Sorabji, had experiences that were important windows into the ways the colonized related to the colonizer. Although their stories are different, they were both from India and had high hopes that British rule would bring social improvements to their country.

As imperialist powers gained control over vast regions of Africa and Asia, there were notable voices rising against them. One of those was Ho Chi Minh, a Vietnamese nationalist who attended the meetings of the Great Powers at the end of World War One and called for the principles of equality and democracy to be extended to his people. When his request was met with silence, Ho abandoned the West and sought liberation in the anti-colonial ideology of Communism. His journey is emblematic of many colonized who fought for independence from colonial rule.

Henry Stanley: Imperialism in Africa

Europe had long been intrigued with exploring and conquering Africa, but a number of obstacles (such as diseases that decimated expeditions and African leaders who were not interested in ceding their lands to outside control) stifled those efforts. During the nineteenth century, however, a combination of factors which included improved medicines, especially quinine to prevent malaria; better technology of conquest—guns, ships and railroads; and political instability in key parts of the continent changed the calculus of European ambition. By the 1870s many European countries were actively seeking to establish footholds and colonies across Africa. They were attracted to the great potential wealth and resources that Africa offered, and the scramble for Africa was on.

European imperial ambitions in Africa were also promoted through the booming businesses of travel literature and journalism. Many nations established national geographic societies which, in turn, sponsored expeditions to become the first to 'discover' something. In Africa, British explorers like Richard Burton and John Speke raced to find the source of the Nile then hurried home to receive the accolades and rewards that came with discoveries. (Speke would ultimately get the credit but died of a shooting accident before he could claim the fame.) Henry M. Stanley, a journalist writing for the *New York Herald*, was subsidized by the paper to report on his harrowing and heroic journeys through mysterious and dangerous lands; the more harrowing and heroic the better, and Stanley knew how to embellish the truth to sell newspapers.

Stanley's most famous reports came in the early 1870s when he traversed Central Africa in search of Dr. David Livingstone. Livingstone was a doctor and Christian missionary who went to Africa to save lives and souls. After he had not been heard form for a quite some time the *New York Herald* hired Henry Stanley to find him. In 1871 Stanley caught up with Livingstone on the shores of Lake Tanganyika. Uttering a carefully constructed phrase, "Dr. Livingstone, I presume," Stanley walked into camp.

Eager readers around the world devoured the account of Stanley's adventure; it was the beginning of his famous and infamous career as an Africa explorer. His tales described the vast wealth of diamonds and gold waiting to be collected and further encouraged European governments to launch wars for colonial control across the continent.

Although he portrayed himself as a selfless adventurer bringing tales of unknown lands to the world and civilization to its peoples, there was another side of Stanley. His writing made it quite clear that he disdained Africans. The titles of his two most famous books *Through the Dark Continent* (1878) and *The Darkest Continent* (1890) were not only about undiscovered lands but a moral commentary on what Stanley thought of African people. He described organizing caravans of porters in Africa and noted that "the dark brother, [was as] wild as a colt, chafing, restless, ferociously impulsive, superstitiously timid, liable to furious demonstrations, suspicious and unreasonable. . . . The savage only respects force, power, boldness, and decision." His stories often gloat about his willingness to use force to make Africans see the superiority of white civilization. (Fellow explorer Richard Burton once said of Stanley, "He shoots negroes as if they were monkeys.") Based on his writings Stanley often backed up his words with actions against the porters and carriers who worked for him.

In 1876 the King of Belgium, Leopold II, chose Stanley to lead his mission in the Congo. European leaders who were now anxious to create legitimate claims for their growing colonial ambitions awarded King Leopold exclusive rights to 'civilize Central Africa.' He promised to abolish slavery, build schools and hospitals, end wars and bring the light of Western civilization to the jungles of the region. Given Stanley's pejorative and condescending views of Africans, it may seem odd that he was Leopold II's choice for a humanitarian mission. More likely, Leopold II was more interested in how his image might benefit from partnering with the famous explorer, albeit overlooking his egregious behavior and attitudes toward Africans.

Leopold II did indeed outlaw slavery in the Congo (for which European leaders honored him as a 'liberal hero'), and Stanley did build schools and hospitals. But the trappings of humanitarian work were far outweighed by the horrific realties of exploitation that unfolded in the Congo under Leopold II's reign. The new system of labor production established to replace slavery was every bit as exploitative as any slave system. Congolese people were expected to provide quotas of ivory, rubber or copper to the king every year. When Congolese laborers did not or could not meet quotas, Stanley directed his military police forces to get them to meet their obligations by whatever means necessary. Killing a few villagers to capture the attention of the rest was one option, and physical dismemberment, often the chopping off a hand, was yet another. (Cutting off hands was sometimes preferred as it saved bullets for the police forces, and laborers could, supposedly, still meet their quotas with one hand.) While Leopold II basked in the glory of his reputation as a 'liberal hero' and reaped the riches of exports, some six million Congolese died because of the brutality.

Stanley's work in the Congo made him fabulously wealthy. He returned to his native England a hero and toured the country giving lectures about his journeys. He was knighted and elected to Parliament. Stanley died in 1904.

As discoveries were made about how rapacious Leopold II's exploitation of the Congo was, European leaders stripped him of his claim in 1908 and relinquished control of the colony over to Belgium itself. The actions perpetrated by Stanley and Leopold in the Congo are now referred to as a genocide. In 2020, as global recognition of the history of racial violence exploded in the aftermath of the George Floyd murder in Minnesota, Belgians began to tear down and deface the King's statues and Stanley's hometown of Denbigh, Wales, continues to debate whether to memorialize or deny its native son.

Ota Benga: Africa on Display in the United States

There is another part of the Congo story. In the year that Stanley died a hero for 'civilizing' the Congo, a young Congolese man, Ota Benga, was brought to the United States and put on display at the World's Fair in St. Louis, Missouri. He had been 'voluntarily' brought, according to the missionary Samuel Varner, who arranged the exhibit along with twelve other pygmies who, Varner said, he freed from slave traders. They were one of the hits of the show. Playing to American expectations of 'savage Africa' they put on ritual battles. (Interestingly these displays were modelled on ritual battles being enacted by Native Americans at the fair.)

After the fair, Benga returned to the Belgian-controlled Congo for a short period, but his village had been destroyed by fighting and so he returned with Varner to the US, where he was sent to the Bronx Zoo and exhibited in the monkey house. Bones were scattered in his cage to make it look 'more authentic.' A *New York Times* article that covered the exhibit noted that Benga was "a Bushman, one of a race that scientists do not rate high on the human scale." African Americans vociferously complained. James H. Gordon, a leading African American in Brooklyn wrote, "Our race, we think, is depressed enough, without exhibiting one of us with the apes. . . . We think we are worthy of being considered human beings, with souls." Eventually Benga was released to Gordon's care. Several years later, sad and depressed, he committed suicide. It was only in the last few years that the zoo officially apologized for this outrageous display.

Domesticating the Empire: European Women in the Colonial World

In the late 1820s Emma Roberts, a young English woman visiting her sister in India, set off on a trip across the northern plains. Her journals describe the journey and who was part of the entourage. The English family of three was accompanied by servants, attendants and their family members who, she noted, "will not consist of less than a hundred individuals." In addition to the numerous servants and guards, there was "the bazaar" of traveling merchants who could provide their every need. Each night as they neared camp for the night, a mini-city was erected. The china and glassware were laid out for dinner. There were facilities for bathing, and elephants used to flatten the ground so that the tent areas would be nice and flat. "All who have been employed in fatiguing offices are buried in profound response."

In many ways her journey across India is a metaphor for European imperialism and colonialism in nineteenth century Africa and Asia. Imperialism was a numbers game in which relatively few Europeans utilized the labor of the colonized people to further their own interests. The nature of the trip also reflected the very hierarchical nature of colonialism. Europeans were the superior group, and the colonized clearly the inferior subjects. Whether in imperial armies, bureaucracies or households, Europeans occupied the key positions of control and depended on colonial subjects to handle the tasks necessary to run an empire.

The notion of women like Roberts traveling during this time was relatively unusual. For much of its early history, imperial expansion was a man's job, focusing on military conquest and economic subjugation. Over time, more women and families traveled to the colonies. Some did so with the hopes of meeting their future spouses, others were looking for adventure. Many were motivated by the desire to participate in the mission of 'civilizing' colonial subjects.

One example is Mary Carpenter, a British educator and reformer. In the 1830s she had met the famed Bengali writer and social reformer, Ram Mohan Roy, and dreamed ever after of visiting India and bringing British civilized society to the colony. In the 1860s her wish came to fruition, and she went to India to visit schools and hospitals. Her notes of that trip reflected that the British were indeed playing an essential role in bettering the subcontinent.

Observing the expansion of the railway there, for example, she proclaimed that:

> Habits of punctuality and attention to duty are also taught, both directly and indirectly, by the railway. At first passengers were constantly too late, or arrived just when the train was starting. . . . While, then, we were frequently annoyed by the inconveniences and discomforts on this journey, we could not but feel that under the circumstances the Indian railways are very wonderful, and show the possibility of improving even the inferior portions of the native races, under judicious government and proper training.

Overwhelmingly, women who traveled to the colonies assumed the bourgeoisie (Victorian) roles that were expected of them back home; that meant that their job was to help manage the domestic sphere so that the colonial men could manage the public fora. This often meant that they were in charge of the servants and, given the size of some colonial households, this was no small task. Fanny Parkes, an English woman who lived in India for twenty years from the 1820s to mid-1840s, noted that fifty-seven servants were required to run "a quiet household;" another twelve to fourteen in the hot, dry season needed to be added to the roster to fan the English family day and night.

While living in close proximity to the servants, colonial women were expected to maintain their superiority over, and social and racial distance from, them. Male and female colonists saw this both as a way to protect the colonial woman's virtue in a foreign land and as a way to represent the superiority of the colonizer to the servant. Christina Sinclair Bremner, a British woman who spent time in northern India in the 1880s, exemplified this attitude. Traveling along the Grand Trunk Road in a palanquin, a covered sedan chair carried by porters, she noted that "like small boys my coolies varied conversation with much giggling. To get out of step . . . to change the *dandi* pole, which often creates painful swelling on the shoulder, on the outer edge of the precipice, causing great alarm to the occupant . . . any of these mishaps would amuse a coolie and make him laugh violently for ten minutes." Bremner was not amused, and after one incident "retained enough presence of mind to rebuke the malefactor with my umbrella, so that there might be no mistake on the part of the most stupid."

Bremner's description of the porters struggling to carry her along as "small boys" and "the most stupid" clearly demonstrated a denigrating attitude toward her servants, and her willingness to "rebuke her malefactor with my umbrella" was, to her, a reasonable action given her sense of superiority. (Even as she admitted that carrying her resulted in "painful swelling on the shoulder," they were to blame.)

Bremner's account does not give any sense of how the porters perceived the circumstances. Was the slip of the poles intentional? Was their giggling a joke at her expense or a nervous response knowing that indeed the whack of the umbrella may follow? Travelers like Bremner provide valuable insights into the mindset of the colonizer, however they largely leave the voice of the colonized muted. Just as colonialism was an unequal numbers game with a few outsiders largely controlling power, so too is the history of colonialism an unequal story with the experiences of the colonizer often dominating the narrative over those of the colonized.

Some argue that accounts like Bremner's can be read through or 'against the grain' to at least speculate on how such encounters may have been experienced from the perspective of a porter. This approach, known as Subaltern Studies, employs a variety of theories and approaches to include the largely voiceless colonial subjects in history. (The term *subaltern* refers to a person of lower rank or position and, applied to colonial studies, it generally refers to all colonial subjects who were in this subordinate position.) Perhaps, given what we know about the agency and resistance of colonized peoples against unequal and often harsh treatment, a subaltern read of this incident may be that the porters jostled the palanquin intentionally as an act of defiance against their colonial master. Bremner's chastisement of her porters may also have reflected a growing fear amongst the colonizers that subjects were not willing to passively accept their fate.

In 1857, Indian soldiers in the colonial army rebelled against low pay, unequal treatment and harsh punishments. The soldiers' rebellion quickly escalated to a larger attack against the British presence in India. British civilians, including some four hundred men, women and children living at Cawnpore, were killed. Gradually the British were able to rally their own forces as well as those of Indian loyalists, and by the summer of 1858—while pockets of resistance remained—the British were back in control. Property damage was extensive, and the British lost some 11,000 soldiers. Indian deaths were in the hundreds of thousands.

Women writers penned heroic accounts of attack and survival that sold well back home. The British novelist, singer and actress, Florence Marryat, wrote a "sketch of Anglo-Indian life" in 1868 in which she speculated on the death of some friends: "Whether poison had been mixed in what they drank by the natives, will never be ascertained; but knowing what I do of the eastern character, I should never feel satisfied, when losing friends in so mysterious a manner."

The Colonized in the Land of the Colonizer

One essential, albeit limited, window into the experiences and thoughts of the colonized came from subjects who travelled to the metropole, or land of the colonizer. They were mostly privileged in that they had the resources and connections to journey abroad. Often they identified with the colonizer's efforts in some ways, often hoping to bring Western values and policies to bear on problems they identified at home.

Behramji Malabari and Cornelia Sorabji, who traveled from colonial India to England, are examples of these cross-cultural commentators. Their experiences offer perspectives of Indians who identified with and tried to assimilate into British culture. As Antoinette Burton said when analyzing Sorabji's autobiography, "I treat Sorabji not as a subaltern figure but as an elite, educated, England-returned Parsee Christian woman—not, in other words, as a self-evidently resistant actor but as a particular example of the female cosmopolitan traveler who can tell us much about. . . 'the complex interaction of local and colonial structures' on the ground in India."

Behramji Malabari was a Parsi Indian from Bombay who spent several years in London. His book about his time there became a runaway bestseller, both in England and in India. Malabari referred to the title of his work, *The Indian Eye on English Life* (1896), as a "rather uninviting title against which neither entreaty nor protest could avail." His preferred title was the subtitle, *Rambles of Pilgrim Reformer*. He defined himself as "a pilgrim, born for the service of others," and saw his journey to London as a chance to continue his "study of human progress. . . . And where could one find a wider scope for exercise of his observation than the metropolis of the world?" The two titles of Malabari's book reflect how the travel of the colonized to the land of the colonizer shaped the experience of colonialism for both parties.

In the book Malabari does not describe himself as a colonial subject. Rather, he saw himself as every bit the equal of the British. He was a reformer, just as many of his English friends in Bombay were reformers. He was, in his own mind, as much British as he was Indian. He went to London to learn what he could learn about English society and customs, many of which he thought were worth studying, but he did not go there feeling inferior in any way. Bombay Parses had seen themselves as mediators between the British colonizers and the Indian colonial subjects. As a religious minority in the midst of the Hindu and Muslim majorities, Parses had often self-identified as outsiders in South Asia. It was a vantage point that made some, like Malabari, feel especially suited to critique the failings of the dominant culture.

Attitudes toward women and children, child marriage, seclusion of women (harems) and the prohibition of widows from remarrying were the social ills that Malabari identified as regressive and repressive practices amongst the Hindus and Muslims of India. British customs, which emphasized "equality among all its members, [t]his means openness and mutual confidence," were superior. He wanted to study the British family in its 'natural setting.' This world, he wrote on English family life "is practically a sealed book to us," and he was determined to open it up for Indian eyes to see.

Many are justifiably critical of Malabari's views on both Indian and British family life. (He exaggerates both the extent of regressive attitudes toward women and children in India and the progressive equalities of the English home.) Even though his social observations are questioned, the historical value of his perspective representing colonial subjects who traveled to the colonial capital is not, and the title of Malabari's book, *The Indian Eye on English Life*, tells another side of the colonial experience. He was the face of India in the streets of London, and for his Indian readers, the eyes of insight into English life. "Travel to Britain enabled colonial subjects like Malabari," summarizes one historian, ". . . to lay claim to a kind of imperial citizenship: to insist that they were mobile subjects at least partly of their own making rather than fixed objects of colonial reform projects."

Malabari's claim to imperial citizenship was on display as he walked the streets of London. "The street arabs of dirty London, little urchins out at elbow" hassled as we strolled. Malabari's description of these youth as 'arabs' denotes that he saw these poor London street waifs as foreigners in ways he did not see himself. He goes on to write about encountering ladies/women who apologize for the street kids but then ask for a photograph of him. "But I'd rather not give them a setting," he replies, suggesting that he too was exoticized by these women as the foreign other. His answer captures the frustration he must have felt as these women failed to see him as an equal but only as subject of imperial rule. Overall, the scene suggests that there were clearly limits to how someone like Malabari was seen by the British; he was never to be their equal despite his intention.

The story of Cornelia Sorabji was, in many ways, similar. Born in 1866, in the aftermath of the rebellions of the late 1850s when the British crown assumed direct rule over South Asia, Sorabji was educated in a missionary school in western India. Given the support of her influential parents and their friends, she petitioned to attend Bombay University. Established during the anti-colonial riots that roiled northern India, the school's primary mission was to educate teachers who could, in turn, help educate a generation of Indians loyal to the crown and willing to support its colonial mission. Sorabji excelled at her studies and dreamed of continuing her education in England at Oxford. It was a lofty goal, but Sorabji was well-connected and committed to bringing the values of English law and social policy to her people. Eventually she became the first woman to pass the British Civil Law exams. She went on to become the first woman to practice law in India, where she focused her work on advocating for girls' education and women's rights, especially women secluded in *purdah*, or isolation as a result of the death of their husband.

To this point Sorabji's story was of integration into and support for the British colonial project. However, there was more to her story. Despite her strong identification with British culture and its laws, she was never accepted as an equal. Even though she had credentials, she was not allowed to actually try cases because women were simply not allowed to do so. (The law was changed in 1923, but continued prejudice against women barristers kept her from trying cases.)

Sorabji's pro-colonial views also alienated her from her homeland. By the 1920s, still aligned with the British, she was actively opposing the Indian National Congress and Gandhi's civil disobedience movement. Because of her outspoken stance, her voice was effectively stifled, and by the early 1930s she moved back to London, where she resided for most of the rest of her life. Like

Malabari, Sorabji's story highlights challenges the colonized faced in navigating the world.

Ho Chi Minh: the Beginning of the End of Colonialism

Noting that he used at least some fifty different pseudonyms tells you much of what you need to know about the complex life of the Vietnamese independence leader Ho Chi Minh (1890–1969). His life path illuminates the trajectory of anti-colonialism in the early twentieth century.

As a young boy Ho hoped to take advantage of new opportunities afforded by Vietnam's French occupiers. Like many young people, he envisioned a colonial education and some sort of bureaucratic career as a path leading to a good life. Life circumstances played out differently. Although records are sparse, it appears that around 1908, he also began to identify with other young Vietnamese who were increasingly critical of French rule. In 1911 he got a job working in the galley of a French steamer; the life of the itinerant laborer and emerging revolutionary had begun.

Ho wound up in the United States around 1912 and worked in New York and Boston. Some biographers speculate that during that time he became interested in the Pan-African movement of Marcus Garvey, and that may have prompted thoughts of becoming politically engaged with Vietnamese independence. By the end of World War One, he was in Paris, the epicenter of the post-war world powers conference. Ho, and many colonized subjects around the world, closely followed the proclamations made by the United States President Woodrow Wilson, who had argued that peace could only be achieved by broader reorganization of international affairs and rethinking colonialism. In his speech Wilson highlighted Fourteen Points needed to reshape geopolitics:

A free, open-minded, and absolutely impartial adjustment of all colonial claims, based upon a strict observance of the principle that in determining all such questions of sovereignty the interests of the populations concerned must have equal weight with the equitable claims of the government whose title is to be determined.

Such sentiments appealed to Ho, who by this time, was a leader in the Vietnamese community and prepared to present his people's concerns to the international assembly of victors. He authored a one-page pamphlet entitled *Demands of the Annamite (Vietnamese) People* that reflected the aspirations outlined by Wilson. For instance, it did not demand independence for Vietnam, only a greater degree of autonomy within the French colonial empire. It also advocated greater democracy by asking for freedom of the press and association and the end of the hated forced labor system.

Ho personally delivered the document to key leaders of the peace delegations meeting in Versailles. Colonel House, Wilson's senior advisor, did write Ho thanking him, and he promised to bring this issue to the attention of the president himself. Ho never heard another word from the US delegation. He also never received an official reply from the French leaders after he presented it to them.

Ho's efforts to gain an audience for his nationalist agenda were not unique. As one reporter in Paris commented:

> Chinamen, Japanese, Koreans, Hindus, Kirghizes, Lesghiens, Circasians, Mingrelians, Buryats, Malays and Negroes and Negroids from Africa and America were among the tribes and tongues forgathered in Paris to watch the rebuilding of the political world system and to see where they "came in."

Many, like Ho, found that they could not "come in." W.E.B. Du Bois (1868–1963) was an African-American leader in the United States who urged African-Americans to support the war effort. In his appeal to Wilson he urged the president to consider the fate of African nationalism in the post-war era. Germany lost its colonies in Africa, but Africans were not granted control over these lands. Instead of independence many of the African colonies were still controlled by European powers as mandates until the peoples there "could stand on their own."

Egyptians, who were increasing angered by unfair treatment by the British, were further embittered by a lack of interest in their concerns in Paris and eventually revolted in 1919. Men and women, Christians and Muslims, peasants and intellectuals banded together, as the Wafd Party staged massive demonstrations against British rule. At first the British tried to suppress the revolts, but faced with continued resistance they eventually negotiated a settlement in 1922. Egypt became independent but under certain conditions. Significant British forces would remain in Egypt, and the Suez Canal remained under British control. Egypt was quasi-independent. Few on either side were happy with this status, but it did position Egypt to become a leader of both African and Arab independence movements after World War Two.

The Chinese government lead by Sun Yat-Sen was also made painfully aware that it too, despite its contributions to the war effort, would not be allowed to 'come in' to the community of great powers. Instead, Japan was the big winner from Asia in the Paris accord. Japan was given control of the former German territory of Shandong. The Chinese delegation was furious, so they refused to sign the treaty. Many Chinese who felt both betrayed by the allies and disappointed in the efforts of their government to promote Chinese nationalism were so angry they took to the streets to protest, and demonstrations erupted across China the day the treaty was announced. Led by students and intellectuals, the May Fourth Movement, as it became known, called for the removal of foreigners, especially the Japanese, from Chinese soil. Many of the movement's leaders began looking for a new ideology that would lead to Chinese independence. Betrayed and abandoned by Western democracy, they increasingly looked to the emerging Communist movement as their liberating dogma. The decisions made at Versailles weakened the Chinese Republic and fueled animosity against the Japanese that eventually erupted into full-scale war by the early 1930s.

Ho had already shown an interest in the Marxist critique of colonialism, but the lack of interest in Versailles toward Vietnam clearly drove him further toward an ideology and a movement to advance national liberation. In 1924 he left Paris and made his way to Moscow. His path to independence followed Leninist Communism. Many others, frustrated by the vast void between Wilson's theories and international practices, followed in step.

Conclusion

The beginning of the end of colonialism was well underway by the end of World War One. However, for the most part Europe and the United States retained control of their colonies until well after the end of World War Two in 1945. The actions of colonists like Henry Stanley in the Congo convinced many that colonialism was an evil to overturn. Even Indian subjects like Malabari and Sorabji, who saw the benefits of British rule, were frustrated by the lack of support of the British for treating them as partners in the colonial enterprise. When the allied powers rejected the aspirations of men like Ho Chi Minh, it set new geopolitics into motion. Wars of decolonization erupted around the world in the 1950s and 1960s. They largely ended colonial rule, although the legacy of such movements have taken years to address. (The removal of the statues of King Leopold II and delayed apologies for the caging of Ota Benga in the Brooklyn Zoo continue to remind us that the legacies of colonialism still shape our world today).

End Materials Chapter 9

Works Quoted

Bremner, Christian Sinclair, *A Month in the Dandi: A Woman's Wanderings in Northern India* (London: Simpkin, Marshall & Co., 1891).

Burton, Antoinette, "'The Purdahnashin in Her Setting': Colonial Modernity and the Zenana in Cornelia Sorabji's Memoirs," *Feminist Review*, vol. 65 (Summer 2000): 145–158.

Carpenter, Mary, *Six Months in India*, vol. 2 (London: Longmans, 1868).

Keylor, William, *The Legacy of the Great War: Peacemaking, 1919* (Boston: Houghton Mifflin Books, 1998).

Malabari, Behramji, *The Indian Eye on English Life; or the Rambles of a Pilgrim Reformer* (Bombay, 1896).

Newkirk, Pamela, "The Man Who Was Caged in a Zoo," *The Guardian* (June 3, 2015).

Stanley, Henry, *Through the Dark Continent*, vol. 2 (New York: Dover Publications, 1988).

Wilson, Woodrow, "President Wilson's Fourteen Points," *The Yale Avalon Law Project*. https://avalon.law.yale.edu/20th_century/wilson14.asp.

Further Reading

Burton, Antoinette, *At the Heart of the Empire: Indians and the Colonial Encounter in Late-Victorian Britain* (Berkeley: University of California Press, 1998).

Burton, Richard, *The Lake Regions of Central Africa* (New York: Dover Publications, 1995).

Clark, Steve, ed., *Travel Writing & Empire: Postcolonial Theory in Transit* (London: Zed Books, 1999).

Duiker, William, *Ho Chi Minh: A Life* (New York: Theiabooks, 2000).

Edgerton, Robert, *The Troubled Heart of Africa: A History of the Congo* (New York: St. Martin's Press, 2002).

Ghose, Indira, ed., *Memsahibs Abroad: Writings by Women Travellers in Nineteenth Century India* (New Delhi: Oxford University Press, 1998).

Hobsbawm, Eric, *The Age of Empire: 1875–1914* (New York: Vintage Books, 1987).

Hochschild, Adam, *King Leopold's Ghost: A Story of Terror, Greed and Heroism in Colonial Africa* (Boston: Houghton Mifflin, 1998).

Lam, Truong Bun, *Colonialism Experienced: Vietnamese Travel Writing, 1900–1931* (Ann Arbor, MI: University of Michigan Press, 2000).

Louise Pratt, Mary, *Imperial Eyes: Travel Writing and Transculturation* (London: Routledge, 1992).

10 Cars, Planes and Cargo Ships

The Twentieth-Century Transportation Revolution

Introduction

If the nineteenth century was the century of the steam engine, then the twentieth century was the century of the internal combustion engine and, later, the jet engine. The development of the internal combustion engine by Karl Benz followed by the emergence of the industrial production of cars in the early twentieth century by Henry Ford were transformational. The emergence of oil as the new fuel transformed not only transportation technology but reshaped global politics. This era also saw the introduction of planes, as the first commercial flight took off in 1914 from St. Petersburg, Florida, and landed in Tampa some 24 miles away. Cargo ships restructured the global economy, making the movement of goods easier and cheaper.

Cars, planes and cargo ships defined the twentieth century in profound ways beyond simply how people got about. Cars determined where people lived and worked. Cities and their surrounding regions were redesigned to account for the growing dominance of the automobile. Planes linked the world together. Travel across oceans to different continents, once a novelty, was a common occurrence. Trips that once took weeks and even months now happened in hours.

As was the case when new technologies were introduced, they also provoked wide social and cultural debate and divide. Some embraced new technology as a step forward. People were able to do what they had never done before. Others rued the encroachment of new technologies dictating our lives in undesired ways and wondered whether we were driving the machine or the machine was driving us to our demise.

As Gijs Mom noted in his important new study, *Globalizing Automobilism*, cars and planes were dominant forms of mobility for some, those with the means to afford them. Outside of the western world, for the majority of people, walking, bicycles or animal transport remained normative. In many places, a lack of infrastructure (roads, access to fuel and repair stations, among other issues) hampered the adoption of cars, and in similar ways limited air travel. For many, existing systems worked and they saw little reason to change for something less certain and certainly more costly.

DOI: 10.4324/9781003168690-11

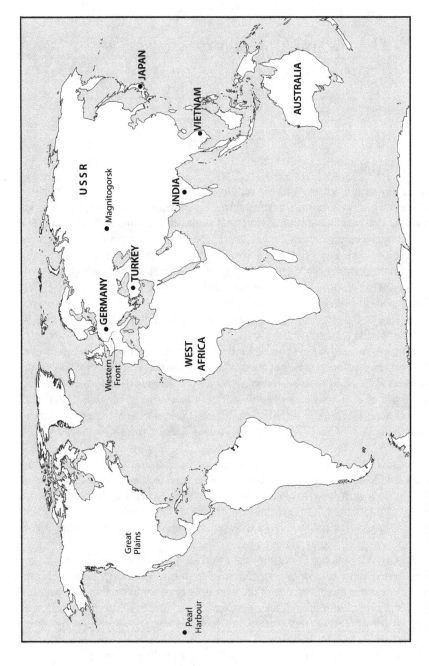

Map 6 Key Places, 1900–1945

The Coming of the Age of the Automobile

Versions of horseless carriages bounced around cobbled roads throughout the nineteenth century. Then in 1885, a German engineer by the name of Karl Benz developed the internal combustion engine, a concept that launched the automotive age. (A couple of years later, Karl's wife Bertha had the first joy ride when she 'borrowed' an improved version and, with her two kids, took off on a 180-kilometer jaunt to visit her visit her hometown. The scandal caught the attention of the press and helped to really launch the Benz Motor Company.) His first automobile was not particularly practical. Its engine was not very powerful or reliable, and it only had three wheels, which made it a bit unstable. Initial attempts to build vehicles with four wheels often crashed because they couldn't turn efficiently.

Within a few years of Bertha's jaunt, her husband had further refined the design. He gained horsepower in the engine, and he figured out a way to steer it as a four-wheel vehicle, making it something closer to the modern car. It was called the *Velo*, and Benz made 1,200 of them between 1894 and 1901. The Velo is considered the first mass produced car; earlier autos were hand-crafted and labor intensive. Eventually, it was American businessman Henry Ford who truly revolutionized the mass production of cars. The Ford Company launched a Model T in 1908. Priced at $825.00 (about $24,000 today), it was a luxury that only the wealthy could afford. Nonetheless, the standardized model made it easier to produce and cheaper to fix. It had higher ground clearance that made it useful on the often-rutted roads it traveled, and its ease of driving quickly caught on. By 1913, Ford had introduced the moving assembly line and reduced the time of production even further, and ensuing costs plummeted. By the eve of World War One, Ford Motor Company was cranking out 250,000 cars a year, and by 1920 more than half of all the cars in the world were Fords.

The first "horseless carriage race" was organized in 1894 by a Parisian newspaper. (Technically there was an earlier race in 1887, but only one contestant showed up.) It was to be seventy-nine miles long, from Paris to Rouen. The newspaper did not bill it as a race but rather as a test of the viability of the new technology. "Rather than speed, cars would be judged on whether they were easy to operate for the competitors without any dangers and not too expensive to run." Most cars actually competed that mission with the first-place car averaging a cautious twelve miles per hour. Not long after, in a race from Paris to Vienna in 1902 the winner, driving a French Peugeot, averaged thirty-nine miles per hour. Within years cars would be going eighty.

The car craze accelerated in the post-World War One era, as there were more manufacturers, and a resurgent post-war economy made the dream of owning a car more of a reality for ordinary people. Automotive technology was also translated into heavier farming equipment. The United States, for example, became increasingly reliant on tractors and combines able to work more efficiently the massive farms of the Plains states. This expanded production, but it also meant that those with smaller farms who could not afford these technological upgrades were marginalized.

By the mid-1920s it is estimated that three-quarters of all cars, and most farming equipment, was bought on credit. By the end of the decade, this debt would help precipitate the Great Depression. This global economic collapse decimated the auto industry, as people could no longer afford what was increasingly seen as a luxury not a necessity. Auto sales fell by over seventy percent during the first years of the Great Depression in the United States.

The next wave of growth in the automobile industry came after World War Two. Economic recovery, the development of suburbs, especially in North America and the construction of interstate highways were all vital to the expanding car market. By 1949 car sales returned to pre-Depression levels, and between 1950 and 1970 global vehicle production doubled every decade. The sale of cars, in turn, drove the development of the interstate highway system. In 1956 President Eisenhower signed the Federal-Highway Act, "the greatest public works project in history." By 2018 there were some 48,000 miles of interstate highway across the United States. (In Germany the Nazis had launched a similar massive highway project when they came to power in the 1930s, partly to create jobs, partly to help modernize their transportation infrastructure to move military equipment if war should come. While these *autobahns* were popular, the system was never built out enough to impact before World War Two.)

As of 2020, there were about 1.4 billion cars in the world, and what was largely a Western phenomenon has become truly global. China, which only a couple of generations earlier was characterized by workers trundling to factories on bicycles, now leads the world in car sales and produces almost one-in-three cars in the world. India, which only a few decades ago had relatively few cars relative to its massive population, now ranks as the fifth-largest car market in the world, followed by Brazil. Both countries have significantly increased vehicle production and export to other countries.

Oil: The Fuel of the Twentieth Century

Coal fueled much of the early Industrial Revolution, but oil became the fuel of the internal combustion engine and the jet airplane engine. In many ways potential energy from oil preceded the car and plane, a classic case of the resource spurring innovation.

Oil had been spurting up from the ground since humans first walked the earth. Marco Polo remarked about it when crossing by the Caspian Sea in 1271 on his way to China. He noted that it was "good for burning," although in its natural state it really isn't viable; it only provides low energy release, which is okay for a lamp perhaps but little else. Polo seemed more impressed with its potential medicinal properties. It is a "salve for men and camels affected with itch or scab." Others used it as an adhesive or as a waterproofing agent.

Oil was largely used for these purposes until the middle of the nineteenth century, when entrepreneurs refined it and turned it into a critical resource.

First came the development of kerosene, a distilled product that was mostly used for lamps. Kerosene came at a critical time, replacing whale oil, which, because of catastrophic overharvesting, was facing shortages.

As the demand for kerosene grew, businesses moved aggressively to develop ways to extract it and build refineries to produce it. In 1859 the first oil corporation was founded in Pennsylvania, and for most of the next half-century the United States dominated the booming oil business. By the beginning of the twentieth century, it produced more oil than the rest of the world combined.

Gasoline, the fuel of the internal combustion engine, was originally a byproduct of distilled kerosene and often discarded; but as cars were invented, so was the need for fuel to run them. At first, many cars used fuels derived from coal tar, kerosene or other products; however, these fuels were inefficient and caused excessive engine knocking. By the 1890s, engineers decided to try using gasoline rather than simply throwing it away. It burned at higher heat, creating powerful, more efficient engines, and a revolution was born.

By the onset of World War One in 1914, gasoline had replaced kerosene as the fuel for both the automotive and aeronautics industries. The war accelerated demand for oil as tanks, planes and ships with oil-fueled engines were called into action. Post-war expansion of car and plane production made oil a globally desired commodity. The victorious powers after World War One argued that Middle Eastern countries should remain under Western protection, in part, so the West could have access to their massive oil reserves. All over the world the lands and seas were poked and prodded to see if they held this invaluable resource. By the end of the twentieth century oil production had risen to over 85 million barrels per day (in 1900, by contrast, global production was still measured in the low thousands of barrels per day).

The critical importance of oil in fueling the global economy meant that access to, and control of, it became a major geopolitical concern. The Organization of Petroleum Exporting Countries (OPEC) was founded in 1960 to give its member countries (initially Iran, Iraq, Kuwait, Saudi Arabia and Venezuela) a greater role in the pricing and production of oil. In 1973, when the United States backed Israel in a war against its Arab neighbors, OPEC flexed its energy muscle and embargoed shipments to the US. Oil prices doubled, then doubled again. Countries dependent on oil imports faced long lines at the pump. Siphoning gas from cars became common petty theft. The US federal government imposed 55 mile per hour speed limits on highways to save gas. The embargo was lifted a year later, but its effects continued to reverberate as the need for oil security became a concern for most nations and still remains an issue today.

Taking to the Skies: The Age of the Airplane

The technology of the bicycle and the internal combustion engine both played a key role in the emergence of the twentieth century's other radical new form of transportation: the airplane. The Wright brothers, who are credited with the first successful flight of a heavier-than-air machine in 1903, had made their career as bicycle builders and repairers in Dayton, Ohio. Both the bicycle and the airplane required balance and dexterous steering control. Design concepts needed to be both strong and lightweight, and the aerodynamic ratio of power-to-weight ratio was critical. As James Howard Means noted in an 1896 article in *The Aeronautical Annual*, "It is not uncommon for the cyclists to remark . . . Wheeling is just like flying!"

Airplane designers also had to have a good grasp of engines, since they had to be powerful enough to provide the lift and air speed to take off and light enough to stay in the air. As the Wright brothers applied their ideas of bicycle design to airplanes, they studied engines and decided that none on the market would work, so they built their own. It was built out of aluminum, a light-weight metal but also one more difficult to shape and machine.

After several years of designing and testing, the brothers took their airplane to Kitty Hawk, North Carolina, a sandy dune area along the coast used for testing gliders. On December 17, 1903, Wilbur (he won the coin toss over his brother Orville) successfully took off from a dune, stayed aloft for fifty-nine seconds and managed to travel slightly under 100 yards. In less than a minute, a new era of travel had dawned.

For the first decade, planes were mostly used as a modern version of the Pony Express, carrying mail across the sparsely inhabited lands of the United States. The first commercial passenger flight took place in Saint Petersburg, Florida, on January 1, 1914, when a floatplane with one passenger flew to Tampa. It took twenty-two minutes and covered 18 miles. As humble as those numbers sound, it would take the better part of a day at that time to get between those cities by steamship and over twelve hours by train.

Early on, passengers were often seated on top of the mail with little more to protect them from the elements than a pair of goggles and a leather coat. Lavatories were tin cups stowed in the side door. Passenger safety amounted to a parachute strapped to the traveler's back. (Instructions how to use it were rarely given.) The first airplane designed specifically to carry passengers was not built until 1920; it was used for the first international flights between Key West, Florida, and Havana, Cuba.

The romance of flight took off in May of 1927 when Charles Lindbergh successfully completed the first nonstop transatlantic flight. The *Spirit of St. Louis* (his flight was sponsored by the city) was stripped of anything considered nonessential, including a parachute, and any communication and navigation equipment. In order to carry enough fuel he had a tank crammed in between his legs, which meant there was no room for a front windshield; he used a periscope to see over the fuel tank. By the time he landed in Paris after taking off from New York City thirty-three hours earlier, he was so tired and bleary eyed that he imagined seeing ghosts in the cockpit. Amelia Earhart became the first woman to match Lindbergh's accomplishment five years later. Tragically, she died attempting the longest flight around the world in 1939. Questions of how and where her plane went down in the Pacific Ocean remain to this day.

As with almost everything, airplane production shifted from commercial to military use during World War Two. After 1945, airplane plants like Boeing were able to pivot back to commercial production. Airline companies also took advantage of the many long runways built for bombers and the increased numbers of military airbases now converted to civilian airports to expand their route options. The post-war period saw a dramatic increase in people taking to the skies. Before the war about three million Americans flew annually; by the mid-1950s that number had increased almost eighteen fold.

After the war, transoceanic flights became a daily occurrence. Trips that had taken the better part of a week by ship could now be done in hours. Along with the increased affluence of the post-war period there was an increase in tourism, as Americans could now reasonably visit Europe on vacation. The Concorde, a supersonic jet, started transatlantic service in 1976. While it enchanted many with the idea that you could now jet over to Paris for drinks and be back to work on Wall Street in the morning, it proved too noisy (those living around airports where it took off and landed complained about the sonic booms) and expensive to be viable.

Beginning in the 1960s, passenger planes became weapons in various conflicts around the world as terrorist groups began to seize them and hold passengers as collateral when negotiating. The most horrific example of planes as terror weapons came on September 11, 2001 (9/11), when three planes were hijacked by members of Al Qaeda, an Islamic terrorist group, and flown into the Twin Towers of New York City and the Pentagon (The third plane was brought down by its passengers in Pennsylvania before it could reach its target). Thousands were killed.

As hijackings became more common, governments responded with increased X-ray detection security in airports. In the aftermath of 9/11, stricter measures were imposed with passengers often required to remove shoes, belts, hats and coats as part of their pre-screening. Air travel, once seen as a luxury and a time of relaxation, became part of the anxieties of the modern age.

The Commercial Revolution of Container Ships

The global movement of goods was revolutionized in the second half of the twentieth century by the development of container ships. The basic idea, credited to US entrepreneur Malcom McLean, was to make the movement of goods more efficient by allowing the same transport containers to be easily moved between rail and ship lines. Gone were the days of stevedores lining the quays of ports around the world, unloading the cargo from ships and then lugging them to trains or trucks. McLean's system was designed to move by cranes containers laden with cargo from one ship to another quickly and efficiently. Over the course of the second half of the twentieth century, ships were redesigned to carry these containers, ports were refitted with massive cranes to move cargo and carefully aligned with rail lines to handle the growing capacity.

The first container ship in the mid-1950s carried about a dozen containers. Supersized ships now carry up to 24,000 containers. Costs of global shipping plummeted from close to $6.00/ton when McLean first started this new process to about $.16/ton today. Seven hundred million containers are moved annually; and they carry some ninety percent of all the goods transported around the globe.

The economics of shipping low-cost goods, like textiles or cheap consumer toys, which were once prohibitively expensive to transport, changed dramatically. Now countries around the world lowered production and labor costs, and could make these goods and ship them profitably around the globe. East Asian countries, especially China, leaned into these new opportunities. As profits from those industries grew, they began to manufacture cars and appliances. Within a half century the centers of global production shifted away from Western countries toward Asia, in no small part because of container ships.

The increasing global dependence on cargo ships comes with challenges. In March of 2021 a massive cargo ship turned sideways in heavy winds and got stuck in the Suez Canal. For six days the canal was closed, and the losses to the global economy were estimated to be in the billions of dollars. This incident raised issues about the security and reliability of a global supply chain dependent on the movement of goods in these massive ships.

The Futurist Movement: An Artistic and Political Reaction to Cars and Planes

Technological innovations are embraced by some who cheer the liberating possibilities that they bring, while others rue the changes that will result. This was the case with trains and bicycles, and it was certainly the case with the development of automobiles in the twentieth century. One example of both the enthusiasm and the skepticism of the automobile was a cultural movement, originated in Italy, known as Futurism.

Futurism was an artistic movement that emerged in Italy in 1909 when an unknown Italian poet, Flippo Thommaso Martinelli, was driving his new car along the road. He swerved to avoid a pair of bicycles, and his car wound up in a ditch, destroyed. Martinelli was, as he later claimed in in article, "transformed by the experience." For this poet the crash was not simply an accident but symbolic of the bicycle trying to deter the future of the car. Shortly afterward he published an essay in *La gazzetta dell'Emilia*. The essay, titled the *Manifesto of Futurism*, promised to wipe away the old and stale world of Italy's past with the speed and power of the future. The poet sought to glorify the new technology and use that technology as an artistic vehicle to transform his country. Futurism was symbolized by the car and the plane.

Time and space, Martinelli argued, were dead—killed by the endless possibilities that the new automobile age offered:

> We declare that the splendor of the world has been enriched by a new beauty: the beauty of speed. A racing automobile with its bonnet adorned

with great tubes like serpents with explosive breath . . . a roaring motor car which seems to run on machine-gun fire, is more beautiful than the Victory of Samothrace [a classic Hellenistic statue of Nike, the Greek goddess of Victory].

Martinelli invoked the image of a machine gun as a metaphor for the engine, framing his belief that the car and plane would be machines that would help lead mankind's liberation from the past through war and violence. "We want to glorify war—the only cure for the world—militarism, patriotism, the destructive gesture of the anarchists, the beautiful ideas which kill."

Futurism struggled to find its moorings as an artistic movement. It did however, shape ideas of how war could benefit from these new transportation technologies. Its greater impact was shaping the ideas of the positive benefits of war that would help spur a willingness for fighting in World War One. Benito Mussolini, Italy's post-war Fascist leader, was inspired by the idea that new technologies could transform society. Mussolini reveled in being a man of action; Futurism emphasized speed, and the excitement of movement matched the future he envisioned. Not only would he make the trains run on time, as he once promised, but he would bring Italy to a future of speed, power and military strength.

Initially, Martinelli and Mussolini were a perfect match. The poet thought he found his political muse in the politician, but egos and differences of strategic direction intervened and they fell out by the time Mussolini had consolidated his power in the mid-1920s. Mussolini did, however, continue to embrace the ideas of the Futurists. Even though the romance between Futurism and Fascism was brief, the impact of the movement the on shaping politics points to the revolutionary ways cars transformed thinking in this period.

How Cars Changed Society in the Post-World War Two Era

The end of World War Two saw the automobile revolution accelerate exponentially. Economic recovery, the development of suburbs, especially in North America, and the construction of interstate highways were critical to the expanding market. Between 1950 and 1970, global vehicle production doubled every decade. By the 1980s, global production, which had been dominated by US car makers, began to shift as Japan and to a lesser extent Korea became players in the field.

In 1956, US President Dwight Eisenhower signed the Federal-Highway Act, "the greatest public works project in history." Eisenhower saw it as both a boom for post-war economic growth and as a strategic military asset facilitating the movement of tanks and weapons across the country in case of an invasion during the Cold War. In fact, its official designation was the Dwight D. Eisenhower System of Interstate and Defense Highways. Today in the United States there are over 47,000 miles of interstate crisscrossing the country.

Cities were also transformed to meet the needs of the car. "It is estimated that as much as one half of a modern American city's land area is dedicated to streets and roads, parking lots, service stations, driveways, signals and traffic signs, automobile-oriented businesses, car dealerships, and more." "In 1970," historians David R. Goldfield and Blaine A. Brownell, would later announce, "America became a suburban nation." Goldfield and Brownwell's analysis was based on the 1970 census, which demonstrated the shift from urban to suburban living. Urban core density declined in many areas as cars facilitated the growth of suburbs and commuter cities, often well away from a major metropolitan core, where people would live but not work. Areas like Los Angeles became megalopolises extending from San Diego to Santa Barbara 200 miles north. Houston became a 600-square-mile sprawl. As one historian noted, "The automobile was the perfect mode of transportation in this terrain, and if it was not responsible for causing sprawl, it certainly fed the impulse. Sprawl became synonymous with the automobile." These trends were most prominent where existing cities were small and the space for expansion was available.

Car ownership was significantly a Western phenomenon until later in the twentieth century, but many parts of the world, especially Asia, have rapidly caught up. China is certainly a good example. Until the late 1980s cities like Beijing were still defined by the bicycle. They were mass produced and affordable; cars were not. The image of hundreds of thousands of Chinese riding their work horse "flying pigeon" bikes in their drab work uniforms was a metaphor for China's period of economic stagnation. But today that image is gone. Bicycles have largely disappeared from Beijing. Massive ring roads surround the city, cutting wide swaths through what used to be quaint *hutong* districts that once dominated the city. Pollution from cars stings the eyes and aggravates the throat. Traffic accidents are now the leading cause of death in the city for people under age forty-five. In 2013 there were more cars sold in China than any place ever, and today half of all the cars sold worldwide are sold in Asia.

Because the number of cars has risen so dramatically, causing issues around congestion among other things, many countries are turning back to travel by trains. New generations of trains, which can travel at hundreds of miles an hour, now connect much of Europe. China is rapidly expanding its high-speed rail system as well. In 2011, a new line between its two most important cities, Beijing and Shanghai, became operational. Travel between the two megalopolises, which had taken over fourteen hours, was now done in four. Shanghai now also has a maglev train between the downtown and the airport. Using magnetic fields to allow the train to float and therefore travel without friction, it can reach speeds of 270 miles per hour.

The Social Impact of the Automotive Revolution:
A Critique

The explosion of cars and suburban housing developments in the US during the 1950s led to a backlash in the 1960s as environmentalists began to deride the crippling impact of car pollution on the planet and social theorists began to analyze the often racially divisive and seclusionist nature of the suburbs. The critique of both is perhaps best encapsulated in Kenneth Packard's *Autokind vs. Mankind: An Analysis of Tyranny, A Proposal for Rebellion, A Plan for Reconstruction* (1971). The car as a vehicle of individual liberation, *automobility*, he calls it, is a myth. "Automobility gradually permeates the daily behavior of people, the purpose of institutions, and the structure of the cities and countryside. This tyranny has been promoted under the cunning popular myth of expanding freedom and affluence." He goes on to say that cars do not liberate; they entrap and do so in a way that literally chokes humanity to death with its noxious fumes. Mankind, he concludes, needs to go to war against Autokind; to lose could mean the end of the human race as we know it.

Packard's hyperbolic treatise was an argument ahead of its time. Published in the early 1970s, it remained a fringe document, never finding a significant audience. Since then, the ideas he espoused did become mainstream for many worried about the deleterious impacts of the growing global dependence on the car. In 1996 a work of similar sentiment, *The Ecology of the Automobile*, two sociologists, Peter Freund and George Martin, introduced their analysis with this provocation: "More than seventeen million people have been killed on roads since the automobile first appeared. An incalculable number have been seriously hurt. In the future, half the world is likely to be run over by a terminal squabble for oil. For today we are possessed by a mindless monster which threatens the planet itself."

The impact of fossil fuels on the planet has also become (according to many) an "existential threat" to global survival. Calls for more electric vehicles and more efficient public transportation are heard in all corners of the globe, yet much of the world remains as addicted to cars as ever with an estimated 1.4 billion cars on the world's roads today (and that does not include cars in junk yards). Oil exploration, distribution and control remain as central to the global economy. Whether the car will be an instrument of liberation, as it was seen for much of its history, remains to be seen. The future will likely include fleets of electric cars, driverless cars and charging stations built in tandem.

The Social and Cultural Impact of the Airplane

Air travel, like the proliferation of automobiles, evoked strong reactions. For some it promised a new era of connectivity, freedom and mobility. For others it was a new age of increasing social stratification, an age of speed and movement but not alienation. In short, airplanes reflected the social and cultural tensions of the modern world.

During the early 'golden days of air travel' most planes had only one cabin, which meant that everyone traveled by the same standard of luxury. Douglas D-C 3s, a common commercial plane of the 1930s, for example, expected that all passengers would be able to lie down. Pan-Am flights from San Francisco to Honolulu had bunk bed sleeping berths for all travelers, who could now wake up refreshed for their island adventure.

As air travel increased during the post-war period, planes changed. They were configured with compartments: first class and coach/tourist. Those with means could travel in luxury in the front of the plane. The Boeing 747 jet, built in 1968 for transoceanic travel, brought air travel to a new high. It had an upper deck where certain passengers could lounge at the bar sipping martinis, dine on restaurant quality food and chit-chat their way to their distant destination. Those in the main cabin, however, were increasingly crammed into smaller seats. A package of pretzels and a neighbor's elbow in your side now seem to be standard fare. The stark divisions between those at the front of the plane and those sitting in the rear demonstrated for many the realities of social divisions and inequalities of the modern age.

Planes also represented globalization and connectivity. The sumptuously filmed National Geographic documentary *Life in the Age of Airplanes* (2015) is one example of how the plane has evoked these images. Starting with a quick overview of human travel, it quickly gets to the central theme of the film: the airplane has truly revolutionized the human experience, bringing the world together in marvelous and unimagined ways. As the narrator, Harrison Ford, tells us, airport gates are "portals to the world." And not only is our present world now brought to us at the cost of a ticket, but "the airplane is the closest thing we've had to a time machine." It gives us access to the wondrous history of the planet and humanity as no human invention has done before.

The plane, according to the documentary, not only gives us a portal to the world, but it brings the world to us. In one of the memorable sections, the documentary follows the story of roses grown in Kenya. The fragile flowers are shipped around the world, adorning vases across the globe and in the scene's climax a dinner table in Alaska. They are still fresh and beautiful.

One critique of the argument that air travel has brought the world closer together comes from the travel writer Pico Iyer in his book, *The Global Soul: Jet Lag, Shopping Malls, and the Search for Home* (2001). In this series of essays, Iyer explores the meaning of our modern age of global travel and, while acknowledging a sense of shared common experience that comes from travel—jet lag, and the airport food and shopping malls—he also critiques the idea that travel is making us closer. In some ways, he argues, it deprives a lack of connectivity by stripping a sense of place, a sense of identity. "Our ads sing of Planet Reebok and Planet Hollywood—yet none of us necessarily feels united on a deeper level." We slog through airports lines and perhaps chat up the passenger in the next seat, but we do not make connections that move us beyond the superficial. Sophia Coppola's movie *Lost in Translation* (2003) explores similar themes through the story of an aging movie star, played by Bill Murray, who struggles with a sense of alienation and cultural disconnection while working in Tokyo.

Conclusion

Cars, planes and container ships have remade the modern world. They have changed not only how we get around and how fast we can get there, but they have reshaped the global economy. They now significantly dictate where we live and the types of jobs we have. They greatly influence how we spend our leisure time. Because of their enormous energy requirements, they have they altered global strategic policies and the geophysical systems. We now live in a world where transportation technology promises a new age of abundance, freedom and interconnectivity and, at the same time, we face a future of global peril brought on my climate change. In many ways our future will be dependent on how we balance the benefits and challenges of the modern transportation revolution.

End Materials Chapter 10

Works Quoted

Coppola, Sophia, *Lost in Translation* (2003). https://en.wikipedia.org/wiki/Lost_in_Translation_(film).

Fisher, Marc, "Cruise to Oblivion," *Washington Post* (September 2, 2015).

Freund, Peter and George Martin, *The Ecology of the Automobile* (New York: Black Rose, 1993).

Holsten, Hilda Hartmann, "How Cars Have Transformed China," *Partner Science Norway* (September 28, 2016). https://partner.sciencenorway.no/cars-and-traffic-forskningno-norway/how-cars-have-transformed-china/1437901.

Iyer, Pico, *The Global Soul: Jet Lag, Shopping Malls, and the Search for Home* (New York: Vintage Books, 2000).

Martinelli, Flippo Thommaso, *The Manifesto of Futurism*. www.societyforasianart.org/sites/default/files/manifesto_futurista.pdf.

Melosi, Martin, "The 'Footprint' of the Automobile on the American City," *The Automobile Shapes the City*. www.autolife.umd.umich.edu/Environment/E_Casestudy/E_casestudy2.htm#popsugrue.

National Geographic Films, *Life in the Age of Airplanes* (2015). https://en.wikipedia.org/wiki/Living_in_the_Age_of_Airplanes.

Packard, Kenneth, *Autokind vs. Mankind: An Analysis of Tyranny, a Proposal for Rebellion, a Plan for Reconstruction* (New York: W.W. Norton, 1971).

The Wright Brothers: The Invention of the Aerial Age, *Smithsonian National Air & Space Museum*. https://airandspace.si.edu/exhibitions/wright-brothers/online/who/1895/biketoflight.cfm.

Further Reading

1885–1886: The Frist Automobile, *Daimler Company*. www.daimler.com/company/tradition/company-history/1885-1886.html (Accessed February 8, 2021).

Andrews, Evan, "The First Automotive Competition Held 120 Years Ago," *History*. www.history.com/news/worlds-first-automotive-competition-held-120-years-ago.

Mom, Gijs, *Atlantic Automobilism: Emergence and Persistence of the Car, 1895–1940* (New York: Berghahn Books, 2014).

Mom, Gijs, *Globalizing Automobilism: Exuberance and Emergence of Layered Mobility, 1900–1980* (New York: Berghahn Books, 2021).

Seiler, Cotton, *Republic of Drivers: A Cultural History of Automobility in America* (Chicago, IL: University of Chicago Press, 2008).

11 War and Revolutions in the Early Twentieth Century

Introduction

The beginning of the twentieth century saw people on the move as never before. The technological revolutions of train and steamship combined with the surge of migration as a result of industrialization and colonialism led to millions traveling across borders and oceans. That tidal wave of travel came to an abrupt halt as borders closed when war erupted in Europe in 1914. European countries no longer wanted people to leave; they needed their military service at the front and their labor to support the cause. Tourist travel, which had grown exponentially in previous decades, came to a halt. Relatively safe journeys across the Atlantic were now fraught with peril, as ships carrying cargo and humans were attacked.

World War One started in 1914 when the assassination of the heir to the Austrian throne by Serbian nationalists quickly precipitated a continental crisis as countries across Europe rushed to align with side or the other. By the beginning of August, most of the major powers of Europe were involved: Germany and Austria-Hungary were the major belligerents on one side; France, England and Russia were on the other. Italy would soon join the fray, and within months the Ottoman Empire entered the war as well.

What had started as a regional European conflict quickly escalated into a global war when colonial powers like Great Britain and France recruited soldiers by the millions from their various colonies. Great Britain sought out support from their Commonwealth; soldiers and nurses from Canada, New Zealand and Australia answered their call. Fighting also erupted between colonial armies across Africa and even in the Far East.

The need for labor in Europe and the Near East brought hundreds of thousands from China, Vietnam and Africa to unload the ships and dig the trenches on the Western Front. In 1917, the United States agreed to fight on the side of Great Britain, France and Russia, further extending the global nature of the conflict. Countries around the world raced to supply materials, and the economies were restructured accordingly.

As nations and generals struggled to find victories amidst the horrors of trench warfare, technology continued to change the way wars were fought;

DOI: 10.4324/9781003168690-12

new, more destructive weapons were introduced. Tanks, planes and submarines were critical in many battles, and warfare caused massive causalities. By November 1918, when the war finally ended, close to 20 million people had died. Half of those who perished were non-combatants, civilians caught in the crossfires and fallout. Even more soldiers and civilians were wounded and permanently disabled.

By the end of the war in November 1918, the world was shattered and transformed. Old empires were no longer in power, and many people were displaced. Revolutions in some countries continued even after the armistice. Millions were left without a country or home. Soldiers trying to return home and refugees seeking shelter carried a virulent disease home: the Spanish Flu. A pandemic raged across the world for two years. By the time it ended, an estimated 50 to 100 million people across the world were dead from this virus; a staggering addition to the death tolls of the war.

Technology and Warfare

Technological developments that were key to the transportation revolutions of the nineteenth and early twentieth centuries also transformed warfare during World War One and other wars that followed. Submarines, tanks and airplanes all played a role in the evolution of war strategy and heralded a century in which wars were no longer fought along static lines but across vast sweeps of land, oceans and air.

World War One was a confluence of the old and the new. Horses and mules were literally the working horses of the early war. Cavalries, while used less on the Western Front where trench warfare became the norm, continued to be used across the Eastern Front and in battles across the Near East. Horses and mules dragged munition and cook wagons to the front lines. According to British sources around 120,000 horses were immediately requisitioned by the military when war was declared in 1914. Between 1915 and 1917, it is estimated that the United States shipped one thousand horses a month across the Atlantic to be used on the Western Front. By the end of the war some eight million horses and mules had perished in the fighting.

As the war dragged on, all sides looked for new technologies to aid the war effort. Tanks were introduced by the British in 1915. Known as the Little Willie, they constantly overheated and got stuck in the trenches they were supposed to be breaching; they were more dangerous to those who used them than to the enemy they fought. Not long after, Big Willie replaced Little Willie as a heavier, more reliable, successor. It was an improvement, but it took time to incorporate it into military strategy, and only near the end of the war were tanks efficient enough to be effective. By the end of the war, France and Britain had produced 7,000 units; Germany only twenty.

This discrepancy in tank production between the Allies and Germany was also reflected in the use of airplanes. Like tanks, planes were initially not very effective as military weapons. Early on, they were used for reconnaissance missions; however the engines were bulky and the armaments minimal. By the end of the war, Britain and France were making five times the number of planes as Germany, and air battles and ultimately the use of planes to drop bombs on distant lines were becoming more and more common.

The Germans mastered the art of building and using submarines. As the war evolved from the military offensives of 1914 into the long, drawn-out conflict of 1915 and beyond, it was apparent to all sides that whoever controlled the seas, and accessed the most material and personnel, would likely survive and win. In the beginning, Great Britain clearly had the superior navy and used it effectively to stop supplies from getting to Germany and its allies. Germany, in turn, decided to use submarines to attack the British navy and its supply lines, hoping to both open their own sea-lanes and disable British ships along the way. Submarines proved effective, but in 1915, the sinking of a British passenger liner, the *Lusitania*, which carried American passengers as well as armaments in its hold, threatened to bring the US into the war and compelled Germany to dock its fleet. As food deprivations decimated the home front and lack of materials crippled the military front, Germany decided to redeploy submarines in 1917. Records indicate they were able to sink over 2,000 allied ships that year, but growing fears that the US would no longer remain neutral soon proved correct, and in April 1917, the United States declared war on Germany and its allies.

World War One: A Global Conflict

War fought on the scale of World War One required endless supplies, soldiers and laborers to fuel its insatiable machine. Hundreds of thousands of soldiers were thrown into the no-man's land of the Western Front, and tens of thousands of casualties followed. Great Britain, France, Russia and their Allies enlisted close to 40 million to their cause; Germany and its allies almost 20 million. Many of the British and French forces were colonial soldiers. Because Germany and its allies, for the most part, were landlocked during the war, they lacked access to their colonies and the resources they could provide.

At Ypres in October 1914 and later at Verdun in 1915, the German army faced a contingent of Indian soldiers who had recently arrived from South Asia. By the war's end, almost 1,250,000 Indian soldiers served in Europe and the Middle Eastern campaigns, accounting for almost ten percent of the British army. They joined tens of thousands of other colonial and Commonwealth soldiers from Africa, Australia and New Zealand. They were also joined by some 450,000 soldiers from Morocco, Algeria, West Africa and Southeast Asia who fought for the French. In many ways the experience of war for these soldiers was the same as it was for their European counterparts. The bullets, gas and artillery shells (and the lice and the fleas) did not discriminate among victims. But, in other ways, the experiences of colonial soldiers fighting in this largely European war were unique and had long-lasting impact.

Historians face the several challenges attempting to understand the experience of colonial soldiers in World War One. Traditionally, colonial soldiers were recruited or conscripted for service from the ranks of the illiterate peasantry. Colonial governments did not want these soldiers to become discipline problems, so they chose soldiers who could not read or write. Nonetheless, some colonial corps did have professional letter-writers whom soldiers could hire to help them keep in touch with home, and some of these letters have been preserved. Although censorship of wartime correspondence complicates an analysis of this type of evidence, such letters still provide a window into the mind of the colonial soldiers. Other soldiers left oral testimonies of their experiences that historians can also use.

For some colonial soldiers, the horrors of war started with their 'recruitment' into the army. For many Africans, this experience recalled old villagers' tales of the brutalities of the Atlantic Slave Trade centuries before. In Senegal in West Africa, for example, young men were sometimes kidnapped by armed agents working for the French and forcibly dragged into service. If they tried to run away, parents or relatives might be seized and held until the young men returned and 'volunteered.' If these tactics failed, agents began to torch the villages, destroy the crops and livestock, and even kill hostages until they were able to meet their quota.

Whether coerced into military service or joining voluntarily, many had never been out of their home region, much less aboard a ship. Suddenly they were lowered and packed into the massive hold of a cargo ship. Voyages could take weeks, although the experience of the sailing varied tremendously. Many colonial soldiers recall it as a brutal time.

As colonial soldiers unloaded at their port of call, many recall being warmly greeted by English and French women and children. Others noted the special care by European officers to accommodate their religious customs and dietary needs. But racial prejudices born of a firmly established colonial mindset persisted. For example, an African soldier traveling on a truck to the front recalled that he was not allowed to sleep for three days because the French soldiers he was traveling with were afraid that he might accidentally move and touch them. One Indian soldier wrote that "the hatred between Europeans and Indians is increasing instead of decreasing, and I am sure the fault is not with the Indians."

The extent to which racial attitudes affected battlefield strategy is an area of historical contention. Many colonial soldiers report that they were integrated into units with European soldiers and fought alongside them without prejudice. At times officers who handled a colonial soldier roughly were punished, a situation that was unheard of in the colonies. Other evidence, however, points to a conscious effort on the part of officers to treat a colonial soldier's life as less valuable than that of European counterparts. General Robert Neville, who assumed command of the French army shortly after the battle of Verdun, pleaded with his staff in early 1916, "It is imperative that the number of [African] units . . . should be increased as much as possible. . . . [This will] permit the sparing—to the extent possible—of French blood."

Not all colonial soldiers fought and died in the European and Ottoman theaters. Battles raged across Africa. Large swaths of territory were scorched and destroyed to rob the enemy of materials. Locals starved miserably. According to some estimates, as many as one million people died in East Africa during this time. "The war changed some regions to such an extent that they needed decades to recover, if indeed they did recover," sums up one historian. In Asia, Japanese forces attacked German colonies in China. Mutinies against British rule brought the war home to Singapore.

Many soldiers suffered the brutalities of the Western Front because they expected that service to their colonial masters would be rewarded. They hoped that the end of the war would land them a secure job back home. The more politically motivated soldiers hoped that by serving they would gain greater rights in the empire. One Indian soldier wrote to his local Imam as he prepared for depart to Europe in 1916, "Leaving Hindustan, to take part in the work of helping the Government, I arrived in France, and today this honour has been conferred on me that I find myself in the field of battle. . . . I hope that my presence here will find favour for me in the eyes of the Government." Did he truly feel this sense of support and commitment, or was he simply putting on a heroic face? Did he know his letters were potentially censored by government officials? We do not know for sure, but it does seem that many colonial soldiers, at least before they faced the horrors of battle, expressed similar sentiments.

In other cases, soldiers rejected the commands of their colonial officers and, overall, the war further exacerbated anti-colonial rebellions, especially in regions where Muslims were asked to fight against Muslims in the Ottoman Empire. In January 1915, three companies of Indian soldiers stationed in Rangoon refused to embark when they were ordered to go to the Middle East to fight fellow Muslims. A few months later, a largely Muslim regiment stationed in Singapore opened fire on their officers when given orders to fight in the Middle East.

When the United States entered the war in 1917, the conflict further escalated into a global conflict. It took almost a year for US forces to organize and train, but by the spring of 1918 they were arriving in France at a rate of 10,000 per day. Within months there were close to two million US doughboys on the ground; about half of them saw active combat. The US army proved to be a huge boost for the Allies and convinced the Germans that victory was unattainable. By November 1918, Germany and its allies surrendered.

Women and the War

While the vast majority of those dragged into the war efforts from abroad were men, women certainly played important roles as well. Some participated in the military theater as nurses and clerks. Often these women came from middle- and upper-class society. For them, the war afforded a chance for a new public role and a chance for personal liberation from the structures of traditional society. One such woman was Olive King, the 29-year-old daughter of a prominent Australian executive who served as a nurse in the Balkan theater. Although King was never in combat, her work put her in close contact with the grim realities of war. During one Bulgarian offensive, she helped evacuate her field hospital. As she waited for the final wounded to be prepared for travel, thirteen ambulances took off attempting to escape by crossing a hazardous mountain pass. They were captured by Bulgarian forces; most were killed, drivers and wounded alike. King managed to load her ambulance onto a train. As the freight car pulled out of the station, a Bulgarian howitzer shell smashed the platform she was standing only a few moments earlier. On another occasion, a fire roared through town, and her group barely escaped before their quarters were burned down.

After the war, King stayed in the Balkans for several years overseeing refugee and repatriation camps. In 1923, she returned to Australia and a largely private life. Some of her female compatriots believed their participation in the war qualified them as equals to their male counterparts and earned them equal rights in the economic and political spheres. Britain, Germany, Austria and the United States did pass suffrage laws following the war. Australia had granted women the vote prior to the war, but King did not seem particularly interested in politics. She frequently gave talks about her war experiences but otherwise led a quiet, private life. Her experience was not all that different than many men who had served, and after the war they simply wanted to return home to a 'normal life.'

World War One: The Demands of Labor

Despite the mobilization of women into the workforce, demands for labor quickly outstripped resources. By the end of 1914, all sides were desperately seeking new workers to keep the factories producing weapons and the farms growing food. Germany and its allies conscripted labor from Poles and Russians left homeless from the war. France recruited workers from Greece, Spain, Portugal and Italy. Both France and England continued to enlist labor from their colonies. An estimated 50,000 Vietnamese worked in Parisian factories and domestic jobs. Over 20,000 South Africans joined in labor brigades to serve British needs. Yet, the war demanded more.

In 1916 a new scheme began to emerge for both the British and the French: recruit Chinese labor. The new republic, created after the overthrow of the Qing dynasty in 1911, was very interested in the possibility because it offered a way to gain influence in any postwar decisions in Asia. They hoped that supporting the Allies would increase the willingness of the international community to recognize and support the new government. They also hoped that if the Allies won, China would get control of the German colony in the Shandong province of eastern China. Eventually, the governments of China and the Allied countries worked out an agreement, and young Chinese men began gathering at the quays of Canton and Shanghai to begin their journey to Europe. By the end of the war, close to 140,000 Chinese had made the long journey. Perhaps another 60,000 made their way across Siberia to work in the mines and munition factories of Russia during the war.

It is hard to know what it was like for these Chinese laborers to arrive in Calais, France, or London. Most were illiterate and so left no written record of their experience. Reports from the British and French soldiers and managers who supervised them, however, do provide a window into their experiences. Based on these sources, conditions of labor were difficult for Chinese conscripts. Many assigned to French units unloaded ships at a port or worked in factories, while those assigned to British and American details usually worked closer to the front lines, digging trenches or hauling material. Hours were long and wages low. Daily life was confined to work and camp. Days off were rare. Confrontations with British overseers frequent. A British officer in his report of a confrontation his unit had with these Chinese conscripts reported, "It was a wretched, pitiful business. . . . They were nearly all illiterate peasants without the slightest notion of why they were slaving eighteen hours a day. . . . We were under strict orders to look upon them as rabble. If they showed face in the streets in groups of over three in number they were to be shot like rabid dogs."

World War One and the Plight of Refugees

With over 9.7 million military and almost 10 million civilian deaths, by November 1918 World War One staggered to an end. Peace and stability were far from assured. Experts estimate that at least 10 million people were displaced internally or fled internationally over the course of the war. Well over a half a million fled from Belgium to Holland, France and England shortly after the German invasion in 1914. At the height of the war, close to two million Belgians were displaced by the fighting. In some places they found shelter and work, and in other areas, local municipalities were already overstretched by the burdens of war and they were 'encouraged' to move on. In Holland, authorities set up temporary encampments (they called them 'Belgian Villages' to avoid the pejorative connotation that concentration camps had become associated with during the Boer War in South Africa) that could be quickly torn down if not needed. In Italy some 400,000 civilians fled south after the defeat of their army at Caporetto in the north. War forced about one-third of Serbia's pre-war population to leave their homes.

An estimated three million people living in the western regions of Russia fled as the Germans advanced and the war escalated on the eastern front. The large Jewish population that lived in this region often found open hostility wherever they went. Some Jews went east, eventually finding refuge in Shanghai, a city that because of China's weak government had become a global city and a place of refuge for many. About 400,000 Jews moved to Palestine during the early twentieth century.

Many refugees never found safety. Around 140,000 Serbian refugees died trying to get to Albania as the fighting erupted in the Balkans. Tragically, well over one million Armenians, men, women and children were brutally slaughtered by Ottoman forces after they were forcibly expelled from their homelands in Eastern Anatolia when war erupted between the Ottomans and Russians. Ottoman leaders claimed they were resettling these Armenians to safe havens in Syria, but that was not the case, and most either died of starvation and dehydration in the searing desserts or were murdered by military forces en route. Many around the world refer to this event as genocide, but Turkish leaders still claim that the elimination of these Armenians was simply a tragic result of the 'fog of war.'

At the end of the war, the task of trying to figure out what to do with these millions of displaced people, as well as the millions of prisoners of war captured during the fighting, largely fell to the newly created League of Nations and a Norwegian explorer turned humanitarian, Fridtjof Nansen. Besides establishing and overseeing numerous committees to deal with the displacement crises wrought by the war, Nansen devised a refugee passport system that gave them legal standing to settle in new lands. Nansen was awarded the Nobel Peace Prize in 1922 for his humanitarian efforts.

As millions of soldiers and laborers boarded ships to return home, and millions of refugees and prisoners of war wandered the roads of Eurasia and the Near East seeking some kind of new start, disease traveled with them. In 1918, a highly virulent form of influenza, which become known as the Spanish Flu (because the Spanish press first wrote about it) appeared amongst soldiers and quickly spread around the world. It was especially devastating, for reasons that epidemiologists still debate, amongst young adults. (Flu viruses more often impact children and the elderly.) In the United States this meant that the life expectancy fell by over a decade within a single year. It took decades for the US population to recover.

Within a year, close to one-third of the world's population, almost 500 million people, were plagued by the virus. Estimates are that at least 50 million and maybe as many as 100 million people around the world died before it mysteriously disappeared in 1920. South Asia was the hardest hit region, with as many as 20 million people perishing. Demographers have concluded that the Spanish Flu caused the world's population to decline; and that was the last time that it would do so.

Revolutions in the Post-War World

As if a catastrophic refugee crisis and a global pandemic were not enough, there were revolutions on the horizon. The strains of war fractured already unstable empires across Europe and the Near East. New ideologies challenged old paradigms, and populist movements committed to new national and political identities stormed the barricades and toppled regimes. Germany, Austria,

Hungary, Ireland, the Ottoman Empire (the list goes on) all faced major revolutionary movements and civil wars. The Russian Revolution would be the most important and impactful of these upheavals.

Throughout the first decades of the twentieth century, Russia had roiled with unrest. The disastrous realities of the country's inabilities to sustain the human and financial costs of the war, and the incompetent and seemingly callous reign of the Tsar and his family, pushed the country over the edge. In 1917, Tsar Nicholas II was forced to abdicate, and months of failed attempts to establish a new, stable system followed. Finally, the temporary government, the Provisional Government that replaced him, fell to a coup by the Bolshevik (later renamed Communist) Party in October 1917. The Bolsheviks ruled Petrograd, Moscow and a few other key cities in western Russia, but their control over the vast country was tenuous at best. Nationalist elements, long opposed to rule from Moscow, as well as social groups opposed to the rise of the Worker's Revolution, immediately began to fight against the new leaders. Called the Civil War of the Reds (the Bolsheviks) and the Whites (a wide variety of groups and peoples opposed to the Bolsheviks), the turmoil lasted for at least four years, and conflicts erupted like prairie fires across the vast expanses of the former Russian Empire.

One ordinary man, whose experiences during the Russian Revolution help us understand the brutal challenges many faced, is Jan Kozlowski. Born in 1904, Jan grew up in comfortable circumstances in Riga in western Russia. His father, who was briefly exiled to Siberia in 1905 for political activity, died in 1910. Living at home with his mother, their world was upended when the German army invaded Russia in 1914. Jan's brother, Alexander, ten years older, was conscripted into the Russian army. Jan's mother traveled with him to St. Petersburg (renamed Petrograd to avoid a Germanic ring to the name) where, for the next few years, he lived a fairly normal life.

When the Bolsheviks overthrew the Provisional Government in 1917 and Jan's mother decided their bourgeoisie background could make them enemies of the state, she sent him alone by train to Ekaterinburg in the Ural Mountains to be with his brother, who had recently been released from military service and was living there with his new wife. Jan's mother thought he would be safe there, away from the unfolding revolution. She was wrong. Not long after Jan arrived in the Ural city, fighting erupted as Bolsheviks units tried to take the city and control the key Trans-Siberian Railway lines that passed through Ekaterinburg. With anti-Bolshevik rebellions spreading across Siberia, the Bolsheviks needed to command this key city to transport the Red Army to strategic locations and supply them with critical material.

In September 1918, when Alexander refused to join the Red Army, the Bolsheviks stood him up against a wall and shot him. Jan, only fourteen, was hiding nearby and watched his brother die. He was alone, again and potentially seen as an enemy of the people because of his brother's refusal to support the

Bolsheviks. In survival mode, sleeping in sheds and scrounging for food, he continued to hide for several days. One day he saw a train going east. With no clear plan in mind, he jumped on with only the hope to get away. As Jan journeyed east, disease, starvation and the bitter cold of Siberian winters were constant companions. Together with fellow refugees from across Russia, as well as German and Austrian prisoners of war who had been sent to Siberia, he jumped on trains trying to get away from the fighting. When they were kicked off, and they often were, they begged rides in camel caravans. Sometimes the trains just stopped in the middle of nowhere, and they were stranded in the cold, cramped cars for long periods of time.

After months of arduous, dangerous travel, Jan wound up in Harbin, a key rail city in eastern China. Even though it was thousands of miles from Moscow and St. Petersburg, it too saw constant fighting between Reds and Whites. Shortly after he arrived, he was sick with cholera, an epidemic that ravaged the city. Then, somehow, he got caught up in a firefight between Bolsheviks and White forces that left him injured with a broken back, lying on the street. An older couple dragged him to safety and after weeks of care helped him get to Vladivostok, a port city on the Pacific Ocean. There, he met American troops who were stationed to protect critical military supplies and to prevent the Communist revolution from spreading across the Pacific and into the United States. Through the help of a US solider, Jan garnered passage to the United States. He never returned to Russia and never saw his mother again.

Jan's story is important for several reasons. First, he was an ordinary young man, but his story conveys the extraordinarily painful events that so many who were forced to flee often faced. Second, Jan was my wife's grandfather, and understanding his story helps us understand that we all have connections to history through our own family stories. Revolutions not only changed governments but fractured lives and destroyed families.

Jan's experiences likely mirrored those of many fleeing the civil war that erupted across the Near East after the collapse of the Ottoman Empire. Beyond, sending hundreds of thousands of Armenians to their deaths in the Syrian deserts, Turkish leaders also waged wars of ethnic cleansing against Greeks and other ethnic groups. An estimated one million Greeks were expelled from their homes along the Aegean coast when war between Greece and Turkey erupted. When the Turks won and a peace agreement was reached in 1923, another 1.5 million Greeks were displaced as well. Greece, in turn, sent 500,000 ethnic Turks who had long lived in Greece out of the country.

Poles expelled ethnic Germans when a Polish state was recreated in 1920. Hungarians, Bulgarians and Serbians all tried to forcibly remove ethnic minorities in the 1920s to strengthen, at least as they saw it, their national identity and consolidate their political power. The national and ethnic cleansings that were an aftermath of post-World War One period have continued, and wars of ethnic cleansing are a sad reality of the modern world.

Conclusion

The end of a war often brings, at best, uncertain peace. Certainly this was the case of World War One. It left in its wake an unimaginable loss of life with many more physically and psychologically marred and millions displaced, often with no home or country. It destroyed old regimes and empires. It invalidated many old ideas and values. For some, this represented fear and foreboding, for others optimism and opportunity. For almost everyone there was a sense that things would never be the same, with questions of what was to come,

End Materials for Chapter 11

Works Quoted

1918 Pandemic (H1N1 Virus), *Center for Disease Control*. www.cdc.gov/flu/pandemic-resources/1918-pandemic-h1n1.html (Accessed February 1, 2021).

Africa and the First World War, *Deutsche Welle*. www.dw.com/en/africa-and-the-first-world-war/a-17573462 (Accessed June 15, 2016).

Gatrell, Peter, "Refugees," *1914–1918 On-Line: International Encyclopedia of the First World War*. https://encyclopedia.1914-1918-online.net/pdf/1914-1918-Online-refugees-2014-10-08.pdf (Accessed February 10, 2021).

King, Hazel, ed., *One Woman at War: Letters of Olive King, 1915–1920* (Melbourne: Melbourne University Press, 1986).

Linn, Joe, *Memoirs of the Maelstrom: A Senegalese Oral History of the First World War* (Portsmouth, NH: Heinemann Publishers, 1999).

McKeown, Adam, "Global Migrations, 1846–1940," *Journal of World History*, vol. 15, no. 2 (2004).

Omissi, David, *Indian Voices of the Great War* (New York: St. Martin's Press, 1999).

Summerskill, Michael, *China on the Western Front Britain's Chinese Work Force in the First World War* (London: Michael Summerskill, 1982).

Taylor, Tom, "The Extraordinary Life of an Ordinary Person: Jan Kozlowski and the Russian Revolution," *World History Connected*, vol. 18, no. 1 (February 2021). https://worldhistoryconnected.press.uillinois.edu/18.1/toc.html.

Further Reading

Aksakal, Mustafa, *The Ottoman Road to War in 1914: The Ottoman Empire and the First World War* (Cambridge: Cambridge University Press, 2008).

Audoin-Rouzeau, Stephane and Annette Becker, *Understanding the Great War: 14–18* (New York: Hill and Wang, 2000).

Fitzpatrick, Sheila, *The Russian Revolution* (Oxford: Oxford University Press, 2017).

Grayzel, Susan, *Women and the First World War* (London: Longman Press, 2002).

Kolata, Gina, *Flu: The Story of the Great Influenza Pandemic of 1918 and the Search for the Virus That Caused It* (New York: Farrar, Straus and Giroux, 1999).

Remak, Joachim, *The Origins of World War I, 1871–1914* (New York: Harcourt Brace, 1995).

Richards, Michael, *Revolutions in World History* (New York: Routledge Books, 2004).

Stevenson, David, *1914–1918: The History of the First World War* (New York: Penguin Books, 2013).

Tooze, Adam, *The Deluge: The Great War, America and the Remaking of the Global Order, 1916–1931* (New York: Penguin Books, 2014).

Trotsky, Leon, *The Russian Revolution* (New York: Doubleday Books, 1932).

Winter, Denis, *Death's Men: Soldiers of the Great War* (New York: Penguin Books, 1978).

12 Dictatorships, the Great Depression and World War Two

Introduction

The fragile recovery underway after the devastation of World War One and the Spanish Flu was shattered in the late 1920s by a crash in the global financial market—the Great Depression. As banks in the United States closed in October of 1929 and stock values plummeted, the global economy, increasingly tied to the US financial system. 'crashed.' Within months, governments shut their borders to foreign trade and workers. Unemployment hit record highs. The 1930s saw millions of people around the world unemployed, desperately on the move, with little or no place to go.

For some, opportunities emerged where they least expected. In 1932 a young American welder, John Scott, unable to find work at home, headed to the Soviet Union in pursuit of work. Scott's journey to Magnitogorsk in the Ural Mountains came at a time of great change in the Soviet Union. He found work, but also suffered through the upheaval of political arrests and purges that Stalin unleashed across the country.

The chaos and disarray of the Great Depression drove many countries to seek radical political solutions. In Germany it led to the rise of Adolf Hitler, leader of the Nazi Party. He promised hope and a return to normalcy along with work, vacations and affordable cars for all Germans—but only if you were a true German, not a Jew or anyone deemed not part of "the community." Those categorized as "others" were ostracized and persecuted and later eliminated by the Nazis. Two such programs—the Nazi Strength Through Joy vacation program and the Volkswagen, or 'people's car'—were instrumental to the Nazi goals; indirectly, they both also revealed the repressive and ominous politics of fascism. They also foreshadowed the horrors of World War Two and the Holocaust that followed.

Japan responded to the social and political strains of the Depression by turning to a more authoritarian government. It responded to the decline of global trade and labor by aggressively expanding aspirations for its colonial empire, particularly in China. In 1937, Japan launched offensives into central China, and soon war engulfed the whole region. Japan promised to liberate Asia from Western powers, but its true intentions became apparent. Chinese, Koreans,

DOI: 10.4324/9781003168690-13

Filipinos, Chinese and others were forced to become state laborers, some as sex slaves for the Japanese army. Asia experienced a racial war as brutal as the Holocaust unfolding in Europe.

The new technologies—planes and tanks, ships and weapons—were used on an unimaginable scale. They left cities destroyed and millions of refugees displaced. By the end of the war in 1945, the newly created United Nations was faced with the immense challenges of trying to bring order and a future to this shattered world.

Travel and the Great Depression

For a time, World War One largely put a stop to transatlantic migration as countries closed borders to immigrants and restricted the ability of their own citizens to leave. Given the demands of wartime they needed their own populations to support their own needs for soldiers and labor. By 1924 numbers of immigrants coming in the US returned to pre-war levels, although their place of origin shifted as the US imposed restrictive quotas on immigration from South and Eastern Europe. Growing ethnic prejudice against people from these regions likely played a role. Donato and Gabaccia note in their study of gender and international migration that the number of women, as a percentage of the immigrant population, increased as trends shifted from labor, which had been predominantly male, to family unification and women were now encouraged to join their husbands.

The economic recovery of the post-war period came to a crashing halt on October 22, 1929, when the United States' financial system plummeted. Overvaluations of stocks and property, excessive borrowing and debt spurred a run on the banks. The Dow Industrial Average, the key indicator of the stock market, fell almost forty percent that day. Thousands of investors, from the great banking baron to the single-family investor, saw their savings wiped out in a day. When banks and other borrowing agencies called in loans to cover their own losses, the financial system collapsed and like a tidal wave devastated economies around the world. When US banks called in their loans from Germany, England and France, the economies in those countries contracted by a third within months.

Countries that supplied the raw materials to the world's industrial giants were quickly left adrift. For example, Japan's silk export industry collapsed, as women could no longer afford fine stockings. Three million people lost jobs, and income dropped significantly. A study of how the Depression impacted rural Egypt suggested that in the early 1930s food consumption among the rural population dropped by as much as twenty-six percent—a figure that indicated widespread malnutrition, chronic illness and likely starvation. In Cuba, the collapse of the sugar economy was catastrophic for the millions of farm laborers who survived by cutting and processing the cane. By the early 1930s, one-fourth of the Cuban population did not have any income, and those who did work saw wages slashed by seventy-five percent.

As the Depression deepened, many industrial countries began to impose tariffs on imports to protect their industries. Immigration into the United States almost stopped. In 1929, records showed 279,678 immigrants entered the United States, but in 1933 there were less than 25,000, a decline of over ninety percent. During the early 1930s, when the Depression was at its lowest point, the United States actually had more people leave than enter.

Mexicans who had originally fled north to escape the chaos of the Mexican Revolution during the early twentieth century returned to Mexico. Some left the United States on their own volition as jobs became scarce in the American South and Southwest. Others left under pressure from people who saw them as taking their jobs (jobs they had not wanted before the Depression hit). Cities like Los Angeles worked with federal officials to conduct deportation raids and negotiated with railroads to establish a 'charity rate' for those who wanted to 'voluntarily' return to their mother country. President Hoover issued executive orders restricting immigration from America's southern borders.

The United States not only experienced a financial collapse, but it also experienced an ecological collapse. A large expanse of land across the Central Plains became known as the Dust Bowl. Over the late 1920s and 1930s, drought, over plowing by new types of tractors and overproduction of crops across many parts of the central United States—Oklahoma, northern Texas, and Kansas especially—caused massive dust storms to blow across the land. Farms literally blew into the sky, and the lives of many who had depended on that soil blew away with the dust. As millions of unemployed industrial workers took to the highways and railways in search of work, they were joined by thousands of farmers in a desperate search for survival.

The stories of these Hobos and Okies, as those fleeing economic and environmental disaster in the US were called, were captured in the novel *The Grapes of Wrath* by John Steinbeck. The protagonists, the Joad family, poor tenant farmers from Oklahoma who saw their farm blow away in the dust storms, loaded everything they had into a creaky, rickety truck and headed west. "The moving questing people were migrants now. Those families which had lived on a little piece of land, who had lived and died on forty acres, had eaten or starved on the produce of forty acres, now had the whole West to rove in." As they crawled west, their jalopy constantly breaking down, their few pennies disappearing, they were followed by "streams of people. Behind them more were coming." At each town they'd stop, hoping to find a little work. Instead, they were often greeted by large billboards on the city line that said, "Keep moving, no work here."

John Scott and the Soviet Union

While many parts of the world closed their borders to protect their workforce, a few countries, notably the Soviet Union, welcomed immigration in the 1930s. Its strong command economy, under the direction of the country's dictatorial leader Joseph Stalin, allowed it to control labor and production. It was also desperate, after the purge of many engineers during the Russian Revolution, for skilled workers to help build its industrial capacity.

One of those workers who decided to try his luck in the Soviet Union was John Scott. In the fall of 1932, he went to the USSR for much the same reasons that most of the one or two thousand Americans did; he was young, idealistic, twenty years old, single, in search of adventure and in need of work. He began to read about the Soviet Union and, he later wrote, "decided to go to Russia to work, study and lend a hand in the construction of a society that seemed to be at least one step ahead of the American."

Scott was a welder, and after arriving in the Soviet Union he was assigned to ply his trade in Magnitogorsk on the eastern slopes of the Ural Mountains. A few years before, Magnitogorsk had been a small town in the middle of nowhere. Although its rich deposits of ferrous metals were well known (in Russian, *Magnitogorsk* means "Magnetic Mountain"), its industrial potential had never been exploited. By the time Scott arrived in the fall of 1932, plans were in place to make it the home of the largest steel plant in the world. Thousands were already there, living in tents and hovels, creating the future out of little or nothing. Steel plants needed to be built, so housing and a city would have to wait.

Many Soviet citizens, like Scott, were there voluntarily. The boomtown of Magnitogorsk promised work and decent pay, and for many peasants and unskilled laborers, it offered a chance to learn a trade and to be part of something special. Not all were there of their own accord. Scott estimated that of the 250,000 people living and working in Magnitogorsk in the mid-1930s, about 50,000, around twenty percent of the population, were there, as he said, "under GPU [security police] supervision." *Kulaks*, better-off farmers, mostly from the Ukraine, who Stalin labelled 'enemies of the people' were forced into labor exile. So too were other enemies of the state, such as those considered political opponents or labor saboteurs. These forced laborers (exact numbers are unclear), many arrested on dubious or false charges, were essential to Stalin's industrial drive. According to one researcher, "The bookkeeping of Stalin's terror is an inexact and contentious science." We do know that prior to the twin policies of Collectivization and the Five-Year Plans, started in the late 1920s, there were likely under 200,000 Soviet citizens in exile; by the onset of World War Two in 1939, there were probably over two million.

In the beginning, Scott reported, conditions were brutal. The southern Urals in winter received the bitter winds that roared out of Siberia, and temperatures plummeted. Men and women froze in their tents at night. Despite these difficulties, he wrote, "The work went on much faster than the most optimistic foreigners anticipated, although more slowly than the chimerical plans of the Soviet government demanded." In February of 1932, the first iron was smelted.

Scott married a local woman and they had a daughter. They moved out of their dorms and into an apartment. "It was no longer necessary," he confessed, "to steal in order to live." Magnitogorsk began to resemble a modern city, with streets and a streetcar line, shops, schools, clinics and movie theatres.

Just as things seemed to become normal, however, the Soviet Union was shattered by yet another wave of arrests and purges. This time fearful of rivals in his own Communist Party, Stalin launched a brutal attack on his perceived enemies. Fellow comrades during the revolution were now accused of trying to assassinate Stalin and overthrow his regime. Trials were staged and many were convicted, often on the flimsiest of evidence. Punishments were swift and often involved execution or long sentences in exile.

The Great Purge, as this period in Soviet history was known, also extended far beyond the party elite in Moscow, as local police officials and citizens exposed 'enemies of the state' in their midst. Millions of upper- and middle-level officials throughout the country were exposed and brought to trial. "The purge struck Magnitogorsk in 1937 with great force," Scott wrote. "Thousands were arrested, incarcerated for months, finally, exiled. No group, no organization was spared." Local leaders were taken away in the dead of night, never to return. Their families and friends were often rounded up afterward.

Scott, like many foreigners, eventually came under suspicion. He was lucky enough to be able to leave the Soviet Union and, after a long period of separation, got his wife and child out. Yet, Scott concluded, it would be wrong to assume that the massive attack of the party apparatus fundamentally altered the average citizen's view of the state. Russians, he said, overwhelmingly took the Great Purge, "more or less as it came without allowing it permanently to influence their attitude toward Soviet power." It is also the case that, for many, the full extent of the horrors of Stalin's gulag system were only realized long after he was dead and the Soviet Union collapsed.

Travel and Leisure in Nazi Germany, 1933–1939

A pillar of the Nazis' dogma when they came to power in Germany in 1933 was creating a *Volksgemeinschaft or* "people's community." This community promised to end the divineness and rancor that had dominated German public life during the Depression and political unrest of the late 1920s and early 1930s. It also served the state's interests by assimilating every aspect of German life into the structures of the Nazi system. What the 'people's community' meant for Germans was succinctly summarized in a speech given by the Nazi minister of propaganda Joseph Goebbels shortly after Hitler was appointed chancellor. Goebbels assessed the significance of the moment:

> We must develop organizations in which the individual's entire life can take place. Then every activity and every need of every individual will be regulated by the collectivity represented by the party. There is no longer any arbitrary will, there are no longer any free realms in which the individual belongs to himself. . . . The time of personal happiness is over.

For Goebbels this speech defined the Nazi revolution, namely that the nation, the collective spirit of the German people, was everything, and individual personal welfare was important only to the extent that it helped fulfill the goals of the whole. Individual rights and liberties were not important; the state and the party were and consequently, personal happiness would come through collectivity.

The Strength Through Joy program (*Kraft durch Freude* or KdF), launched in November 1933 by the Nazis, was promoted as state-sponsored initiative that would bring these benefits of the community to ordinary Germans through vacation and recreation opportunities. Through trips to Baltic Sea resorts or the Bavarian mountains, average Germans could enjoy the healthy benefits of fresh air and exercise often denied to them in their taxing work and urban living conditions. A Nazi pamphlet summarized the goals of the program as follows: The "value [of the program] lies neither in the type of transport nor in the destination of the journey, but solely in the community experience." Moreover, they could experience the joys of Germany with their fellow citizens from around the country and, at least in theory, everyone helped promote the central goal of the Nazi party of creating a 'people's community.'

The Volkswagen or 'the people's car' was another part of this Strength Through Joy program. Symbolically, it was intended to convey that the Party was making the good life, in this case cars, affordable and available to all. At the German auto show of 1934, Nazi leaders proudly proclaimed that they would begin building this simple, efficient automobile with which all Germans could then travel throughout the country on the beautiful *autobahns*, or highways built by the state. In a country still locked in the depths of economic depression, this dream, along with vacations offered by the program, was taken as a clear demonstration that the Nazi state was making life better for ordinary Germans. (While studying abroad in Germany in the 1970s, the owner of a small restaurant told me, "Remember, Hitler gave us the Volkswagen!" Trying to understand what she meant became a major focus of my graduate work later on.)

The travel program and the Volkswagen also reveal the darker side of the Nazi social and economic agenda. The vacations facilitated the state's ability to create a monolithic, state-structured society in which individual autonomy was subservient to state control, as on most trips propaganda sessions were as essential as visits to historic sites or boat rides on a lake. In the end, many average Germans rejected the state-controlled vacations in favor of their own solitary getaways. An underground dissident analyzing these programs wrote in 1939 that "People now look for place where there are no KdF visitors. 'Not visited by the KdF' is now a particular asset for summer vacations."

Even though the Volkswagen idealized the economic populism of the Nazi movement, few private citizens ever actually got to drive them during the Nazi regime. By the time the first Volkswagen factory was built in 1938, its main use was not to produce cars for the common person but cheap, efficient military transport for war. During World War Two 'the people's car' was built by slave labor from the prison and death camps of the Nazi empire, and over seventy years later the Volkswagen company and the German people continue to live with how they were complicit in the barbaric history of the Nazi state.

The other dark side to these Strength Through Joy programs was the Nazi ideal that the 'people's community' was a community of exclusion. Some people, because of their ethnic and/or religious heritage, were marginalized and excluded. The story of Victor Klemperer shared through the extensive diaries he kept reveals how these policies of exclusion impacted ordinary people. Klemperer was born into a Jewish family in 1881. In 1912 he converted to Protestantism, but when the Nazis came to power he was deemed Jewish. His distinguished military service during World War One did not spare him and, in 1933, he was removed from his university position because of his heritage. His wife, who was 'Aryan,' faced persecution and was encouraged to leave him; she refused. As Nazi control intensified in the mid-1930s and their lives were further restricted, the Klemperers turned to driving. Victor got his driver's license and they bought a car. It was not an easy process; the state stifled their every effort to do so, but because he was legally married to a 'German' woman, in the end they relented.

For a few precious years the Klemperers were able to drive around their city of Dresden and get out in the countryside. Their drives symbolized independence and gave them a sense of normalcy in a time when policies against Jews were becoming more oppressive and virulent. In 1937 their freedom came to a crashing halt. A small accident gave the local Nazis police an excuse to label him a danger to society and to take away his license and his car. Without a vehicle their lives were more and more confined to their house to avoid the probing eyes of the Nazis, looking for any excuse to harass them. Tensions escalated, and in 1939 Germany launched a brutal war of aggression, a horrific, calculated racial war against Jews and others deemed not part of the German nation.

World War Two and the Technology of Destruction

World War One provided a glimpse into the destructive capability that the technology—tanks and planes, ships and submarines—could levy through war; World War Two unleashed this horrific reality with full force. When Germany invaded Poland in 1939, thousands of tanks rolled in front of the infantry. Planes bombed indiscriminately. Warships attacked the coastal cities and submarines mined the harbors. As the war turned to the West and Germany attacked Belgium, France and England, these weapons inflicted unimaginable damage. And when Germany invaded the Soviet Union in 1941, the horror of this war was put on full display as tank units swept across the plains demolishing anything in their path while fighter planes and bombers flew overhead attacking soldiers and civilians.

When Japan launched its offensives into central China in 1937, it followed by sending fleets to attack islands and archipelagoes across the Pacific. In December of 1941, when Japan attacked the US Naval base Pearl Harbor in

Hawaii, the war was truly a world war. Aircraft carriers carrying bombers, submarines sinking hospital and transportation ships, and massive battleships pummeling coastal fortifications and towns swept across the Pacific waters.

Shortly after the Japanese bombed Pearl Harbor and brought the United States into the war, British Prime Minister Winston Churchill noted that Japan's defeat was certain—given these new technology of weapons of war. "As for the Japanese," he said, "they would be ground to powder. All the rest [of the war in the Pacific] was merely the proper application of overwhelming force." What Churchill meant when he predicted the defeat of Japan shortly after Pearl Harbor in December 1941 was that modern warfare was a war in which the fate of belligerents was significantly determined by their industrial-military capabilities and by how much and how fast countries could produce materials for war. He reasoned that the US, with its massive industrial capabilities, could simply out produce the Japanese. He was correct, and by the war's end the US had made over three times as many planes as Japan, and, as the war spread across the vast regions of the Pacific, this advantage proved decisive.

One way that new technology of destruction (planes and bombs) was used was to attack cities and industrial centers. The goal was to cripple the industrial capabilities of their enemies and, at the same time, weaken the morale of those at the home front. After Germany failed to defeat Great Britain through their assaults in 1940, the Allies in Europe sent squadrons of bombers to destroy cities in Germany. Hamburg, Dresden, Frankfurt and Berlin were incessantly attacked, first by bombs intended to break apart buildings and then by incendiaries that would turn that rubble into a horrific conflagration of fire. People suffocated in bomb shelters, and the fires robbed the air of oxygen. As the United States gained control of the Pacific, it deployed similar tactics. Tokyo, a city largely made of wood, was almost completely burned to the ground.

The defining moment came on August 6, 1945, when an American bomber, the *Enola Gay*, carried one bomb, an atomic weapon, which eviscerated the Japanese city of Hiroshima. Between 70,000 and 130,000 people literally disappeared in the bomb's searing flash. Tens of thousands more died over the weeks and years that followed as a result of the lethal radiation the bomb left behind.

While it was the military technology of the twentieth century—tanks, planes and ships—that defined the battlefields of World War Two, the train also played a critical part in facilitating the transport of people into concentration camps and ultimately to their death. Prejudice against Jews was a central part of Nazi ideology since its inception. As World War Two unfolded, Hitler and his henchmen strategized over how to use the fog of war to annihilate their enemies. Jews were the vast majority but not the only victims of Hitler's war. Homosexuals, Roma and Jehovah's Witnesses and anyone who played a part in harboring 'enemies' were also targeted, persecuted and executed. As the Nazis conquered Poland and other territories in Eastern Europe, they built ghettos in major cities to confine the large Jewish populations. Construction of labor/death camps to extract every bit of energy from these trapped populations was part of the systematic effort to eventually eliminate them as a people: the Holocaust.

To transport Europe's Jewish population to these camps, the Germans employed the vast railway networks of their expanding empire. Passenger and freight cars were requisitioned and crammed with as many humans as possible; maybe eighty to one hundred people in a space less than 200 square feet, with no food, water, ventilation or sanitation provided. If these people died en route, it only made work at the camps easier. During the darkest days of the war, these trains rolled day and night to the death camps of Auschwitz, Treblinka and others.

Charlotte Delbo, a French Communist captured by the Nazis while trying to foment anti-German resistance in Paris in 1942, was one of the millions who were forced on a train to Auschwitz; she was also one of the few who survived. After the war she did her best to write about the experience, to capture the often inexplicable horrors of what it was like to be crammed in cattle cars and carried across Europe to the death camps. The result was a poignant poem: *Arrivals/ Departures* that captures, as well as words can, the horror and humanity that she and millions of Jews, Roma and others faced: It captures the reality, she writes, of those who knew what they faced "and yet they did not believe. . . . They had no idea you could take a train to Hell but since they were there they got their courage up and got ready to face what was coming."

The magnitude of the deportation of the Jews and other minorities deemed expendable by the Nazi state required the detailed coordination by almost every element of the Nazi state and the collaboration with many of their allies. This coordination obviates any arguments that the Holocaust was carried out by a few individuals or that the larger population did not know what was going on. So central was the Holocaust to the Nazi leaders that they continued to order the trains to roll even when the war was turning against them and military leaders were begging for more transportation and resources. Winning the war against a race was every bit as critical to these leaders' aims as winning on the military front.

Caught Up in the Conflict: Civilians and the War in Asia

The Japanese had claimed at the start of the war that their primary goal was to liberate Asia from western imperialists. It soon became apparent that they intended to forcibly colonize most of the East. As the war advanced, Asians and Westerners living in colonies across the region who were unable to escape the rapid Japanese advance became prisoners of war and were forced into serving the Japanese military machine. It is difficult to know with any accuracy, but the number of forced laborers was estimated to certainly be in the millions. Approximately 750,000 Koreans were shipped to Japan to work in factories; they comprised over one-third of all labor in Japan during the war. Other forced laborers built railroads and defense fortifications in searing jungles. Others had to dig and haul ore in mines for twelve to fourteen hours each day in dire conditions. In the rubber plantations of Indonesia, many natives found circumstances worse than they were under the harsh policies of the Dutch colonizers.

Some 200,000 young women, mostly Korean but also from the Philippines, China and many other territories, faced a horrific fate as they were kidnapped or 'drafted' into forced prostitution as 'Comfort Women' for the Japanese army. Taken from their homes, these women were shipped to distant military outposts throughout the Japanese imperium, often raped and then shut in buildings for days, months and agonizing years to have sex with Japanese soldiers. Kim Tokchin, a young Korean woman sent to Shanghai in 1937, recalled having to serve thirty to forty men a day, six days a week. Fifty women lived with her in her brothel. Beatings, tropical diseases, unsanitary living conditions and malnutrition claimed many, and those who survived faced social ostracism. Adding to the tragedy has been the longtime denial by the Japanese of the brutal treatment these women experienced.

Japanese-American citizens living in the western parts of the United States were sent to internment camps, forced to leave their homes after the Japanese attack on Pearl Harbor. This came about on February 16, 1942, when President Roosevelt signed an executive order that ostensibly was designed to prevent espionage; what it did was remove some 120,000 mostly American citizens from their homes. Canada and Mexico passed similar versions of this order. Once the orders were passed, these citizens were given six days to load what belongings they could and report to assembly centers, where they were loaded on buses and trains and sent to internment camps to spend the duration of the war. When finally allowed to leave, many of these citizens found that their homes and property had been taken away, and they could not get it back. It was not until 1988 that the US government offered a formal apology and finally gave reparations to those who were incarcerated.

The End of World War Two and the Refugee Crisis

It is difficult to know how many people were forced from their homes to flee the horrors of World War Two, but the numbers are staggering—in the tens of millions. Peter Gatrell, in his analysis of refugees during the war, estimates that as many as 45 million Chinese were internally displaced by the Japanese invasion of their country and that some put the figure as high as 100 million—a quarter of the entire population. Others cite the numbers of refugees in Europe as also in this range. The fighting and the physical and psychological destruction of their homes meant that many had nowhere to turn at the end of the war. Forced laborers and camp survivors often found themselves hundreds or thousands of miles from home with no way to return. They had no material possessions except perhaps a ragged prison uniform hanging on an emaciated body, no identity papers to prove who they were or where they once lived. Adding to the chaos were millions of prisoners of war from both sides who sought repatriation.

Tens of thousands of women forced into sexual slavery or raped by enemy forces faced discrimination even by their own families. Conventions stipulated that these prisoners of war should be treated "in an orderly and humane manner," but that was often far from the case.

Refugees faced the bitter politics of the post-war era. Many Jews wanted to immigrate to Palestine, but Great Britain controlled the territory and was reluctant, fearful that it would further enflame ethnic unrest in the area. People of German heritage who had never lived in Germany were expelled from central and eastern Europe and had to find countries that would take them in. It is estimated that 11.5 million ethnic Germans were expelled from the countries they had long lived in after the war. Poles, Ukrainians and peoples from other ethnic groups were sent to the Soviet Union to help rebuild that country. Dutch, French and British colonists who tried to return to their colonial homes faced military opposition by indigenous peoples throughout Asia.

The millions of Chinese who were internally displaced by the war faced a violent civil war between the Communists and Nationalists. That war lasted four long bloody years and left many frantically searching for safety. When Mao Zedong led the Communists to victory in 1949, some two million Nationalist supporters who had lost the civil war fled to Taiwan, where they set up a rival government, the Republic of China (ROC). Communist China (mainland China) some seventy years later claims that the ROC is illegitimate and that its now 34 million citizens are really part of Communist China.

Even before it was officially founded after the end of the war in October 1945, fifty-four countries that would become initial members of the United Nations agreed to the creation of the United Nations Relief and Rehabilitation Administration (UNRRA). They were tasked with to try to bring some coordination to what they knew was unimaginable misery. Operating mainly in Europe, the UNRRA set up displacement camps, provided food and shelter and tried to help many of the war's orphans find homes. By 1947 it ran some eight hundred camps and had served over 70,000 people. It was impressive but also clearly lacking, given the scale of the global refugee crisis.

Conclusion

The Great Depression forced untold millions to leave their homes in search of work. Many, like the Joad family in *The Grapes of Wrath*, found they were not welcomed. So they kept moving, kept searching and hoping. The Great Depression had global economic, social, political and psychological impact. The chaotic crisis of uncertainty prompted some countries to seek radical solutions. The Nazi Party in Germany offered false promises of a return to normalcy, leisure and vacations, but those false promises soon gave way to war and genocide. When World War Two broke out in Europe in 1939, millions were once again on the road, either fleeing the Nazi onslaught or perishing in their death camps.

The war also engulfed much of Asia and the Pacific and was equally brutal. Japan, decimated by the Depression, intensified its efforts to colonize China and eventually much of Asia. Brutal acts of war followed, and men and women alike were forced into serving the growing needs of the Japanese army.

When World War Two ended in 1945, millions of refugees and prisoners of war found themselves far from home many with nowhere to go. One solution proposed to fix a broken world was the United Nations. Nations were called to come together in association, to prevent future conflicts and serve those who are caught in war's crosshairs. The post-war world would give it too many chances to fulfill its mission.

End Materials Chapter 12

Works Quoted

Blyth, Stephen, "The Dead in the Gulag: An Experiment in Statistical Investigation," *Journal of the Royal Statistical Society: Series C (Applied Statistics)*, vol. 44, no. 3 (1995).

Delbo, Charlotte, *None of Us Will Return, vol. I: Auschwitz and After*, Rosette Lamont, trans. (New Haven, CT: Yale University Press, 1992).

Gatrell, Peter, *Forced Migration During World War Two: An Introduction.* https://www.gale.com/intl/essays/peter-gatrell-forced-migration-second-world-war-introduction.

Klemperer, Victor, *I Will Bear Witness: A Diary of the Nazi Years*, vol. 2 (New York: Random House, 1999).

Noakes, J. and G. Pridham, eds., *Nazism: A History of Documents and Eyewitness Accounts, 1919–1945* (New York: Schocken Books, 1983–1984).

Rothermund, Dietmar, *The Global Impact of the Great Depression* (London and New York: Routledge, 2000).

Scott, John, *Behind the Urals: An American Worker in Russia's City of Steel* (Bloomington, IN: Indiana University Press, 1973).

Steinbeck, John, *The Grapes of Wrath* (New York: Viking, 1939).

Tokchin, Kim, "I Have Much to Say to the Korean Government," in Keith Howard, ed. and Young Joo Lee, trans., *True Stories of the Korean Comfort Women* (London: Cassell Books, 1995).

Further Reading

Brook, Timothy, ed., *Documents on the Rape of Nanking* (Ann Arbor: University of Michigan Press, 1999).

Davies, Sarah, *Poplar Opinion in Stalin's Russia: Terror, Propaganda and Dissent, 1934–1941* (Cambridge: Cambridge University Press, 1997).

Goda, Norman, *The Holocaust: Europe, the World and the Jews: 1918–1945* (New York: Pearson, 2013).

Koonz, Claudia, *The Nazi Conscience* (Cambridge, MA: Belknap Press of Harvard University, 2003).

Rothermund, Dietmanr, *The Global Impact of the Great Depression, 1929–1939* (London: Routledge, 1996).

13 Cold War Conflicts, Youth Rebellions and Decolonization Movements

Introduction

By February 1945, as many cities of Europe and Asia been burned and millions of people suffered and died, the leaders of the Allied powers—the Soviet Union, the United States and Great Britain—met and signed the Yalta Agreement to officially end the war. They discussed the fate of liberated lands across Eastern Europe. Yet, even as these leaders warmly shook hands and sat for photos, it was apparent that unity would likely fade. Not long after, the onetime allies were locked into ideological and military struggles around the world that defined geopolitics for most of the rest of the century. Most notable was the very adversarial relationship between the United States and the Soviet Union that came to be known as the Cold War.

Cold War tensions led to wars and conflicts across the globe. They shaped political ideas and inspired revolutionaries. Che Guevara was one revolutionary. Journeying across Latin America he was deeply affected by the deleterious impact that Western governments and corporations were having on the poor of his continent and indeed the world. What he saw led him to communism and the life of a global revolutionary.

Tensions were also growing between the older and younger generations after the war; their differences ranged from politics and economics to hairstyles and musical preferences. The younger generation was emboldened by growing numbers as the world's population swelled after the war's end. Baby boomers, as they were known, were also motivated by what they thought to be the inability of the older generation to address the ideas and animosities that had led the world to war. The Beatles, arguably the most famous musical group ever, became an inspiration and political voice for these generational wars. Their influence peaked around the Vietnam War and, in many ways, reflected the baby boomer generation grappling with their place in the world.

Colonial regimes were no longer accepted, and independence movements gained traction. India separated from Britain with the Partition of 1947, the French left Vietnam in 1956 and Ghana was the first country in Africa to achieve independence in 1957. The country's leader, Kwame Nkrumah, promised that his country would become a beacon of hope for Africans and the

DOI: 10.4324/9781003168690-14

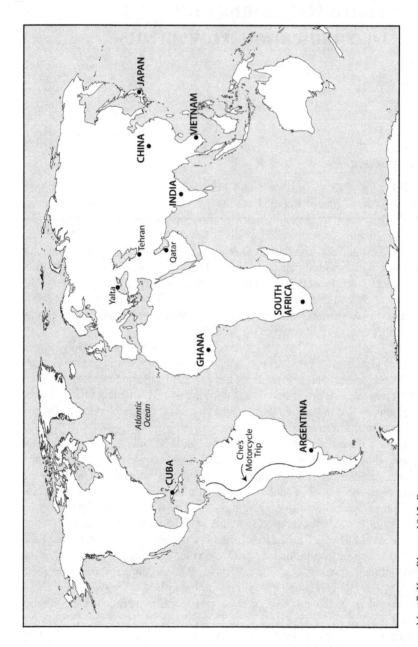

Map 7 Key Places, 1945–Present

diasporic African communities around the world. Two prominent African-Americans, Maya Angelou and Malcom X, answered his call to come home and help build a new Africa. Their stories tell of decolonization after the war and help us understand issues of racism that deeply divided the United States and other countries.

The Meetings of the 'Big Three'

Joseph Stalin, the leader of the Soviet Union during World War Two, did not like to travel. In order to do so, he would have to leave the security of the Kremlin and expose himself to enemies he imagined lurking in every corner. By the end of 1943, he had to travel. The Allies—Russia, Great Britain, and the United States—needed to coordinate their offensive against the Nazis. They also needed to plan the post-war world, given that Germany and Japan were beginning to retreat. Stalin needed to sit down with the President of the United States, Franklin Delano Roosevelt, and the Prime Minister of Great Britain, Winston Churchill, and begin the delicate dance of diplomacy. Reluctantly, he agreed to travel, but only to Tehran (modern Iran), where occupying Soviet troops could ensure his safety.

The meetings in Tehran mostly focused on how to defeat the Nazis. The Soviet Union was regaining territories from the Germans, but the costs were astronomical and Stalin wanted help; he wanted a second front to split the German forces. For his part, Roosevelt was especially interested in forging a "special relationship" with Stalin (or "Uncle Joe" as he was now called in the United States during the war), one that he hoped would lead to cooperation not only in Europe but against Japan and into the post-war era. Churchill was less concerned about a long-term alliance; he wanted a clear understanding about who would control what once Hitler's Germany no longer existed. He did not want a Communist dictator simply taking over for the Nazi dictator. The Tehran Conference concluded with promises of an Allied landing in France in the late spring of 1944 and cooperation in dealing with Germany and the post-war order.

By the time the 'Big Three' met again in February 1945, the situation had changed dramatically, and concerns about the post-war order had sharpened significantly. American and British troops were in Germany, and Soviet troops were only 40 miles from Berlin. Germany's defeat seemed eminent; resolving its fate and that of the rest of Europe was crucial. Stalin again insisted that they convene in a place controlled by his forces, and Yalta, a port town in the Crimea, was chosen. For an increasingly weak and debilitated Roosevelt, the trip was arduous, but Stalin liked being in control on his home turf and Roosevelt, still interested in cooperation, acquiesced.

Besides the fate of Germany, the major issue on the table was Poland. It was, in a sense, the canary in the coalmine—the warning signal for problems that lay ahead. Stalin's forces controlled the country, but Roosevelt and Churchill had promised the London Poles, i.e. Polish leaders in exile, that they would have a strong voice in any post-war government. Both men wanted Stalin's assurance that he would allow for a democratic Poland, and both believed that Poland's fate would determine the fate of all other liberated countries in Eastern and Central Europe. In the end, they agreed to a statement promising that the exiled leadership "would be included" in a post-war government and that free elections would be held "as soon as possible." The questions surrounding the details of such promises remained unanswered. The alliance stayed together, but it was clear that implementing these vague agreements could lead to serious rifts.

Stalin met with the other Allied leaders one more time, at Potsdam, a Berlin suburb, in July 1945. Once again he agreed to travel only where his troops offered protection and, with Germany now defeated, Soviet forces occupied the region. Churchill arrived, but just as the conference was getting underway he was voted out of office and replaced by the leader of the British Labour Party, Clement Attlee. Roosevelt was not there. He died in April and was succeeded by President Harry Truman, who was less inclined to placate Stalin. He did not need Stalin to win the war in Europe. As he was sailing to the conference, the atomic bomb was successfully tested in New Mexico. He realized that he did not need Stalin's forces to defeat Japan. Both sides hardened their stance toward Poland and the rest of Eastern Europe. Truman demanded immediate democratic elections in all of Eastern Europe. Stalin insisted that he could not allow anti-Soviet regimes adjacent to his borders. The lines were drawn, and the alliance effectively ended. Nine months later, when Churchill toured the United States, he proclaimed, "an Iron Curtain had descended" across Europe.

The meetings of those leaders in Teheran, Yalta and Potsdam defined the trajectory of geopolitics for much of the rest of the twentieth century. Tensions between the United States and its allies, and the Soviet Union and those under its sphere of influence, divided Europe and much of the world for the better part of four decades. Alliances came through financial and military support and sparked proxy in many corners of the globe.

Che Guevara: The Globalization of the Communist Revolutions

Che Guevara's road to Communism started in his home country of Argentina. Much of Latin American was rife with challenges following the war. While Argentina had benefited economically during the war by supplying food and material, its economy slowed dramatically after the war ended. Unemployment spiked and unrest grew. Members of the government were found to have connections to the fascists during the war, and the ideologies of the Cold War divided the populace.

Che grew up in a comfortable middle-class household and as a young man had little interest in the issues facing his country. He was skeptical of Argentina's populist president, Juan Peron, who promised to modernize the economy, support unions and promote social welfare. In 1948 he began to study medicine. Three years into his program he decided to take a break. Along with his close friend, Alberto Granado, they took off on motorcycles to see Argentina and a bit of South America before settling down to finish exams and start a career.

Leaving the capital, Che and Alberto made their way across the pampas to the mountains of Patagonia. The bikes fell apart in Chile, but they continued to make their way north up the spine of the Andes, passing into Peru, Columbia and eventually Venezuela. Along the way they stayed with local Indians and visited the massive copper mine of Chuquicamata in Chile, where labor battles were underway. Che's interest in medicine took him to hospitals and a leper colony located on an isolated tributary of the Amazon River.

The trip became legendary, and many of these legends were constructed by Che himself. He kept a diary on his trip, but it is unclear how much he or his family embellished before it was eventually published as *The Motorcycle Diaries* (1995) long after his death. Aside from the historical accuracy of the diary, there is no doubt that his journey was instrumental to awakening a call to the plight of Latin America's poor, indigenous and working-class populations that would become his life's work.

Within a year after returning from his adventure, Che finished his exams and headed back out on the road. His vague plan was to head to Venezuela and work in a leper colony, but he seemed equally interested in continuing his political education. He spent five weeks in Bolivia talking with locals and intellectuals about the state of labor problems in the country's mines. During those conversations he became more concerned about the role that US businesses played in these mines, prospering at the cost of the working-class people.

By the time he got to Mexico City, Che was committed to leading a revolutionary life. Fortuitously, he met the man who would help him channel his revolutionary fervor: Fidel Castro. Castro was living in Mexico City in exile while organizing resistance against the dictatorial government and backed by US businesses in his native Cuba. The lucrative sugar industry was largely controlled by US companies, and the working conditions faced by the cane workers were deplorable. Intense periods of low-wage labor followed by long periods of unemployment left most of the island's population destitute. Havana was awash with casinos for the island's few rich and their US partners, but most of the country suffered short life expectancy and poor health.

In 1956 Che, Castro and eighty fellow revolutionaries snuck into Cuba. Their goal was to overthrow the Batista regime and introduce sweeping land and social reforms. After three long years, much of which found the revolutionaries isolated in the island's eastern mountains, they finally succeeded in ousting the dictator, prompting fearful middle- and upper-classes to flee the country. The United States watched the new revolutionaries with a skeptical eye. Questions about how to deal with the domestic chaos and the international community divided Che and Fidel. Che was fully committed to a Communist revolution and an anti-US stance; Castro seemed to be more cautious on both fronts. It may have been these differences that convinced Castro to send Che abroad on a diplomatic mission in 1960 that took him to China.

By the time Che got back to Havana after spending months touring the Communist world, Cuba's relationship with the United States had deteriorated. In April 1961, barely three months after assuming office, the young President John F. Kennedy ordered a group of anti-Castro Cubans who were exiled in Miami to collaborate with US CIA intelligence and military support to invade Cuba and overthrow Castro's government. The Bay of Pigs Invasion, as this became known, failed miserably. It also ended any of Castro's ambivalence about Cuba's future. The US was the enemy, and Communism was the answer.

Cuba sought Soviet backing to defend itself against any future US threat, and Khrushchev answered by agreeing to send nuclear missiles to the island. The Cuban Missile Crisis followed and was the most dangerous period of the Cold War, given the threat of a Soviet nuclear arsenal within 100 miles of US shores. In October of 1962, US President Kennedy confronted Castro and Khrushchev in a televised speech to the world. He ordered a blockade of Cuba and demanded removal of all nuclear bases from the island. The question was how would Castro and Khrushchev react? Would the Soviet ships try to run the blockade? Were missiles already in Cuba or only in transit? Was Kennedy bluffing? Would either side really use weapons of mass destruction over Cuba? For almost two weeks the world watched with fascination and fear.

By the 1960s nuclear weapons had become astronomically more powerful than the atomic weapons that shocked the world in 1945. The threat of nuclear war was a high-stakes game played out on a global stage. In the end, both sides decided against going all in, and after tense negotiations the Soviets agreed to remove their missiles in return for Kennedy's promise not to try another invasion. The world let out an exhausted sigh of relief.

Che felt betrayed. It seemed to him that the USSR had sold out the Cuban people. More and more he saw the world divided not between Communists and capitalists but between the militarized imperialists of the northern hemisphere and the exploited masses of the Global South. In 1965 Che left Cuba to support resistance movements against Western interference in the Congo. Freed from Belgium control in 1960, the country had descended into regional and civil war. Western powers, fearful that left-leaning leaders may take control, sent in aid and advisors to make sure they did not succeed. Che hoped to stop these interventions and help the Congo and Africa chart a new path free of Cold War interventions. He stayed two years. His plans in Africa were foiled when military dictatorship took control of the country, and he returned to his home continent. In 1967, while trying to spark anti-Western revolution in Bolivia, he was captured and executed.

More than a half century after his death, Che remains a symbol for many reformist movements hoping for radical social and economic change while avoiding the crippling dependencies of alignment with the world's great powers. (I have seen Che's visage everywhere, from T-shirts on my students in Seattle to campaign posters for the Indian Communist Party in Kerala, India, to barn walls painted to show support of the Zapatista movement in Chiapas, Mexico.)

Vietnam and the Youth Movements of the 1960s

Che's death in 1967 came during a time of great global turbulence. The post-war baby boom had resulted from a shift in demographics; young people in unprecedented numbers came of age in the 1950s and 1960s. They saw the world through a different lens. They demanded access to opportunities in education, employment, social and cultural expression. They also sought out political access that often conflicted with the expectations and ideals of their elders. They came of age at a time when global conflicts, especially the war in Vietnam, confirmed that the older generation was intent on continuing the disastrous conflicts that had so dominated the twentieth century, and they were determined to find a new path.

One of the most important, if somewhat reluctant, voices of this youth movement were the Beatles, a rock-and-roll band from Liverpool, England. The four boys—John Lennon, Paul McCartney, George Harrison and Ringo Starr—exploded onto the world stage in early 1964 when they accepted an invitation from the most popular variety show in the United States hosted by Ed Sullivan. Wearing black suits and skinny ties, with floppy hair and boyish charm, they had already taken Europe by storm. Their appearance on Ed Sullivan played to one of the largest audiences ever watching a non-sports event on television; they were a global phenomenon. Over the next two years the Beatles played to crazed audiences who often screamed so loudly that they could not even hear what the band was playing. Beatlemania was born.

As the Beatles traveled around the US and to other global venues, they found themselves becoming arbiters of the new global youth culture. They began to change their clothing styles from black suits to loud, funky clothes. They wore rose-colored glasses, and their hair styles went from floppy to long shoulder length. Millions of rabid fans from around the world followed suit. As they began to participate in the growing drug culture of the 1960s, millions of young people joined them. (In 1967 Paul admitted to trying LSD, although the band insists that the song "Lucy in the Sky with Diamonds" was not about the drug.) They became embroiled in the major social and political turmoil of the 1960s, and millions listened. More than any other band at the time, it was the Beatles who pushed youth culture to the center stage.

The Vietnam War soon took center stage. As George Harrison put it, the early 1960s were fun, fame was intoxicating "and then we bumped right into Vietnam and realized there is more to life than being noddy-head Beatles." Like many youth around the world, they increasingly saw this war as a war of politicians acting against the wishes of its citizens, a war that was driven by the outdated thinking of the older generation who were willing to let the young generation pay the price for their Cold War follies. "We were all on a ship in the Sixties," said Beatles guitarist and singer, John Lennon in the band's official anthology, "Our generation [was on] a ship going to discover the New World. We were in the crow's nest of that ship."

The year 1968 was a pivotal year. Vietnam had been embroiled in war for over a decade between the Communist north and the US-backed republican south. As Communist forces gained footholds further south, the United States committed more troops to stop them. For a while it looked like US military power would win the day, but then a surprising attack by North Vietnamese troops deep into the south turned the tide. The attack, named the Tet Offensive, took place on the Vietnamese New Year, January 31, 1968, in Danang. It convinced the American public that promises the US government made about winning the war were simply not true. Televised reports of the brutal fighting made reports of the US Army's "body counts" seem to be callous lies. More grotesque was the mass reprisal initiated against the Vietnamese village of Mai Lai when a US military unit committed rape and murder in a village inhabited by mostly women and children. Although Mai Lai was kept quiet for a year, it became for many the moral turning point in which the US promises of protecting freedom and the innocent were no longer believable.

The South Vietnamese and US government responded to the Tet Offensive by calling for more and more young men to be drafted into the army. In both countries, riots against the draft became endemic. The Democratic Party Convention staged in Chicago during the summer of 1968 was disrupted by a radical student group, Students for a Democratic Society (SDS). The riot provoked massive unrest and police retribution as it played out in front of a wide TV audience of millions.

University students in Europe, Mexico and many other parts of the world, while not directly impacted by the Vietnam War, identified with what they saw to be increasingly autocratic, outdated governments acting against their will. Concerns over overcrowded universities, with outdated curricula, run by people who seemed to care little about students, also produced massive riots. In May, Parisian university students took over university offices at the Sorbonne. In Berlin the leader of the radical arm of the student movement, Red Rudi Dutschke, was shot and severely wounded by a right-wing extremist.

In Mexico City student protests against overcrowded universities and the stranglehold of the National Revolutionary Party on political life merged with growing frustrations over the enormous amount of money the government was spending to host the Olympics in October. Students were gathered in Tlatelolco Square, on the campus of the national university, when protesters were met by armed police and snipers fanned out on the rooftops. Three hundred protesters were killed that day, and the government hurriedly cleaned up the streets so no one would know of the incident when the games opened a week later. The games themselves became a scene of global protest when two American sprinters, John Carlos and Tommie Smith, raised their fists in a Black Power salute during the medal ceremony.

The generational wars were also fueled by long-standing gender discrimination. One reason for student unrest in Paris was the fact that women were only allowed marginal roles at best in politics. Political, cultural and social move-ments demanding equal rights for women had been underway for decades, but the unrest of the 1960s amplified the call to action and convinced many that one solution to the problems of the Vietnam War was to put women in charge.

The Beatles were increasingly drawn into the growing anti-war, anti-establishment protests of 1968. John and George felt that the band needed to take an even more active role in these events. John's political evolution was certainly influenced by Yoko Ono, a Japanese artist and feminist he met in 1966. Ono encouraged John to take a visible role in leading the youth move-ment; the question was how. John rejected the violence against 'the Establish-ment' by organizations like the SDS. He saw it as fruitless and believed that it would ultimately only destroy those who perpetuated it. He turned to music to explain his views and wrote the song "Revolution." "We all want to change the world; But when you talk about destruction; Don't you know that you can count me out."

The strains of political activism as well as the burdens of Beatlemania took a toll on the Fab Four, and in 1968 they decided to go to India and practice transcendental meditation. They hoped these non-Western practices would be an alternative to the crass materialism and pressures of Western culture that increasingly weighted on them. Paul wondered about John's politics and his relationship with Ono, both of which, he thought, were ruining the band. As he mulled over his friendship and the fate of the group that that had been so much a part of his life, he penned one of the most popular songs of all time, "A Long and Winding Road." The song was a reflection on the band's journey; it was also a rumination on the band's future. For the Beatles it was a road that would begin to take them in different directions. Within a year the band broke up, and they went separate ways. Years later, John Lennon, known as a peace activist, was shot dead outside his apartment in New York in 1980. A crazed, obsessed fan pulled the trigger. The next day his widow, Yoko Ono, addressed the press: "John loved and prayed for the human race. Please do the same for him."

The Vietnam War ended with the Fall of Saigon. The last helicopters carry-ing personnel took off from the US embassy roof on April 29, 1975; the next day the North Vietnamese rolled into Saigon and took control of the embassy and renamed the city Ho Chi Minh City. The war obliterated much of the coun-try and, in the end, the United States left defeated. Estimates are that as many as 800,000 Vietnamese fled South Vietnam; many took perilous boat journeys to find safety in neighboring countries. Estimates are that a quarter of them never made it, perishing in the rough waters of Southeast Asia. Those who did survive often faced years of life in refugee camps and eventually sought homes in new places. Close to 150,000 eventually settled in the United States.

The Space Race

In October 1957, a Soviet satellite, *Sputnik* (a Russian word meaning "travel") was launched into space. It was the first man-made object put into orbit around the earth. It not only ushered in a new era of human achievement, but it ignited a race for control of space that escalated the Cold War rivalry between the US and USSR for the next two decades. While it really did not have a specific purpose (it emitted radio signals, but its batteries died after only three weeks and it fell back to earth), it demonstrated that the Soviet Union was winning the battle of new technology. The United States was quick to respond and within in a year US President Eisenhower announced the creation of the National Aeronautical Space Administration (NASA) to coordinate and accelerate the country's efforts to travel into space (and keep up with the USSR). While ostensibly a civilian program, it was clear that NASA's efforts to put satellites (and later men) in space could have clear military applications in particular satellite surveillance.

Not to be outdone, the USSR took the next major step forward, putting the astronaut Yuri Gagarin into orbit in 1961. The Americans followed with Alan Shepard a few months later, and within a year John Glenn became the first person to orbit the earth. Ratcheting up the stakes, US President John F Kennedy established the Apollo Mission. Its goal was to put a man on the moon. "If we are to win the battle for men's minds," he said in his speech to Congress announcing the initiative, "the dramatic achievements in space which have occurred in recent weeks should have made clear to all of us the impact of this new frontier of human adventure."

On July 20, 1969, the tremendous efforts of the US Apollo program paid off when Neil Armstrong became the first man to set foot on the moon. As he hopped off the lunar landing module and on to the moon's surface he said that it was "one small step for man, one giant step for mankind." Images of the earth taken from space conveyed a hopeful sense that these voyages could herald a new era of cooperation.

In 1972 the Cold War rivals US President Richard Nixon and USSR President Leonid Brezhnev met in Moscow and signed the Strategic Arms Limitation Treaty (SALT). The treaty halted the escalation of the production of nuclear weapons. It gave a world a chance to catch its breath after a long period of uncertainty. And, while direct US and USSR Cold War tensions moderated, both sides continued to sponsor proxy wars across the globe. The Soviet Union invaded Afghanistan in 1979; the United States backed anti-Communist movements across Central America. Both sides took their fingers off the nuclear trigger, but the Cold War continued to unsettle the world.

Decolonization Struggles: The Case of Ghana

Independence movements had been building for decades, but after 1945 Western powers were more willing to relinquish their colonies in Africa and Asia, and colonized people no longer wanted to be governed foreign imperialists. British rule in South Asia ended in August 1947, and the area was partitioned into Pakistan and India. (East Pakistan separated from Pakistan in the early 1970s and become an independent country, Bangladesh.) As the British left, a number of issues moved forward: How would borders be created? How would these countries treat their minority populations (Pakistan was predominantly Muslim and India Hindu)? Violent clashes led to the killings of between 200,000 and 2 million people, with 10 to 20 million more displaced from their homes in the months that followed. In a similar way, the wars that consumed North and South Vietnam in the 1960s began when northern forces pushed the French out in 1956, creating a struggle between competing factions for control of the regions formerly occupied by the French. In Indonesia and the Korean Peninsula, organized resistance to colonial rule began during World War Two and strengthened in the following years. Decolonization movements percolated across Africa in the post-war period as well. Algeria, Egypt, Morocco and the Sudan in the north gained independence in the early 1950s. Ghana was the first country in sub-Saharan Africa to achieve independence from Great Britain in 1957, and it would become one of the most important in shaping the trajectory of Africa in the decades to come.

The new president of Ghana, Kwame Nkrumah was a leader of the Pan-African movement and promised to promote cultural and intellectual advancements that would make all Africans proud. Part of his efforts to promote Ghana's role in the cultural reawakening of Africa was to encourage Africa's diasporic community to return home and help build that new future. After all, Ghana had been one of the key slaving regions during the era of the Atlantic Slave Trade, and many in the Americas traced their roots back to that region. Many had never felt at home amidst the racism so prevalent in the United States and other countries; they hoped that Ghana could finally be a place they could call home and help to contribute to something important.

One person who answered Nkrumah's call was Maya Angelou. By the late 1950s she was already a well-known writer, actress and political activist in the United States. In 1960 she had met Dr. Martin Luther King, Jr. and became inspired to help his civil rights work. A year later she met a South African anti-apartheid activist and moved to Cairo, Egypt. When their relationship ended a year later, she decided to travel to Ghana. Like many African Americans, Angelou had never felt that the United States, the country of her birth, was home. After all, her ancestors had been kidnapped in Africa and forcibly taken across the Atlantic. She grew up in Saint Louis, Missouri, and later Oakland, California, during a period of deep racial segregation and prejudice.

Angelou arrived in Accra, Ghana's capital, in 1961 and was immediately integrated into the African-American community. "I was one of nearly two hundred Black Americans . . . who hoped to live out their biblical story [of return from exile]," she noted in her autobiography of these times, *All God's Children Need Walking Shoes*. W.E.B Du Bois, the long-time Pan-African activist was also there.

At many levels Ghana liberated Angelou and the other ex-pats. It was a liberation from a sense of the inferiority that racism had imposed on their blackness. Entering the government buildings in Accra on one of her first days she noted, "Seeing Africans enter the formal building makes me tremble with an awe I had never known. . . . Black and brown skin did not herald debasement and a divinely created inferiority. We were capable of controlling our cities, ourselves and our lives with elegance and success."

In 1964 Angelou met another ex-pat from the United States in Accra, Malcom X. He had been on a global tour working on issues of Pan-Africanism and civil rights, and he convinced her to return to the US to help him develop a new initiative, the Organization of African-American Unity (OAAU). It was to be a US-based organization that emulated the efforts the Organization of African Unity established in by Nkrumah. Shortly after his return to the US, Malcom X was assassinated by members of the Nation of Islam, a group he had recently split from.

In 1966 Nkrumah was ousted as president of Ghana. His initial embrace of democracy had become more authoritarian and while on a trip abroad, military leaders took control. It started a cycle of political unrest that would plague Ghana and many African countries for decades as independence leaders struggled to translate the end of colonialism to political stability and economic prosperity.

Malcom X's murder and Nkrumah's fall and the subsequent political turmoil that ensued deeply saddened Angelou, but eventually she channeled her grief into activism. Through writing, teaching and acting she used her political activism to raise issues of racial justice and African-American pride. In 2008 she proudly witnessed the election of the first African-American President of the United States, Barrack Obama. "Finally," she said, "we are growing up beyond the idiocies of racism and sexism." (Recognizing Ghana's importance in the liberation of Africa and African Americans, President Obama made a point to visit the country on one of his first international visits in 2009.)

Political independence often did not translate to economic independence for the former colonies. Decades in which their economies had been monopolized by the interests of the colonizer left many underdeveloped. Long and costly wars of independence left new nations with few resources to rebuild. Colonial rulers had often intentionally left colonial populations uneducated, making it difficult for new leaders to find the intellectual capital they needed to rebuild.

Ethnic, tribal, geographic and/or religious divisions also complicated the burden of rebuilding. Some groups, who had become privileged by colonial rulers in their game of divide and conquer, now became objects of post-colonial retribution. Such was the case in Rwanda, where the Tutsi minority, which had been favored by the Belgians, became the object of suspicion under a new government dominated by the majority Hutu group. After independence, violent attacks escalated between these groups, and animosities continued to build, culminating in the horrific genocide that swept through the country in 1994.

Conclusion

In 1989 the wall dividing East and West Berlin, the symbol of the Cold War for decades, came tumbling down by the hands of people it separated. Within months the Soviet Union that had dominated post-war geopolitics broke apart. The Cold War between the USSR and the US was over. Some boldly predicted that the end of the Soviet Union meant that the world would be dominated by Western-style liberal democracies and free-market capitalism. In reality, the tensions between competing ideologies was far from over. Major nations, most prominently China, remain staunchly Communist and concerns about the dominance of the United States both militarily and economically still animate politicians and protest movements around the globe. Although Africa and Asia were largely independent of colonial legacies, challenges of underdevelopment, social and political division remained.

According to demographers the baby boom ended in the mid-1960s. Its impact on the world remains strong. Aging baby boomers now shape elections and economies in much of the world. The post-World War Two era continues to cast its long shadow of historical events over our world today.

End Materials Chapter 13

Works Quoted

Angelou, Maya, *All God's Children Need Traveling Shoes* (New York: Vintage Books, 1986).
The Beatles, *The Beatles Anthology* (London: Apple Corps Books, 2000).
"Che" Guevara, Ernesto, *The Motorcycle Diaries: Notes on a Latin American Journey* (Melbourne: Ocean Press, 2004).
Kennedy, John F., *Excerpts from 'Urgent National Needs,' Speech Before the Joint Session of Congress* (May 25, 1961). https://history.nasa.gov/Apollomon/apollo5.pdf.

Further Reading

Castañeda, Jorge, *The Life and Death of Che Guevara: Campañero* (New York, NY: Vintage Books, 1997).
Hajari, Nisid, *Midnight's Furies: The Deadly Legacy of India's Partition* (New York: Houghton Mifflin, 2015).
Schildt, Axel and Detlef Siegfried, eds., *Between Marx and Coca-Cola: Youth Cultures in Changing European Societies, 1960–1980* (New York: Berghahn Books, 2006).
Stokes, Gale, *The Walls Came Tumbling Down: The Collapse of Communism in Eastern Europe* (New York: Oxford University Press, 1993).

14 Continuity and Change After the End of the Cold War

Introduction

Plagued with corruption and inefficiencies in weakened economies, military rivalries that had drained their resources, repressive policies and lackluster political participation that alienated the majority of people, the Soviet Union and its Eastern European allies were, by the late 1980s, weakening and fragmenting. In 1989 governments in Hungary and Poland were beginning to lower their guard, ignoring the growing numbers fleeing across their barbed wire borders to the West, and Mikhail Gorbachev, leader of the Soviet Union, proclaimed to Eastern European leaders that he would no longer intervene in their internal affairs.

In the midst of these seismic events Gorbachev went to China. He ostensibly went to reaffirm the solidarity of the two Communist superpowers amidst the growing demands for reform but in reality, his visit energized protests in China. Students and workers were gathered in the gargantuan Tiananmen Square in central Beijing under the imposing gaze of Chairman Mao's portrait, making placards calling for reform and erecting statues of Lady Liberty. Journalists from around the world were watching the summit and the protests. What Jan Wong, a Canadian-Chinese journalist, saw unfold in the coming days would shock the world.

In Africa, independence movements that had swept across the continent after World War Two had, by the 1980s, largely ended outside, minority control. In South Africa, however, whites tenaciously held on to power against the will of its black majority population. But, even there the winds of change were blowing. Crippling international economic sanctions and mass domestic protests called for an end to segregation. As the unrest spread, Nelson Mandela, who had been imprisoned on Robin Island for twenty-seven years for anti-government activities, was set free. It was the final stage, he would later say, in not only his own long, personal walk to freedom but also a critical step in the eventual liberation of his people, his country and, in some ways, the whole continent.

The collapse of the Soviet Union and the ending of apartheid in South Africa were transformative historical events but also limited in their impact.

DOI: 10.4324/9781003168690-15

The Soviet Union broke apart, but Communism survived and in many ways is stronger than ever in China. Apartheid ended in South Africa when Mandela was elected president of a new South African republic in 1994; however, amidst the cheers of his election were the realizations that the roots of the apartheid system were deep and difficult to dig out.

History is the story of continuity and change. Significant changes in travel continued to develop throughout the end of the twentieth and into the twenty-first centuries in particular: the tourism industry, humanitarian refugee crisis and issues around global migrant labor. After World War Two, tourism and global travel increased significantly. Budget travel, travel for business, travel for pleasure and access of travel to new places that used to be inaccessible made travel the largest industry in the world.

Continued political instability, war, inequity and discrimination sadly fueled a global refugee crisis during the late twentieth and early twenty-first centuries. The staggering number of refugees around the world reached historical proportions. Furthermore, economic globalization prompted an increase in the travel of migrant labor. Statistics estimate that over 150 million men and women work outside their country today. At the same time, more and more governments are raising concerns about influxes of 'foreigners' and closing their borders. Many of the debates about these issues seem to hearken back to immigration policies a century before. Recent decades have seen more global integration, and, at the same time, strong reactions to it.

Communism and Consumerism in China in After Mao

Jan Wong first traveled to China in 1972 as a bright eyed, idealistic Canadian student of Chinese descent, anxious to find her ethnic roots and alternatives to intellectual and political alienation that were so prevalent in the West. Communist China was in the midst of the Cultural Revolution and, from her perspective, it seemed to be a vibrant movement full of youthful activism, egalitarianism and idealism. It appeared to offer students a voice in shaping their world. At a time when students were frustrated by the lack of rights and opportunities in the West, "China," she would later write, "was radical-chic."

Wong left China as a student and returned eight years later, in the early 1980s, as a reporter for one of Canada's leading papers, *The Globe and Mail*. The China she returned to had changed. Mao, the great captain of the Communist ship, died in 1976 and after a period of internal purges and succession struggles, the diminutive Deng Xiaoping (all 4 feet 11 inches of him) had eventually emerged as the new head of state. Once arrested by Mao during the Cultural Revolution, Deng seemed to be charting a new course for China. He repudiated the Cultural Revolution and investigated Mao's mistakes. Instead of Mao's dogmatic and rigid Marxism, Deng encouraged people to "get rich." Instead of Mao's isolationism, he promoted international contact and trade, and promoted an opening of China to the world.

While many in China and around the world embraced Deng's new China, Jan Wong watched, wrote and wondered. After having spent time in China, she questioned whether China's rush to consumerism was good. As she traveled around China, it became apparent that Deng's policies were not benefiting everyone. A new elite had emerged, but rural poverty seemed as brutal as ever. New skyscrapers appeared above the smoggy skylines of Shanghai on a seemingly daily basis, but the workers who built them often had no place to sleep. The elite could easily be identified by the expensive foreign cars they drove, safely moving through the hordes of bicyclists. Workers were encouraged to get rich but not demand rights or form unions. No one was to question the legitimacy of one-party rule. The labor camps started by Mao remained full.

Unease crystallized into shock and horror during the spring and summer of 1989 as Wong witnessed attempts by students pushing for pro-democracy reforms turn into a bloodbath. Students, workers and ordinary citizens had been gathering by the thousands in Tiananmen Square at the center of Beijing since spring. They echoed many of the same demands heard across Eastern Europe and the Soviet Union for greater freedoms and openness. When reformist Soviet leader Mikhail Gorbachev arrived in May for a summit of the two great Communist leaders, it heightened calls for change.

Deng squirmed through the summit in mid-May. He did not want to ruin China's image on the international stage and, we know now, he was struggling against members of his own inner circle who felt that the gatherers in Tiananmen should be engaged rather than confronted. However, Deng had also learned during the Cultural Revolution that zealous students and workers were unpredictable.

By the beginning of June, the summit was over and Gorbachev had left China. So too had many journalists who were there to cover the event. Jan Wong was still there. As Deng had proved victorious behind the closed doors of party debate and garnered the support of key military leaders. military units began assembling on the highways ringing the capital. On Friday night, June 2, the troops moved into Tiananmen Square. "The people are all unarmed," Wong scribbled in her notebook. "The army has been firing on them for two hours." The carnage continued all night and into the next day. Hundreds died. Wong was numb as she watched the massacre unfold.

Still numb and almost hallucinating from lack of sleep Jan Wong was roused by her husband the next day. "You'd better get out here," he shouted. It was noon on Monday June 5, 1989. I dashed onto the balcony. A young man had leaped in front of a convoy of tanks. "Oh, no!" she screamed. It was an anguished cry that echoed around the world that day as millions witnessed through pictures and video smuggled out of Beijing, the defiant act of an unknown young man, 'tank man' who stood up to the military tanks on their way to end, once and for all, the anti-government demonstrations in Tiananmen Square for over a month. Paralyzed with fear Wong watched as tank man played chicken with the vehicle, stepping in its path so it could not go forward.

Finally, someone ran out and grabbed tank man and ushered him away. The Communist government continued its crackdown, and those involved fled into exile, if they could. Those caught faced long prison sentences or executions. It is unclear how many died after Tiananmen Square, including the fate of that one man who dared to defy the power of the state.

In the wake of Tiananmen Square, arrests and executions of dissidents increased. So too did the pace of China's economic modernization. Deng died in 1997, but his policies have continued, and they have made China a global superpower. They have lifted hundreds of millions of people out of poverty. They have also kept the Communist Party firmly rooted in control of the political structures of the state. It is not surprising that pictures of 'tank man' are still, over three decades later, banned in China.

Chinese University Students Go Abroad

One of Deng's policies that has continued and blossomed in the post-1989 era is sending Chinese students to universities abroad, especially the United States. "To send Chinese students abroad," Deng proclaimed early in his tenure as party leader, "is a practical step in modernization." Desperate to accelerate his country, Deng felt that foreign universities offered the best and quickest path to make up China's technological knowledge gap. In 1979 he signed an agreement to send fifty-two students to the US. Within a year 2,000 had boarded planes bound for American universities; that number tripled in several more years. Advisors warned him that some students may not return and would become 'Westernized.' Deng reportedly answered that if only ninety percent came back, China would still be way ahead.

Some fears raised by Deng's advisors may have come true. By the end of the 1980s some of those (now close to 30,000) Chinese students who studied in the US did come home, and they also participated in the protest in Tiananmen Square. After the crackdowns, many students who were still abroad feared returning to China, and in the 1990s President George W. Bush signed an executive order allowing many to stay and establish permanent residence in the US. Feeling they no longer had a future at home, many gratefully accepted the offer.

Whatever fears there may have been about the trustworthiness of Chinese students studying abroad was overridden by China's desire for technical training and expertise. Within a few years of the massacre in Tiananmen Square, Deng, arguing now that if only fifty percent returned it would still benefit China, relaxed student visa restrictions. Throughout the 1990s the number of students going abroad once again grew exponentially. By 2010 there were over 200,000 Chinese students in the US. They accounted for over one-third of all international students studying at American universities. Students from India were a distant second.

For US colleges and universities full-tuition paying students were an asset to diversifying revenue needed to manage university budgets. In 2019 Chinese students paid close to $6 billion in tuition and fees. Competition amongst institutions of higher educations for Chinese students became incredibly competitive. American students began to complain that they were now being denied access to key programs because of university commitments to international students. Politicians and pundits renewed old Cold War fears that foreigners coming in were spies and that the US should consider closing its borders to these students. Donald Trump, who was elected President of the United States in 2016, loudly professed these arguments.

Chinese families began to reconsider sending their children to the US given this growing unease; they did not feel welcome. More recently, the global pandemic that swept across the world in later 2019 (known as COVID) ended the possibility of studying abroad as governments closed their doors to travel. Between April and September 2020, as the pandemic spread, the US issued less than 1,000 visas for Chinese students; one year earlier, by the same point in time, they had processed over 90,000 student visas. Some wonder whether the wave of Chinese students studying abroad, which started with the reforms of Deng Xiaoping and continued long after his death, has now come to an end.

Nelson Mandela: The Long Journey to Freedom in South Africa

Sometimes journeys are not measured in miles but rather by life experiences and transformations. Such was the story of Nelson Mandela, who described his remarkable journey from activist to political prisoner to the President of South Africa in his autobiography, *My Long Walk to Freedom* (1994).

Mandela's long walk to freedom began when he was sent to prison for acts of violence against the government of South Africa in 1962. He admitted he was guilty of the crime he had reluctantly committed. Violence was not his preferred or desired strategy to end apartheid, but he felt it was necessary given the repressive policies of the state. *Apartheid* is an Afrikaner word meaning "separateness," defined officially by government policies of segregation that were established after the elections of 1948. All residents of South Africa were identified by their race and that identification in turn, mandated almost every aspect of their life, from where they lived and worked to whether they could vote. Blacks, by far the majority of the population, were denied the right of citizenship. According to the law they belonged to "tribal lands" that were nominally independent. In practice they were forced to live in South Africa as 'guests' of the white ruling minority, Afrikaners.

As member of the African National Congress (ANC), a multi-racial organization opposed to the apartheid government, Mandela preached and practiced non-violence. He was inspired by Gandhi and like Gandhi he advocated massive public protests to oppose laws that the government used to harass and detain blacks. However, in Sharpeville, a black township near Johannesburg when the government responded to a demonstration on March 21, 1961, with violent attacks by police against the protesters, Mandela agreed that armed resistance to apartheid violence was necessary. He decided to head the *Umkhoto we Sizwe*, 'the Spear of the Nation' arm of the ANC, and within a year he was captured, arrested and sent to prison for twenty-seven years. Mandela used these years in prison to continue the struggle against his racist government. Over time he came to realize that in order to bring about systemic change, it was necessary "to liberate the oppressed and the oppressor both."

As Mandela sat in prison in the 1970s and 1980s, protests against South Africa's apartheid policies grew. Newly independent African nations worked to actively support efforts against what they deemed were the colonialist policies of the white South Africans. International condemnations accelerated as private companies and universities boycotted South African products and investments. Most critically, massive protests in South Africa continued. Church leaders like Anglican Archbishop Desmond Tutu developed an activist religious response to apartheid. By the 1980s more members of South Africa's white community joined them in the streets. Mandela's stature as an outspoken voice against apartheid was an inspiration to many.

Protests swelled across his country, and South African President William de Klerk calculated that the only way his country would survive was to deal with Mandela directly. He released Mandela from prison and began to negotiate the country's future. Over the next four years, four long years, apartheid continued, but in 1994 Mandela's dream was finally realized. That year, at age seventy-five, he participated in the country's first multi-racial elections ever, and he was elected President of the Republic of South Africa. He had indeed helped his country take a long walk to freedom. He knew quite well, however, despite progress, it still had a long way to go. "I can rest only for a moment," he wrote at the end of his autobiography, "for with freedom comes responsibilities, and I dare not linger, for my long walk is not yet ended."

During the many years he spent in prison, Mandela contemplated a number of issues that would come if he ever got out and South Africa was able to shed its apartheid regime. He had to deal with the warders and police who had arrested him. Should they be put on trial for crimes against humanity? Should they be forgiven as victims of the system? Should bureaucrats from the old regime work for the new? After all, if they did not, who had the technical expertise to manage the complex affairs of state? How should the state deal with the economic realities of the apartheid system in which the vast wealth of the country was in the hands of a small, white minority? Should lands and property simply be expropriated and redistributed and, if so, would white citizens flee the country and leave it without any means to deal with its vast problems of poverty, population growth and public health that crippled lives and society? The world greatly admired the humanity of a man who could see his prison as a school rather than a jail. It would take all his humanity to help steer South Africa in the very challenging days after apartheid

In his final public act, Nelson Mandela led his country down the path toward a peaceful electoral transition of power. In 1999, after serving his term, he retired from politics. He spent his post-presidential years working tirelessly for the multi-racial and inclusive South Africa he hoped and dreamed possible. In 1993, Nelson Mandela and Frederik Willem de Klerk were jointly awarded the Nobel Prize for Peace. He died in 2013, at the age of ninety-five. To this day, his dream has not been fully realized as South Africa continues to struggle with the legacies of apartheid, but neither has it been abandoned. The long walk to freedom continues.

Tourism: The Largest Industry in the World

Tourism, according to the United Nations, is defined as "the activities of persons traveling to and staying in places outside their usual environment for not more than one consecutive year for leisure, business and other purposes." The second half of the twentieth century saw an explosion of people "staying outside their usual environments." New airports were built to aid the war efforts, and planes were developed to fly further and carry cargo prompting a massive expansion of civil aviation after 1945. Increasing prosperity and a rapidly expanding global population also played a part in growth of the industry. In 1950, the number of tourists was around 25 million. By the mid-70s the number of foreign tourists had increased to over 220 million, and by 2010 there were over one billion tourists moving about annually. According to Elizabeth Becker's book *Overbooked: The Exploding Business of Travel and Tourism* (2013), tourism has become the largest industry in the world. Around ten percent of all workers, she estimates, have jobs tied in some way to the travel industry in transportation, hotels, restaurants, conventions, global events, and working as guides and other service providers.

The overwhelming destination chosen by travelers in the early heydays of global tourism after World War Two was Europe. In 1958, Pan-American Airlines launched the first direct transatlantic routes, from New York to Brussels, and North Americans flocked to France, England and Italy. Paris, London, Rome, Venice and Florence were transformed into tourist meccas with millions of visitors touring the museums and gazing at the castles, and of course eating and sleeping where they traveled. Quantas, the major Australian carrier, initiated the transpacific travel in 1965.

By the end of the century, the industry had evolved to include even wider geographic reach. Rapid economic modernization in many parts of East Asia made foreign travel more feasible to many Asians who had not dreamed of it earlier. It was not only Americans and Canadians touring the Louvre or the Vatican, with cameras at the ready, they were joined by busloads of Japanese and Chinese who were anxious to see the world. Travel destinations such as New York City and Disneyland were increasingly attractive to international tourists.

As global travel increased, many less-developed parts of the world aggressively courted tourism as a way to stimulate their economies. Countries such as Vietnam, Thailand and Morocco saw that tourism brought foreign capital at relatively low cost. It has become apparent, however, that economic opportunities often come with costs. Debates continue about whether tourism in the developing world benefits the local community or the international conglomerates who build the hotels, pay for low-cost labor and reap the profits. Tourism can strain local recourses and have significant environmental impact. Angkor Wat in Cambodia, for example, has seen explosive growth in tourism in recent decades. Large hotels have been built that use such enormous quantities of water that the historic ruins are sinking as water tables drop. Cambodians worry that their treasured history and the economy that has been built on it may literally sink. Countries in the Middle East, like the United Arab Emirates and Abu Dhabi, have also seen notable increases in tourism that has fueled economic growth, but those places also face water shortages among other issues.

The sheer numbers of people traveling to certain places can be the demise of local cultures and communities. Venice, a city of 60,000 now gets over 20 million visitors a year, and many who live off that tourism now feel they may only function as a tourist destination. Tourism has been a major boom for Thailand, however at least some aspects of that industry, especially sex tourism, raise deep concerns. Places like Rwanda, Bosnia and Cambodia have benefited from tourism after horrific genocides that took place, but some worry that this "dark tourism," which focuses on the past, hinders the ability to move forward.

Refugees: A Global Humanitarian Crisis

As the Cold War ended many were hopeful that the world had moved beyond ceaseless warfare; they were wrong. As Communist regimes fell across Eastern Europe, leaders sought to legitimize power by preaching virulent nationalism. Across the former Soviet Union new countries expelled those not deemed part of their national community and aggressively sought to reshape borders. In the Balkans the breakup of Yugoslavia ignited genocidal conflicts pitting Serbs and Croats against Bosnians. Images of emaciated bodies in internment camps, that many had hoped were a relic of the past, appeared nightly on the television during war in the Balkans.

Deep-seeded distrust and antagonisms from the days of colonialism in Africa exploded into violent civil wars. In Rwanda, a history of pitting ethnic Hutus against Tutsis traced back to the Belgian colonial ruler. A war of revenge by Hutus against Tutsis erupted when on April 6, 1994, the airplane carrying Rwandan President Juvenal Habyarimana and Cyprien Nataryamira, the president of neighboring Burundi, was shot down as it left the Rwandan capital of Kigali. What came to follow was a civil war of genocide. Between April 7 and July 15, 1994—over the course of 100 days—at least 800,000 Tutsis were brutally killed by roving armed militias. Similarly, civil war and genocide in Sudan left the lands destroyed and led to the creation of a new state, South Sudan, in 2011.

Civil and national wars, born of poverty and political unrest, have swept across the Middle East and the Americas. Wars between Israel and the Palestinian territories as well as with neighboring countries have displaced hundreds of thousands. Most recently wars in Syria, Iraq and Afghanistan have literally torn countries apart with devastating consequences. State-sponsored wars against minority populations in Myanmar, especially the Rohingya, led many to flee across the borders into Bangladesh and Thailand. Hurricanes and earthquakes in Haiti, El Salvador and Mexico have coupled with man-made havoc caused by gangs, poverty, illegal drug cartels and authoritarian leaders who have perpetuated inequality and violence.

Ongoing conflicts and instability at the end of the twentieth century have resulted in a refugee crisis not seen since the end of World War Two. Estimates are that by the early 1990s, when some hoped that the world would be entering a period of peace and stability, 20 million refugees were forced to flee or were internally displaced. Turkey currently has the highest refugee population in the world, with almost four million people sheltering within its borders; many are from Syria. Columbia is challenged by a tidal wave of refugees fleeing the prolonged political violence and economic chaos of Venezuela. Pakistan has millions seeking refuge from the incessant wars ripping apart its neighbor Afghanistan. Iran has seen many Afghanis coming into their country. In the aftermath of the genocide in Rwanda, millions of Hutus fled into neighboring countries, in particular the Democratic Republic of Congo, overwhelming limited resources and igniting conflicts and unrest. At the end of 2018, there were some 70 million displaced people around the world. Eighty percent of them have been living in exile for at least five years, and twenty percent for over twenty years. Over half of refugees are children.

Living conditions for those displaced are often dire. Fleeing Myanmar, many of the stateless Rohingya have wound up in what is known as the world's largest refugee camp in Cox's Bazar in Bangladesh, where over one million Rohingya live in squalid, flood-prone shanties. The global COVID pandemic has not only decimated the camp's population, but it has also forced non-government agencies working in the region to leave. Reports reflect that serious medical issues along with hunger have collided with violence and insecurity as rival gangs have turned the area into a war zone. Rohingya trying to call out the violence have been targeted for assassination. One activist in the camp living in seclusion for months said when interviewed, "No one will give us protection. Why is my fate to be born a refugee?"

Accurate statistics about refugees are very difficult to obtain and verify because refugees flee, often with no idea of where they are going. While some find aid abroad either through a host country, through UN agency support, or Non-Governmental Organizations (NGOs) like the International Rescue Committee (IRC), many do not. Of these 70 million or so displaced people, less than one percent have applied for asylum. These asylum seekers, whether trying to cross the hazardous waters of the Mediterranean in rickety boats or risking the searing heat of the deserts in the US Southwest, have become central to tense political divisions. Former US President Donald Trump (2016–2020) campaigned on an anti-immigration platform. Boris Johnson was elected prime minister of Great Britain in 2019 in part because he promised exit from the European Union and to secure its borders from asylum seekers. Viktor Orban in Hungary has proclaimed many of the same arguments. They are three examples of many politicians who have been elected based on claims that they will "shut" the borders.

The reality is that most displaced people do not have the means or opportunity to seek asylum. Getting from Afghanistan or Syria to Europe or the United States is an arduous journey, one most people cannot afford or endure. Smugglers who promise transit often rob or abandon their clients.

The story of Abed Alkhalaf from Syria is sadly a fairly typical story. It is typical in the sense of the traumas, the family separation, the arduously uncertain journey of a refugee. It is unique because, in the end, he was one of the rare, lucky ones who found safety and a new home. The father of seven, he left his wife and children behind during the fighting in his city of Deir ez-Zorleft. Unable to get them out, in 2015 he took off alone, hoping that if he could find safety, they could be reunited. Managing to get on a boat, he made it to the Greek island of Chios, though this was only the beginning. For months, he attempted to sneak across borders into Hungary, Austria, Germany and France, usually as part of a small group, traveling at night. He walked much of the way and recalled that "the situation was hell, more than you can imagine."

Finally, Alkhalaf made it to Northern Ireland where an NGO, Together Now, that supports refugees displaced in the United Kingdom helped him secure an asylum visa and began to work on reuniting him with his family, who was still stuck in Deir ez-Zor. Unfortunately, the city was controlled by rival factions, and they could not get out. Finally, by 2017 they managed to travel to the capital of Syria, Damascus. Months of haggling officials for visas followed as Abed tried to convince British officials that they were indeed his family. (They had lost all their papers) and therefore, rights to asylum. In 2019, now across the border in Beirut, they were finally approved after DNA tests proved they were indeed a family. Just as they were close being reunited, COVID hit and borders closed. By 2020, in a rare happy ending, they were all finally reunited in Belfast.

Climate change has been another driving force in the refugee crisis. Global warming is causing disastrous weather trends, rising coastlines, fires and food insecurity. Its impacts are often hitting the poorest and most vulnerable the hardest. The number of climate refugees is rising dramatically. According to a 2021 World Bank report the number of climate refugees could rise to over 200 million by the middle of the century. Bangladesh, a densely populated, low-lying country in the Bay of Bengal is expected to have almost 20 million climate refugees, over twelve percent of the population. Almost ten percent of North Africa's population could be forced to take to the roads and seas seeking safety because of increasing drought and climate uncertainty. Dramatic and immediate climate mitigation, the report hopefully concludes, could reduce these numbers four-fold.

Foreign Workers: The Labors Who Support the Global Economy

Globalization of the world's economy has seen dramatic growth in the number of people working outside their countries or origin. In 2018, according to the International Labour Organization (ILO) 164 million individuals fell into this category, approximately fifty to eighty percent are men. Over half work in so-called high income zones: North America, Western Europe and the Arab states. Foreign workers comprise some forty percent of the total labor force in the Arab States of the Middle East. In the United States it is estimated that almost three-fourths of all those working in the agricultural sector are immigrants. Work in this sector is usually seasonal, and these immigrant farm laborers often find themselves moving frequently, chasing the next job. Consequently, the vast majority of foreign laborers are men, many who leave their families at home.

For many people and many countries, this work in foreign countries is essential for survival. In 2019 (before COVID significantly halted the global movement of labor) it was calculated that $58 billion in work remittances were sent home by migrant labor. These paychecks often support extended families and even whole communities. According to data from the World Bank, remittances from El Salvadoran workers accounted for almost one-quarter of the GDP. Families that received remittances were more likely to have access to running water, a bathroom and electricity than the average household, and children of those families went to school.

Working conditions for migrant labor can obviously be difficult and dangerous. The story of migrant workers helping Qatar prepare for the 2022 World Cup is a case in point. The small country, located on the northeastern end of the Arabian Peninsula, has seen incredible growth in recent decades as oil and tourism have fueled a booming economy. Ninety percent of this booming work force is migrant labor, most coming from countries across the Indian Ocean.

When the country was awarded the bid to host the World Cup, soccer's most prestigious tournament, demands for laborers surged. Seven stadiums, a new airport and hotels had to be built in short order. The 2015 bid was controversial, in part because Qatar had a long history of abusive treatment of foreign labor. As in many countries, workers had to give up their passports for the duration of their contract. Without the ability to travel home, they were at the mercy of their employers, who often crammed them in ramshackle housing, denied wages and forced them into hazardous jobs.

As part of their bid, Qatar promised to reform its labor system, and while many human rights organizations say conditions have improved, the human cost of the glitzy tournament has been significant. It is estimated that as of February 2021 over 6,700 workers have been killed constructing stadiums and other facilities for the 2022 World Cup. Qatar and the World Soccer Federation (FIFA), while not disputing the numbers, argue that most of these deaths were from "natural causes." Their arguments point to the continued challenges of really knowing the experiences of those millions of foreign workers around the world today.

Conclusion

The end of the twentieth and the first decades of the twenty-first centuries witnessed dramatic global changes. Communist states across Eastern Europe and the Soviet Union, which dominated this region for over half a century, collapsed. This came about as the Cold War between the Soviet Union and the US ended. South Africa's difficult legacy of apartheid ended, and a man once imprisoned for being an enemy of that state became its president. People moved around the world in unprecedented numbers. Students from China attending US universities, a phenomenon that once seemed unusual, was now ordinary. Tourism became the largest industry in the world. Foreign laborers moved around the world as never before.

Although this era saw dramatic changes, many issues remained the same. Communism is thriving in Russia and China. Tiananmen Square in 1989 looked like the beginning of the end for Communist rule there, but over thirty years later it remains firmly entrenched and shaping global affairs in ways that few thought imaginable not long ago. A former Soviet secret police operative, Vladimir Putin, has had an iron grip over Russia for more than twenty years. Apartheid ended in South Africa, but the achievement of a truly pluralistic society remains a distant dream. While more people travel globally than ever before, many travel as stateless refugees or as guest workers.

The parameters of modern travel are also being challenged by political movements that are restricting the access of foreigners, whether refugees or students, temporary or permanent workers, into their country. The outbreak of the COVID pandemic reminds us that a virus can move seamlessly and knows no border. A pandemic presents a challenge to science, humanity and to global supply chains. It can equalize, attack and magnify issues as never before.

As Jon Bon Jovi sang in 2010, "The more things change the more they stay the same. Ah, is it just me or does anybody see. The new improved tomorrow isn't what it used to be. Yesterday keeps comin' 'round."

End Materials Chapter 14

Works Quoted

Becker, Elizabeth, *Overbooked: The Exploding Business of Travel and Tourism* (New York: Simon & Schuster, 2013).

Beech, Hannah, "They Warned Their Names Were on a Hit List: They Were Killed," *New York Times* (November 14, 2021).

Clement, Viviane, Kanta Kumari Rigaud, Alex de Sherbinin, Bryan Jones, Susana Adamo, Jacob Schewe, Nian Sadiq and Elham Shabahat, *Groundswell Part 2: Acting on Internal Climate Migration* (Washington, DC: World Bank, 2021). https://openknowledge.worldbank.org/handle/10986/36248 License: CC BY 3.0 IGO.

Fish, Eric, "End of an Era? A History of Chinese Students in America," *SupChina* (May 12, 2020). https://supchina.com/2020/05/12/end-of-an-era-a-history-of-chinese-students-in-america/.

International Labor Office, *ILO Global Estimates on International Migrant Labor: Results and Methodology* (Geneva: International Labor Office, 2018).

Jovi, Jon Bon, *The More Things Change* (2010). https://genius.com/Bon-jovi-the-more-things-change-lyrics.

Kaya, Bülent, *The Changing Face of Europe- Population Flows in the 20th Century* (Strasbourg: Council of Europe, 2002).

Mandela, Nelson, *Long Walk to Freedom: The Autobiography of Nelson Mandela* (Boston: Little, Brown & Co., 1994).

McGarvey, Emily, "Abed's Story: A Syrian Refugee's Journey to Belfast," *BBC News* (September 20, 2020). www.bbc.com/news/uk-northern-ireland-54153398.

Wong, Jan, *Red China Blue: My Long March from Mao to Now* (New York: Anchor Books, 1997).

Further Reading

Coleman, William and Alina Sajed, *Fifty Key Thinkers on Globalization* (London: Routledge, 2013).

Hessler, Peter, *Country Driving: A Chinese Road Trip* (New York: Harper Perennial, 2011).

Manning, Patrick and Tiffany Trimmer, *Migration in World History* (London: Routledge, 2020).

Martin, Philip, *Migrant Workers in Commercial Agriculture* (Geneva: International Labor Office, 2016).

Rosenberg, Tina, *The Haunted Land: Facing Europe's Ghosts After Communism* (New York: Vintage Books, 1995).

Solomos, John and John Wrench, eds., *Racism and Migration in Western Europe* (Oxford: Berg Publishers, 1993).

Spohnholz, Jesse, *Ruptured Lives: Refugee Crises in Historical Perspective* (Oxford: Oxford University Press, 2020.

Stearns, Peter, *Globalization in World History* (London: Routledge, 2019).

Afterword

As I sit down to write this Afterword, I cannot help thinking that I am supposed to be on a ship right now somewhere between Reykjavik, Iceland, and Gdansk, Poland, and from there heading out into the Atlantic and across the Mediterranean. Instead, I am in my basement where I have spent a significant chunk of the last eighteen months. COVID. Of course, I am not unique. The global pandemic that started in the tail end of 2019 has affected every corner of the world. Travel came to a halt and after eighteen months is only haltingly returning. The world's biggest industry, tourism, has almost completely shuttered its collective door. According to the United Nations World Tourism Office, 2020 saw more than one billion fewer global travelers than the year before: a decline of seventy-three percent. The report also said that 2021 would see it go from bad to worse. Huge parts of the world, particularly the Asia-Pacific region that aggressively shut its borders to mitigate the spread of the virus, saw declines of ninety-five percent in international arrivals.

These declines have been felt by big corporations and mom-and-pop businesses alike. Ashish Kadariya, a young Nepalese man, had made a solid living as a guide at Chitwan National Park helping manage the parks' endangered species and guiding tourists. When COVID hit, no one came and Kadariya went off to the United Arab Emirates to work as a hotel guard. "We have to work twelve hours a day, thirty days a month. I miss my country and my profession, but I don't have any options; because of COVID, I was jobless," he said.

In Bolivia, on the shores of Lake Titicaca, a shimmering blue lake sitting at 12,000 feet, Juan Callo now spends his time fixing up his modest place and planting potatoes. He used to spend his days working with his children, helping tourists enjoy the region. "There are no tourists now, and there is no source of work," Callo says. "Not a single person comes here anymore." Four of his five children have left for textile mills in Brazil. He putters away on his guesthouse, hopeful that outsiders will one day return.

Aigul Abdukadyrova, who runs a small guesthouse in the Pamir Mountains of Tajikistan, provides another important perspective. "I miss tourists. When they came to us, we did not feel cut off. On the contrary, I felt like we were part of this world." His comments help us remember that while for many tourism is part of their livelihood, it is also part of their life.

How, when and if the tourist industry recovers from its COVID collapse depends on many factors—variants, vaccines and a host of other variables. The role that this non-living thing, this "infective agent" can play in changing the whole trajectory of global movements is a sobering reminder that the story of travel in the modern world is intimately connected to many other aspects of that world.

The global pandemic is also altering migration flows as countries close borders to prevent the spread of the virus. This is coming at a time when regional instability and economic collapse are compelling many to flee their homelands. Border clashes along the US southern border, or along the European Union's borders, or the surge of migrants trying to make their way across the Mediterranean are all heightening tensions and putting migrants at greater risk as they then try to find other, often far more dangerous, ways to move across borders. A recent report by UNICEF noted that "migration also serves as an important pressure valve as populations respond to different shocks, whether economic, environmental or related to conflict. At a time when the world is facing growing risks, closing off this valve implies greater risks for vulnerable families [especially children]."

COVID is clearly the development that is most shaping travel in the twenty-first century at the moment, but it is not the only development that is impacting travel today; so too is the communication revolution. Recall that when the Jesuits launched their missions in Asia in the mid-1500s, communication between the missionary in Goa, India, and the leader of the Jesuits in Rome was measured in years. Today much of the world has instantaneous connectivity. People pick up a cell phone in Tokyo and casually chat with a friend or colleague in Paris. The internet has provided access to real-time information about what were once the remotest places of the world. Cameras hung in trees allow people to gaze at the mountain gorillas of Rwanda on a morning feed while stretching out on a yoga mat in Los Angeles. Concerts and plays are now live-streamed around the world.

The ability of people to connect instantaneously and virtually has made some wonder whether it is worth it to go through the hassles of physical travel. In 2015, a social historian of cars, Mike Berger, noted that "the automobile just isn't that important to people's lives anymore." Berger was specifically thinking about the appeal of cars to young people in the Western world, where their expense was no longer commensurate with their value as instruments of connectivity. Cell phones, he says, are more treasured for the instantaneous ability to give them access to friends, community and information at a cost greatly below that of car ownership.

The shuttering of offices and classrooms during the COVID pandemic and the ubiquity of Zoom meetings and conferences have many wondering whether these types of communications will remain the norm once the pandemic is over. Educators, parents and psychologists almost all agree that the learning experience of sitting in a room or a closet staring at a screen with twenty other students trying to understand a biology lab is not the same as being in a lab, performing the experiment. On the other hand, many liked aspects of that remote education: not having to take a bus an hour to get to school or the ability to do parts of the class asynchronously at the student's pace and time frame.

Of course, many argue that a Zoom happy hour is not the same as a gathering of friends for a getaway weekend or that watching a concert on your computer is nothing like the experience of being in an arena or a virtual lab is not really doing science. And they are right; but that does not mean that the nature of travel in the late twentieth century, hopping on a plane and jetting around the world, will return full-fold once the pandemic is over. Virtual learning is beginning to seriously compete with the study-abroad experience for college students. Parts of these new modes of connectivity and communication will remain and will change the story of travel in the twenty-first century.

Another development that is changing travel today and will increasingly define the nature of travel in decades to come is the evolution of electric cars and the rapid growth in their sales. The deleterious impacts on the internal combustion engine on our planet are immense. Fourteen percent of the global emissions of greenhouse gases come from the transportation industries. In the United States it the single largest emitter of pollution, accounting for over one-quarter of all emissions in the country and seventy-five percent of all the carbon monoxide pollution.

Curbing this pollution and slowing down the rising tides of climate change have stimulated the move toward electric cars. Better batteries and the construction of charging stations have helped overcome some of the inherent limitations of electric cars, and now sales are climbing. In March of 2021, over 120,000 electric vehicles were sold in the US alone, and sales are projected to rise even more. Government policy is aggressively promoting the switch. While it is way too early to see where these trends are going, it does seem that the age of the internal combustion engine, which has dominated global travel for well over a century, is at least being challenged.

While the move away from internal combustion engine cars is motivated, in part, by fears of dwindling oil supplies, electric cars have their own supply issues. The batteries need particular metals, including cobalt, to handle the intense charges required to operate for reasonable periods. The largest supplies of these metals are located in many of the poorer countries in the world, including the Congo, and controlling them is leading to conflicts and exploitation of labor that remind many of the dark days of colonialism. Cobalt has been called "the blood diamond of batteries" because of the brutal conditions that the miners work in and the corruption of those who control the industry.

Climate change is also affecting where we can travel. The glaciers of Kilimanjaro and the complex coral reefs off Australia's east coast are decaying because of rising temperatures. Desert holidays in Las Vegas or Phoenix, or Dubai or the Sahara are now endangered because temperatures in those places are now becoming literally too hot to handle. Island nations across the Indian and Pacific Oceans, once prime, lifetime destinations for vacationers are now under threat to disappear underneath the rising ocean waters. Tropical jungles are now withering under the intense heat and droughts that climate change is bringing to these equatorial lands. Where tourists can travel and what they can experience in these places is very much in question.

Perhaps a final, whimsical note on the evolving nature of travel in the modern world is the dawn of "space tourism." In 2021, some of the richest people in the world have joined the space race, this time building private rocket ships. On July 20, 2021, Jeff Bezos stepped aboard his private rocket ship, the *New Shepard*, and went into space. A few months later, another of the world's richest men, Elon Musk, followed suit. Both are now offering space rides for anyone who can afford it. Of course, at costs in the hundreds of millions for one jaunt, few can, and it is likely that space tourism will remain a fringe, elite experience for the precious few. Then again, that is what people said when the bicycle, the car and the airplane were first developed. You never know.

Works Quoted

Pattisson, Pete, William Wroblewski, Mehrangez Tursunsoza and Charles Pensulo, "No One Comes Here Anymore: The Human Cost as Covid Wipes Out Tourism," *The Guardian* (August 19, 2021).

UNICEF, *Prospects for Children: A Global Outlook, 2021–2025*. https://www.unicef.org/globalinsight/media/1516/file/UNICEF-Global-Insight-5year-Outlook-2021.pdf.

Index